ISBN 978-0-366-42113-8
PIBN 11349644

1 MONTH OF
FREE
READING

at

www.ForgottenBooks.com

By purchasing this book you are eligible for one month membership to ForgottenBooks.com, giving you unlimited access to our entire collection of over 1,000,000 titles via our web site and mobile apps.

To claim your free month visit:
www.forgottenbooks.com/free1349644

English
Français
Deutsche
Italiano
Español
Português

www.forgottenbooks.com

Mythology Photography **Fiction**
Fishing Christianity **Art** Cooking
Essays Buddhism Freemasonry
Medicine **Biology** Music **Ancient**
Egypt Evolution Carpentry Physics
Dance Geology **Mathematics** Fitness
Shakespeare **Folklore** Yoga Marketing
Confidence Immortality Biographies
Poetry **Psychology** Witchcraft
Electronics Chemistry History **Law**
Accounting **Philosophy** Anthropology
Alchemy Drama Quantum Mechanics
Atheism Sexual Health **Ancient History**
Entrepreneurship Languages Sport
Paleontology Needlework Islam
Metaphysics Investment Archaeology
Parenting Statistics Criminology
Motivational

Signal Success.

THE WORK AND TRAVELS
OF MRS. MARTHA J. COSTON.

AN AUTOBIOGRAPHY.

"Γενηθήτω φῶς, καὶ ἐγένετο φῶς."
"In hoc signo vinces."

PHILADELPHIA:
J. B. LIPPINCOTT COMPANY.
1886.

TO THE LATE

ADMIRAL JOSEPH SMITH, U.S.N.,

WASHINGTON, D C,

MANY YEARS CHIEF OF BUREAU OF YARDS AND DOCKS,

U. S. NAVY DEPARTMENT,

THIS BOOK IS DEDICATED,

AS A TOKEN OF GRATITUDE AND AFFECTION.

PREFACE.

In this attempt to recount my life and some of the varied experiences attendant upon my efforts to perpetuate the name of my beloved husband and to support my children and myself, I am actuated by no idle vanity, nor yet the wish to pose as a writer, but by the honest desire to encourage those of my own sex who, stranded upon the world with little ones looking to them for bread, may feel, not despair but courage rise in their hearts; confident that with integrity, energy, and perseverance they need no extraordinary talents to gain success and a place among the world's bread-winners.

Perhaps, though, it is right for me to add here, that I had a still higher aspiration than that of supplying daily needs, or even the perpetuation of an honored name,—the intense and heartfelt desire to accomplish something for the good of humanity; in some way to lighten the load of watching and responsibility that rests on the shoulders of the brave mariner;

3

and to place in his hands the means of saving not only property but precious human life; to prevent perhaps other women from becoming widows like myself; other children from growing into manhood with no other Father than the wise and all-merciful One above us.

M. J. C.

VILLA COSTON, WASHINGTON, D.C.
May 1, 1886.

CONTENTS.

CHAPTER   PAGE

I.—"Full Well do I Remember" . . . 9

II.—"The Secret is Out" 15

III.—What Coston accomplished . . . 23

IV.—Washington Society "Befo' de Wah" . 29

V.—Bereft—A Discovery 35

VI.—A Struggle and Success 42

VII.—The First Fruits 50

VIII.—Strange Countries for to See . . . 57

IX.—Sir Charles Freemantle 63

X.—John Bull and Yankee Inventors . . 73

XI.—French Procrastination 81

XII.—Before "the War Congress" . . . 86

XIII.—Expensive Patriotism—An Enemy . . 93

XIV.—The Signals in War 101

XV.—The Stars and Stripes vs. the Union Jack 108

XVI.—A Parisian Banquet—Fine Feathers . 115

XVII.—Queen Victoria's Drawing-Room . . 121

XVIII.—Strasburg—Baden-Baden and Tragedy . 129

XIX.—A Quiet Retreat and Cologne . . . 134

XX.—A Letter to the Emperor 139

XXI.—Testimonials from Great Men . . . 143

XXII.—France comes Forward 150

XXIII.—Roma—A Handsome Marchese . . . 153

XXIV.—An Audience of the Pope 160

XXV.—Count Piccolomini 167

XXVI.—The Mystery—The Italian Marine . 173

XXVII.—The Guest of the Government . . . 179

XXVIII.—Coffin and Bones 185

1*   5

CHAPTER   PAGE

XXIX.—The Russian Heel 191

XXX.—In St. Petersburg 196

XXXI.—The King and Queen of Sweden . . 204

XXXII.—The Tomb of Thorvaldsen . . 211

XXXIII.—At the Court of Napoleon III. . . 216

XXXIV.—The Empress Eugénie 223

XXXV.—The Vision in Florence 228

XXXVI.—The Palace of Prince Demidoff . . 233

XXXVII.—Italy Adopts the Signals . . 239

XXXVIII.—À Berlin!—King William . . 246

XXXIX.—France was Lost 252

XL.—Danish Delights—An Interview with
Charles XV. 255

XLI.—The Queen Dowager's Palace . . 262

XLII.—Putting Out my Lights 271

XLIII.—An Interesting Trip—Palace of Peter
the Great 273

XLIV.—Perilous Travelling 279

XLV.—Beautiful Americans Abroad . . 286

XLVI.—"Home Again! Home Again!" . . 291

XLVII.—An Appeal for Justice 298

XLVIII.—What my Son has Done 305

XLIX.—Sunset Cox on the Life-Saving Service 316

L.—Wolves! 327

INTRODUCTION.

WHAT a mirror! Only the mother of us all could have furnished one so suited to a darling of her own, a placid basin of water, azure shot with silver, as the sky smiled or frowned; in a rich frame of wavy ferns and velvety moss sprinkled with violets and reflecting with marvellous clearness the charming figure of a young girl, examining with critical interest the image that peered back anxiously at her. The tall, lithe figure, lacking the soft curves and rounded outlines to come later, was viewed with disdain; but even the owner of it could not gaze with severity upon a face dimpled, radiant, and blooming as a flower. Cheeks convincing one that pink was the loveliest of colors; throat and brow that threatened contradiction in their snowy whiteness; eyes that confounded both snow and roses in their purity of blue; and above all a glory of golden hair, that a thousand fairies seemed to have twisted round their tiny fingers and left in a confusion of tangled curls and tendrils, that, imprisoning the rays of the sun, formed a halo about the daintily-poised head.

The fair maid gazed, meditated, and, bending over the smiling water, suddenly dipped her head, once, twice, thrice into its limpid bosom, playfully shaking her sunny locks until the green moss at her feet was sprinkled with dew; then drawing herself up, shook back her golden mane, opened wide her morning-glory eyes, and beheld—Prince Charming—the very handsomest youth she had ever seen in her life, standing on the other side of the pool and gazing intently at her.

The situation was old enough, but the parties were not, to accept it with cool indifference; and in dismay the lovely wood-nymph fled to join her companions, while the youth, with a thoughtful look in his great dark eyes, slowly followed her.

Ten minutes later society joined hands with nature; and Mr. Benjamin Franklin Coston was formally introduced to Miss Pattie Hunt, one of a merry party of school-girl picnickers from the staid old city of Philadelphia.

This introduction must also serve as one to the remarkable history of the author of this volume, who will relate her later experiences in her own language.

* * *

A SIGNAL SUCCESS.

CHAPTER I.

"FULL WELL DO I REMEMBER."

WHEN I was a tiny little girl, my widowed mother gathered her large family of children about her, and, leaving Baltimore, where for five generations and through many vicissitudes our family had lived, started for Philadelphia to establish a new home that we might have all the educational advantages for which Philadelphia was at that time particularly famous. A pleasant house in the suburbs of the city was chosen, the various relics and bits of furniture brought with us soon gave it a look of home, and my elder brothers and sisters entered at once upon their studies.

Left alone with my dear mother, who found delight in drawing out my childish ideas and preparing my mind for the training to come later, a peculiarly tender affection resulted from this constant companionship, and the society of my brothers and sisters, their gay voices, badinage and amusements, were to me not half

9

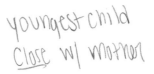

so attractive as the quiet presence of my mother, whose cares and troubles I could not understand, though an instinctive sympathy made me long to share them; and when she called me "Sunbeam," and smiles again graced her lips, my natural joyousness would assert itself, and to divert and amuse her became a charming task.

The years slipped rapidly and happily away, and found me at fourteen unusually tall and mature in appearance for my age, and most anxious to have a more just proportion between my mental and physical development. I went to school and studied with ardor, spending my evenings with my mother in her quiet sitting-room getting ready my lessons for the next day, while my two sisters entertained their young friends and beaux in the drawing-room.

One beautiful summer day, during the school vacation, I went to a picnic with my school-mate and particular friend, Nellie Foster. An unusual excitement took possession of me. I remember now how my fingers trembled as I tied back my wilful curls with a piece of soft blue ribbon, though I did not fail to notice that the ribbon matched in color the sprigs of forget-me-nots on my muslin dress. My cheeks burned, my eyes sparkled, and that singular and unaccountable feeling of "something going to happen" that seizes especially upon impressionable natures pervaded me. However, the fresh air, warm June sun, and the delicious smell of the woods distracted my mind, and when I ran to the pool known as "Clear Pond," to cool my head and make a brief toilet for dinner, I had quite forgotten the "something to happen."

The introduction has told you what did take place, and how, after encountering a pair of brilliant brown eyes, I ran off with a fluttering heart, and for the first time in my life a consciousness of my sex. When the owner of the eyes overtook me, and we were introduced a few moments afterwards, it was a great relief to me to find that my companion Nellie and a young gentleman by the name of Tom Blair (popularly known as "Nellie's beau") both knew him; indeed, the young men were friends.

At that time Mr. Coston, though but nineteen years old, was mature and distinguished in appearance. A Philadelphian by birth, but a Frenchman by descent, his devotion to science and habit of study had not extinguished an inherited vivacity and charm of manner. Rather above the medium height, and erect in carriage, the young inventor's earnest and resolute character was betrayed in the broad forehead, straight brows, and clearly-chiselled mouth. His large, full, brown eyes were singularly expressive, so much so that his gaze embarrassed me.

5 years older

We had all heard of the gifted young inventor, and his submarine boat or torpedo that could be navigated eight hours under water, having no communication with the surface, the necessary air being manufactured by a chemical process; and, to tell the truth, I was a little too much in awe of his genius to be quite at my ease with him.

fangirl of him

A short time after this meeting, Mr. Coston found means to make my mother's acquaintance, and became a frequent visitor to the house; and she, dear guileless soul, felt not a little pleased and flattered at his evident preference for the calm atmosphere of her sitting-room to that of the gayer drawing-room. A new book, the latest number of the magazine, the pleasant chit-chat of the day that he brought with him, made him especially welcome; and the interest he took in my lessons, his faculty in smoothing for me the thorny path of mathematics and grammar, and enlivening the dry data of history by anecdotes and drawings, made him to me a veritable good genius.

became her tutor

So valuable and practical was Mr. Coston's assistance that with it I remained at the head of my classes, and during his occasional absence from the city I invariably went down to near the foot. Unconsciously I learned to depend upon him. When I began to love him I have never known, and this pleasant intercourse might have gone on without revealing, had it not been for the half-real, half-assumed jealousy of my elder half-sisters, who resented the idea of the most gifted visitor we had ignoring their claims to his courtesies.

Foolishly enough, they began to tease me about him, and if it had not been that Mr. Coston had so thoroughly won my mother's respect and liking, the acquaintance would have come to an abrupt end. As it was, the constraint of my manner only accelerated a crisis and an explanation, and one evening when my sister's ridicule and opposition to his visits had stung me to the quick, I refused to leave my room.

Mr. Coston seized the opportunity to confess his feelings to my mother, who was really shocked at finding any one in love with her "baby girl," as she considered me; but influenced by her own regard for me and desire for my future happiness, she promised him if nothing was said, and my education not interfered with, that when I reached eighteen he should have her consent to his suit. Filled with happiness and courage at having gained so valuable an ally, and bent on carving out a future for me and himself, Mr. Coston pursued his studies and experiments with renewed energy, and only his eyes broke the promise of his lips.

In the mean time, however, Admiral Charles Stewart, "Old Ironsides," as he was called, had heard of and made the young inventor's acquaintance, to become his warm friend and advocate. He was particularly desirous of having him enter the navy on account of his nautical inventions; but as he was too far advanced to enter the Naval Academy, the admiral urged him to go to Washington with letters to Mr. Bancroft, then Secretary of the Navy.

The fame of Mr. Coston's inventive genius had preceded him. On his arrival at the capital he at once presented himself to the Secretary, who, struck by his youthful appearance, said, half doubtfully, "Is this *the* Mr. Coston? Why; my dear sir, you are very young."

Fearing that his lack of years might be made to tell

2

against him, the youthful inventor replied, laughingly, "Yes, sir, I am; but I beg you to remember that time will amend that fault, and that age and merit are not always associated."

The Secretary after a few moments' thought said, "I do not see what I can do for you at present, unless you will accept a temporary appointment as a master in the service, until such time as we can create some office which would be more acceptable to you. The admiral evidently wishes you to be attached to the navy."

After much deliberation, Mr. Coston accepted conditionally the appointment of master in the service, and as the head of the laboratory in the Washington Navy-Yard. This position I beg my readers to remember was accepted under protest, and only with the assurance from the Secretary that he would ask Congress to create an office more acceptable to one of his extraordinary attainments.

A separation between us now threatened, and for the first time I realized how much I had grown to lean upon Mr. Coston's help and judgment; and, though not able to define my feelings as a woman might, under the circumstances, I knew I really loved him, and my love was developed not a little by the opposition of my sisters, who, perhaps not unnaturally, resented that a "mere chit" should have an adorer and offer of marriage, which with their superior advantages was more than they could boast of. They also criticised my mother's course of action severely, and for the first time in my life I became really unhappy.

CHAPTER II.

"THE SECRET IS OUT."

WHEN Mr. Coston came to bid me farewell, before leaving upon a two years' scientific expedition on which he had been ordered from Washington, the family antagonism was more pronounced, and, together with the consideration of my extreme youth, and the possibility that in his absence I might be laughed out of love, or my mind distracted by the attentions of others,—in short, that in some way he would lose me,—filled his mind with forebodings and melancholy.

Anxious to fulfil, in spirit at least, his promise to my mother, and at the same time to make me his own, he persuaded me into consenting to a secret marriage, solemnly promising that he would not claim me as his wife until I was eighteen, the age at which my mother had promised to sanction his suit.

The romance of the idea charmed me, the necessary deceit repelled me, but finally the desire—that every woman who has loved must know—to make the beloved one happy, and to send him on a toilsome, lonely path confident and content, conquered, and I consented. It was necessary to have a confidant, and I did not hesitate to make one of Nellie, who had then become engaged to Tom Blair, Mr. Coston's *bon comrade.*

Young and gay like ourselves, they did not realize how momentous the step to be taken was, and willingly joined in the plot, which they thought very good fun.

Little time was left for thought, and the next evening, having gained permission to spend it with Nellie, I donned my best white muslin frock, first taking out a few tucks to give it a more dignified appearance, bound it round the waist with a broad blue sash, and then, with a furtive attempt at a bridal toilet, fastened some starry white jessamine in my curls.

As I ran down-stairs my mother called me to her, and with an air of loving pride surveyed my simple and, her eyes told me, becoming costume. As she bent over to give me a parting kiss, a bitter pang passed through me, and for the first time in my life I felt unworthy of her love, and was glad to hurry away and join the little party waiting at the corner for me. They laughed at me until their raillery brought back the color to my cheeks; and Nellie, in her white cambric and ribbons, seemed to half envy me as the heroine of an exciting drama.

We proceeded at once to the house of a minister, unworthy of the gospel he preached, and willing for the sake of an extra fee to ask no embarrassing questions and agree to make no revelations. Nellie and Tom stood together, at our right, and in a few moments it was over, and I, a sixteen-year-old girl, a wife.

My young husband called me once by that name, so full of dignity and sweetness, and then took leave of me. So much had his agitation and impassioned declarations of love impressed me, that for the time being I forgot the ordeal to come, and rejoiced in the happiness I had conferred and the consciousness of being so beloved. We separated, and I went home and hastened to my room, glad to have a chance of regaining my self-possession.

There is a homely old couplet—

> "Oh! what a tangled web we weave,
>   When first we venture to deceive,—"

that no one can appreciate until they have "ventured." The next morning at breakfast, my mother's simple questions about the amusements of the evening before put me in an agony of shame and confusion. Never before had I feared to look into her eyes, never before had I told her a deliberate untruth, and yet twenty minutes in her presence made me feel a criminal, every word I uttered increasing my sense of enormity. This was but the beginning.

Happily for me, school kept me away from home during the day; but day or night my secret was with me, until the burden of it became almost intolerable. I did not even dare to weep at night, for by my side lay the dear mother I had deceived, and who trusted me. Sometimes I felt I must tell her, for anything would be better than this continued weight upon my bosom; but when even in the cover of darkness I tried to, the words died away on my lips, and I rose the next day despising myself, not only for my deceit, but for my cowardice.

b   2* *She broke that trust w/ her mother*

One afternoon about a month later I had just returned from school, when the maid brought me a note, which read :

"DEAR MATTIE,—Something dreadful has happened ; let nothing prevent your coming here at once. *The secret is out!*

"NELLIE."

I had been pale before, but now the color rushed to my face, and my mother's sweet, pleasant countenance wore an anxious look as she asked, "Why, Mattie! what is the matter ?"

"Nothing, mother, only Nellie has something to tell me, and wants me to go there right away," I stammered.

"Oh, you girls, you girls, with your mighty secrets and your big conspiracies ! But you may go to Nellie, provided you tell me this hidden mystery when you come back."

"Yes, yes," I said, feverishly, "I will." And tying on my hat, I flew rather than walked to the prim mansion where Nellie dwelt with her maiden aunt.

Nellie met me, white and worried. "Pattie," she said, "something has happened indeed, but don't be afraid ; I have not betrayed you. It seems the night you were married the minister's nurse-maid was in the garden, looking through the window to see what was going on. From her position she could not see you and Ben, but she could see Tom and I standing together, apparently before her master, who was reading the marriage service, and she supposed it to be our wedding. This afternoon she came here to visit our cook, and, not knowing she was telling a secret, began gossiping about it. Cook came right to aunt. You know how stern and severe she is, and she pounced on me, and actually shook me in her anger, as she demanded a 'confession.' I have told her nothing, except that I am not married, and that until I had seen another person I could not in honor explain why we were at the minister's house that night."

This was a blow, and I buried my head in a sofa-cushion, unable to speak. "The worst of it is," went on Nellie, piteously, "that aunt has written a dreadful letter to my mother, telling her to come, and she declares that unless this thing is cleared up before night nothing on earth shall prevent her posting it."

This was enough, and, with Nellie's white lips and red eyes, decided me. Jumping up, I gave her a hug, and then seizing her hand, ran across the hall into her aunt's sitting-room. Never shall I forget how grim, how gray, how pitiless Miss Clancarty looked as she sat bolt upright, in her straight-backed chair, knitting with needles as steely and stiff as herself. I don't know how I got it out, but I did, and, in my relief at extricating Nellie from her dilemma, faced fearlessly the lecture that followed, in the course of which the indignant old lady pictured a most horrid doom for me.

I left the house and walked rapidly home. Indeed,

I was in that state of mental exaltation that sometimes follows extreme excitement, that though the distance was long and the day warm, I felt neither heat nor fatigue, and entered my mother's room like one who had been borne along.

"Well, what is the dreadful secret?" said she, brightly, beckoning me to take my favorite stool at her feet.

"Mother," I said, desperately, "I am married!"

"Who is married? not Nellie, I hope," she answered, not understanding me.

"No, mother; *I* am married."

All the color fled from her face, all the light faded from her eyes, as in a low, intense voice she said, "Pray, who to?"

"To Ben!"

"This is a wretched joke; he is away!" she answered.

"Yes; but we were married before he left."

Without a word she, my gentle mother, pushed me away from her with such a gesture of repulsion and contempt that, utterly dismayed, I uttered a sharp cry and rushed from the room, up to the very top of the house, where, in the old-fashioned garret, I flung myself down among the dusty trunks and chests, to give vent to my grief. Heart-broken, I wept until the tears scorched my eyelids. There I stayed until night, and there my mother's maid found me, with the matter-of-fact summons, "Please come to supper, miss."

Then the thought came to me that my eldest sister

with her husband had arrived during the evening, on a visit, that my mother had told them of my terrible deceit, and that assembled together they were waiting to pass judgment upon me. Pride came to the rescue. I summoned up all my resolution, and, after smoothing the tangles out of my curls and bathing my red eyes, I descended to the dining-room in a spirit of bravado.

When I entered the dining-room, my first glance showed me that my secret had not been revealed by my mother, whose manner was gentle, but so cold that I felt she, as a part of my punishment, had left me to announce my marriage. I could not; a lump rose in my throat when I made an effort, and though they all wondered at my pale face and pink eyelids, they left the table still in ignorance.

In the mean time Tom had written to my young husband, giving him a full and sensational account of the *denouement;* and Mr. Coston, supposing that all my family were now aware of the step we had taken, at once wrote to me. The next morning when I came down to my breakfast, in the bravery of a pink and white cambric, with a lot of pink ribbons and an assumed air of indifference, I was startled by finding on my plate a very big letter, directed in a large round hand to—

"Mrs. B. Franklin Coston."

Involuntarily my hand closed upon it, when I became aware that every eye in the room was concentrated upon me, and I suppose something in the incongruity of the title with my short dress, curls, and

married women wore their hair up and long dresses (I think)

childish assumption of dignity, touched them with **a** sense of the ludicrous, for there was a general burst of laughter; that, however, made my confession easier, because it softened their severity.

The next day Mr. Coston came on from New York, from whence he was to have sailed, and after not a little sermonizing, and a great deal of discussion, we were forgiven. My dresses were ordered to be let down, my curls were caught up and fastened with a matronly-looking comb, and I made a huge effort to assume a manner more in accordance with my new dignity.

Through the influence of Mr. Coston's friends the Secretary of the Navy withdrew his orders for the two years' scientific expedition, and, instead, stationed Mr. Coston in the Washington Navy-Yard, giving him at the same time one of the pleasantest dwellings there for our home; and so it happened that before I knew the real meaning of life I entered upon its most serious phase.

Happy to do this

not a long marriage

she played the perfect wife "eye candy"

CHAPTER III.

WHAT COSTON ACCOMPLISHED.

FOUR beautiful years of love and happiness passed swiftly away, and found us the parents of two lovely boys, and the centre of a circle of delightful friends. My husband, who saw in me the very queen of women, and was proud of my youth and of the attention I commanded, found pleasure in society, and together we enjoyed the most agreeable phases of life in Washington.

During this time my husband originated and perfected many inventions of great use and value to the government. A pyrotechnic laboratory for which Congress made an appropriation was built after his plan and under his immediate supervision, with a detached roof in case of explosion. The interior, with its neat and ingenious arrangement, the exhibit of the rocket machine, percussion-cap machine, etc., were the results of his energy and skill. Mr. Coston was also the officer appointed by the Secretary of the Navy to receive the secret of the manufacture of the Hale rocket, as the following letter will show:

"BUREAU OF ORDNANCE AND HYDROGRAPHY,
"Dec. 30, 1846.

"SIR:

"Upon receipt of this, you will repair to the Arsenal, and join Commander Powell, who is ordered to give his attention to the making of Hale's rockets, the right to which has been disposed of by Mr. J. B. Hyde to the War and Navy Departments. You are associated with Commander Powell for the purpose of gaining the information necessary to their complete preparation. As this is a confidential matter, it is necessary to apprise you of the propriety of keeping everything in relation to it secret.

"Respectfully your obt. servant,

"L. WARRINGTON,
Com., Chief of Bureau.

"B. F. COSTON, ESQ.,
"*Master, U. S. Navy-Yard, Washington.*"

The right to use the Hale rocket was purchased by Congress for twenty-five thousand dollars, and Mr. Coston made all these same rockets used by the government during the Mexican war.

One of Mr. Coston's most remarkable inventions was that of the cannon percussion primer. The commander of the yard, Commodore Aulick, and Lieutenant Dahlgren (afterwards Admiral) were very anxious to gain the secret of the composition necessary to manufacture this primer, and wrote Mr. Coston the following letter:

"COMMANDANT'S OFFICE, NAVY-YARD,
"WASHINGTON, Feb. 2, 1846.

"SIR:

"You will please furnish me with a statement of the ingredients, and their proportions, forming the composition of the cannon percussion primers which were tested and approved of by the officers of this yard a few days since; also, the quantity, by weight, of the composition used for a single cap, and an estimate of their cost per thousand when complete for service. As it is deemed proper that this information should accompany the report of the Bureau of Ordnance, etc., of the tests referred to, you will please furnish it me with as little delay as possible.

    " Very respectfully your obedient servant,

" J. H. Aulick,

" *Commandant.*

" Master B. F. Coston,

    " *U. S. Navy.*"

To which Mr. Coston sent the following reply :

" Laboratory, Navy-Yard,

" Washington, Feb. 2, 1846.

" Sir :

    " I had the honor to receive your order of this morning, requesting a statement of the ingredients, and their proportions, forming the composition of the cannon percussion primers which were tested and approved of by the officers of this yard a few days ago. As I consider the composition of the above-mentioned caps as my private property, as much so as the remainder of my private receipts, I must respectfully decline making this composition known until I have seen the honorable Secretary of the Navy on the subject. I have no objection, however, to make any number of caps you may order in the same manner as those mentioned above.

    " In answer to your second inquiry, as to the weight of composition in a single cap, I would state that they contain sixteen grains each, and that their cost per thousand, ready for service, would be as follows :

Composition ready for use . . .	$4.50
Varnish	1.22
Paper	18
Labor	3.41
Total . .	$9.31

" Very respectfully yours,

" B. Franklin Coston.

" Com. J. H. Aulick,

    " *Comd. U. S. Yard, Washington.*"

It will be seen from Mr. Coston's answer that he regarded the primer as his " own private property," and his reason for refusing to make known or surrender the secret of its composition was that the Secretary of the Navy had not, after a lapse of two or three years, remembered his promise to ask Congress to create an acceptable office for him, with just compensation. But after his reply was sent, he at once called upon the Secretary. During their interview that gentleman recommended him strongly to give the secret of the composition of the cannon percussion primer to the navy, promising at the same time that at the next Congress he, the Secretary, would ask by letter that a proper and acceptable office should be created for Mr. Coston, as he was not then in the line of promotion ; and being constantly in danger from explosions, he would not, under these circumstances, be able to leave a proper pension or provision for his family in case of death.

The honorable Secretary of the Navy, then Mr. George Bancroft, kept his word, my husband having on his recommendation given the secret, receipts, etc., of the primer to the navy. The government had been for some time in the full use and enjoyment of the primer, when at the meeting of the next Congress Mr. Bancroft addressed a letter to that Congress, asking that the office of lieutenant-commander, with the pay of three thousand five hundred dollars per annum, be created ; no office of this kind then existing.

A bill to this effect was brought before the Senate, and passed unanimously by that body, which then boasted the brains and genius of Clay, Webster, Cass, Benton, and others hardly less great in intellect. Unfortunately, however, Mr. Coston had a rival in the ordnance line, and the jealousy which had been smouldering for some time burst forth in the active influence brought to bear on the House of Representatives; and when the bill reached that body, for the more perfect satisfaction of its enemies, the office of pyrotechnist, with a salary of fifteen hundred dollars per annum, with no rank and no residence in the navy-yard, was created.

This of course was not so acceptable as the office Mr. Coston then held, the honor, pay, and perquisites being alike less. Mr. Coston positively refused, and never did accept the said office of pyrotechnist; therefore the government had the benefit of his inventions without his receiving any recompense whatever. About this time my husband's health began to be seriously affected by the constant inhalation of chemical gases while experimenting, so he resolved to resign his position as master in the navy, and head of the laboratory.

This he did notwithstanding the earnest entreaties of the Hon. John Y. Mason, the successor of the Hon. George Bancroft as Secretary of the Navy. Mr. Mason fully appreciated the serious loss the government would sustain in Mr. Coston's resignation; he visited my husband at the residence of the succeeding commandant, Commodore McCauley, promising to have the rejected bill reconsidered by the next Congress, adding that rather than Mr. Coston should go, and his services and talents be lost to the government, he would take the responsibility of paying him a salary at his own risk, until it became a law by Act of Congress.

Mr. Coston keenly appreciated Mr. Mason's offer, but his feelings were so deeply wounded at the treatment he had received at the hands of the government that he had already accepted the position of president of a Boston Gas Company, through Mr. David Henshaw, Ex-Secretary of the Navy. This gentleman paid twenty thousand dollars for a share in Mr. Coston's patent,—a portable gas apparatus, the first ever invented, and used by the company at the time. And here I should like to add a fact that will not be uninteresting to my readers: that the first gas ever made or burned in the city of Washington was made at Mr. Coston's own residence in the United States navy-yard, of Washington, after his own patent.

Before resuming my story, I should like to insert here a letter of Commodore (afterwards Admiral) Charles Stewart, of the United States navy, to a friend, which will show the esteem in which that gentleman held my husband:

"PHILADELPHIA, 20th Feb., 18—.

"MY DEAR SIR:

"Five or six years have elapsed since I had the pleasure of shaking you by the hand, but I hope before the session is over I shall have that pleasure again.

"I observe that the Senate has attached an amendment to the Naval Appropriation bill, by providing a salary with rank for a pyrotechnist and chemist. I am truly glad of this, as the service has too long suffered for the want of a properly qualified person to fill such a station. The young gentleman who has been performing that duty for the last three years was at my instance appointed a sailing-master in the navy, in consequence of his entire knowledge of pyrotechny and his competency as a chemist. The various beneficial improvements already introduced into the service by him have saved the government a large sum of money.

"I have taken the liberty of giving him a letter to you in order that you may know him personally. I can only say he is one of the prodigies of the age. He is stationed at the Washington Navy-Yard in charge of the laboratory. I should like you to visit it, and converse with him, and I doubt not that you will then arrive at the conclusion that the service is fortunate in having a person like him attached to it. In which case, I am sure you will readily advocate the Senate's amendment; and wishing you health and happiness,

"I am truly your friend,

"CHARLES STEWART,
"Commodore.

"HON. T. BUTLER KING,
   "*House of Representatives, Washington City.*"

CHAPTER IV.

WASHINGTON SOCIETY "BEFO' DE WAH."

IT was with genuine regret that I prepared to break up our pleasant home in the navy-yard, and the impending departure perhaps heightened my enjoyment of the last season I was to spend for some time in Washington, and impressed more vividly upon my mind the brilliant affairs of which I was about to take leave.

3*

The cabinet parties and the receptions at the foreign legations were unusually gay that winter, but the great crush of the season was at a ball given by the Hon. John Y. Mason, then Secretary of the Navy; and a little incident that occurred that evening stamped it upon my memory. The dazzling illuminations, heavy fragrance of the cut flowers, the gay music, intense heat, and the throngs of people surging to and fro within the drawing-rooms, made me quite faint,—so much so that, afraid of succumbing, I went up-stairs to seek the comparative quiet of the ladies' dressing-room.

As I entered it, I noticed an old lady sitting upright in an arm-chair, and dressed in a rich silk, brocaded with huge gold flowers. Over her gray curls was placed a large crape turban, and there was an air of distinction about her, enhanced by her mode of waving her large feather fan, while she critically surveyed each new-comer in a condescending manner.

After looking me over from head to foot, she said, abruptly,—

" Ill, child ?"

" The heat and the crowd below are too much for me, madam," I replied.

" Too much for any Christian. I was driven up here on that account myself," she nodded approvingly. And then she launched on such a pleasant and amusing dissertation on society, that I forgot my ill feelings, and was highly entertained. Very soon my husband came to the door to inquire after me. The old lady, whom he at once recognized as Mrs. President Madison, beckoned him to enter, and when I introduced him as my husband, she exclaimed, in a horrified voice, "Why, you are not married? You are nothing but children!"

Excitement had left a slight flush on Mr. Coston's cheeks; and his eyes bright with excitement gave him a boyish look, while my own flowing curls and slight figure clad in pure white, ornamented with lilies of the valley, I suppose gave me anything but a matronly appearance. For some reason the old lady seemed to take a fancy to us both, and frequently afterwards came to visit us at our cosey home in the navy-yard, where she treated us to many amusing reminiscences.

In those days before the war society at the capital was of a more refined and elegant character than even now. In a measure I attribute this to the presence of many lovely Southern women, who as a rule were highly accomplished, exquisite in manner, and gave a certain tone to the gay circles of Washington. After the war fortune changed hands; the *nouveaux riche* ruled with a hand heavy with gold, and often ingrained with dirt.

The older population, sensitive and shocked, withdrew from society at large and formed a small and exclusive set of their own. I may be pardoned here for digressing a little, in order to mention that this same set were thrilled with horror when it was known that the wife of President Lincoln had inaugurated the custom of shaking hands with the populace at her public receptions; a custom never before practised by the lady of the White House. Mrs. Tyler, Mrs. Polk, Miss Harriet Lane, would never have consented to it; and

I know Mrs. Grant disliked it, for I remember being present at one of her receptions during the Grant administration and hearing her say in a tone of utter disgust, "Oh, how sticky my glove is!"

To return to my subject; society before the great rebellion was also distinguished by the presence of many brilliant people. I remember at one cabinet party chatting with Henry Clay, whom I had often heard speak in the Senate when the silence was so intense as to become oppressive. Mr. Clay was a great ladies' man, and I can see him now as he entered the drawing-room of the White House, tall, slender, and very dignified. His face was striking, with its lofty forehead, unusually large but eloquent mouth, prominent nose, and electrical blue eyes. His appearance always excited the curiosity of strangers, and the exclamation, "Who is he?" could almost be seen to issue from their lips.

On Mr. Clay's arm on this occasion was leaning one of the belles of Washington, Miss Ada Smith, a daughter of Major Smith, and a dazzling blonde of great perfection of feature and charming manners. Daniel Webster's large, deep-set eyes watched the tour of this exceptional couple round the salon, and as he turned his splendid and massive head to do so, met my gaze, and in his deliberate manner crossed the room and paid his respects to me, with the air of hauteur and reserve he maintained towards even his *intimes.*

We frequently met General Winfield Scott, who was perhaps the most gallant great man in the capital at that time. When I was first presented to him he said, with a profound salute, " I recognize madame to be a Baltimore lady."

As I happened to be one by birth this took me by surprise, for I was too ingenuous to understand that this was merely the general's mode of complimenting, as then, even more than now, Baltimore women were famous for their beauty. Was it not N. P. Willis who wrote, " I have seen the women of every civilized land, the fair Saxon, the dark-eyed Italian, the stately Spaniard, the fascinating Frenchwoman, the classic Greek, the blue-eyed German, and the houris 'of the East, but for grace and beauty the women of Baltimore carry off the crown from the world" ?

I fancy now General Scott must have been very much amused at my simplicity. It was many years before I encountered the stately old warrior again, and then under peculiar circumstances.

Delightful as we both considered society, our real happiness was found in our own home. My husband's inventions were of absorbing interest to me, and many nights we spent the silent hours together in his study, he pursuing his investigations, and I at his side to cheer, encourage, and look after his personal comfort.

Our children were lovely and healthy, and when a third son was born to me on the eve of our departure from Washington, I remember thinking, during my long convalescence, how good God had been to us. Health, youth, fame, a fair share of fortune, many friends, and these three baby angels to crown our happiness. Was this not more than we had a right to?

Before leaving, we received many kind and flattering testimonials from scientific *confrères* of Mr. Coston's, but perhaps none pleased him more than the following letter from his men, to whom he was much attached:

"Navy-Yard,
"Washington, Aug. 7, 1847.

"Sir:

"The undersigned, the workingmen of the department lately under your efficient charge, hereby respectfully express our unfeigned regret of the necessity that separates us.

"The gentlemanly and urbane treatment we have invariably received from you while under your charge will ever be fresh in our minds and held in grateful remembrance.

"Wishing you prosperity in all your undertakings, and health and happiness for the future, we take our leave and subscribe ourselves,

"Very respectfully,
"Your obt. servants,
"Jer. Cross,
"Andrew Martin,
"James Jordan,
"Daniel Kleiss,
"John Pigott,
"John S. Davis,
"George Breast,
"Daniel Carroll,
"W. Bradley,
"John M. McFarland,
"Wm. Harrison,
"Robert Peake,
"Chas. Robinson.

"B. Franklin Coston, Esq."

CHAPTER V.

BEREFT—A DISCOVERY.

FROM Washington we moved to Boston. The first year passed very quietly away. Contrasted with our life in Washington, the city seemed dull, and society stiff and cold. However, I devoted more time to my little ones, and when a fourth son came to us in the very image of his blessed father, he was welcomed as another source of joy and occupation.

Shortly after the arrival of the new treasure, my husband was called to Washington on business; on his way home he was taken so suddenly and severely ill that he was obliged to stop at Philadelphia and be carried to an hotel. His illness, originally caused by cold, developed into a sharp fever, and when I reached his side he was in a dangerous condition. The physicians who had met in consultation agreed upon the necessity of absolute quiet, without which they said Mr. Coston's recovery was impossible. With their sanction, I at once took a small furnished cottage on a quiet street, and with great difficulty removed him to it.

My readers will forgive me, I am sure, for not dwelling on this part of my story, still so exquisitely

painful that in recalling it the paper grows dim before
me. Suffice it to say that after three months of extreme suffering, my beloved husband expired in my
arms, and in the same dear old city which I had left
with him a few years before, a happy child bride.
Absolutely stunned by this blow, which so terribly
ended our brief and beautiful married life, I turned
like some wounded animal to her young for consolation.

At my mother's solicitation I broke up my home,
and with my children took up my residence with her.
Scarcely had we entered upon this new arrangement,
when my beautiful baby boy Edward was taken ill,
and in spite of the tenderest care and nursing his innocent spirit soon fled to join that of his father in another
world.

The dreadful thought that my husband's death was
but the beginning of calamity seized me on this second misfortune, but I tried to defy my presentiment,
and devoted myself to the care of my mother. For a
time I think I must have been so dazed in mind and
so nearly broken in body that I did not realize my
mother's declining health, until all at once I was
roused to the fact that every month found her more
delicate and feeble.

Sometimes, though, one does not recognize in a new
sorrow a blessing. Even in her suffering my mother
retained her angelic disposition, her gentle wisdom, and
power of wise counsel. Throughout her long illness
her words of love softened my heart and soothed my

mind, and I devoted myself with renewed energy to be a comfort to her. My reward came, when with her dying breath she whispered, "My angel child."

When she had passed away, I felt that I was indeed adrift. I had lost both my anchor and my pilot, and was at the mercy of unknown seas. With redoubled yearning my heart turned towards my only treasures on earth, and the pangs of necessity roused me to the need of a better understanding of my business affairs.

The drafts that had been sent to me from Boston had rapidly diminished in number and amount, and I wished to comprehend what resources and income I had to depend upon for the maintenance and education of my dear children. Another and a new shock awaited me. Absorbed as I had been in nursing and caring for my dear ones, and implicitly believing in common honesty, I had not demanded, as I should have done, more accurate accounts of the men who were in business with my husband; nor had I realized the enormous expense illness and death had entailed, and which my husband's business associates insisted had swallowed up the ready capital.

To be brief, through my own ignorance and the duplicity of others, trusting too much to an improvident relative who misplaced my money, I found myself at twenty-one a widow with three little children and penniless. I knew not how to dig, I was ashamed to beg; and long and intently I pondered upon the course I should pursue, and earnestly I wished that *clearly she had some intelligence*

nature had bestowed upon me a little of that brilliant genius so liberally given to my husband.

In thinking of him my mind reverted to a box of papers which, in his last illness, he alluded to as being of considerable value, and the thought came to me like an inspiration that perhaps in that same box I should find the means of retrieving my fallen fortunes.

It was on a dreary November afternoon, the rain was falling on the window-panes heavily, the boughs of the great birch in front of our cottage scraped the walls with a mournful sound; even the canaries in their cages were so depressed by the pervading gloom that they refused to sing, and the children bent seriously over their picture-books.

All these trifles were impressed upon my mind, I suppose because I felt the importance of the next step, which was to decide possibly our whole future. As I unlocked the wooden chest and raised the lid, it was with a prayer in my heart and tears in my eyes. There I beheld numerous packets carefully sealed and labelled. One by one I lifted them out, only to be told by the title of the contents of unfinished inventions, inventions too costly to be utilized, and successful experiments in chemistry to be used in different branches of pyrotechnics.

At last I came upon a large envelope containing papers and a skilfully drawn plan of signals to be used at sea, at night, for the same purposes of communication that flags are used by day. This chart was colored, and showed that to each signal was attached a number

COSTON'S NIGHT SIGNALS.

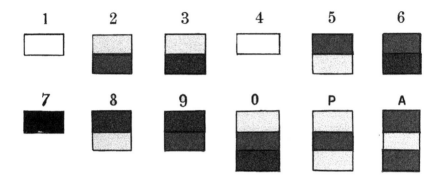

EXPLANATION.

The Signals, while burning, will show the colors and correspond with the numbers and letters as above indicated. EXAMPLE:—No. 1, white light, being shown, followed by No. 3, then followed by No. 6, making 136. See Signal Book.

and letter explanatory of the particular colored fire used, so that in lighting the signals no mistakes should be made. I recognized this idea as one discussed in the days of our courtship, and greatly encouraged by Admiral Stewart.

I also remembered my husband making a few of these signals at the Washington Navy-Yard, and giving them into the care of a naval officer until such time as they could be tried. All at once rose before me like a vision a visit of this same officer to my husband on his death-bed, and his promise that if the invention proved a success he would interest himself in making it public for the benefit of his wife and children.

My course lay clear before me. I closed the box and at once sat down at my desk. I saw the immense value of the invention, and wrote to Captain —— asking what use he had made of the signals.

Days passed; no reply came. I called at the captain's house; he refused to see me. Twice I met him on the street; he turned on his heel and went in another direction to avoid me.

Fortunately for me, just at this time he got into disgrace, and was put upon the retired list. Of course he brought every possible influence to bear to gain his restoration. I seized this opportunity, and wrote Captain —— a peremptory letter, saying if he did not at once return to me the box of signals I should report him to the Navy Department.

Next day the box of signals arrived, much damaged, having been exposed to all kinds of weather, but unac-

companied by the written recipes for their manufacture; the captain declaring in a note that he had not
received any recipes from Mr. Coston. This staggered
me, but my anxiety for the time being was to place the
box in a place of safety, for I had no means of knowing whether the signals were explosive, and would affect
the insurance on the house.

In this dilemma I conceived the idea of asking our
old and stanch friend Admiral Charles Stewart to keep
them for me in the Philadelphia Navy-Yard until I
could secure an order from the Secretary of the Navy
for their trial. The admiral said if they belonged to
the government he had the authority to store them; this
I was willing to certify to, as they were made of government materials, and in the Washington Navy-Yard.
Without further delay they were placed in store.

My old friends in Washington were greatly interested
in my efforts to make known my husband's invention,
and insisted on entertaining me in their homes until
further steps could be taken. The Secretary of the
Navy, Mr. Isaac Toucey, listened with interest to my
appeal, and replied that I certainly had a right to my
husband's brains, even when put into government materials, and that anything coming before the Navy Department with the prestige of Mr. Coston's acknowl-
edged and brilliant inventive genius would be favorably
received. He readily consented to a trial of the signals,
and asked me where I should like it to be made. I
replied, "in the Home Squadron."

The order was given, and the Assistant Secretary

suggested that I should write to the officers of the flag-ship "Wabash" and make myself known. I knew none of them, but thought the Secretary's advice good, and wrote at once to the commanding officer. To my surprise I received an exceedingly kind letter by return mail from Commodore (afterwards Admiral) Paulding, to the effect that though I did not compliment by re-membering him, he had once had the pleasure of escort-ing me and my little ones from Washington to Phila-delphia, my friends having put me in his care.

I at once recollected the circumstance, and also the fact that under the impression that his name was Bald-win I had been unable to identify him afterwards, his delicacy deterring him from correcting my mistake at the time. I remembered his exceeding courtesy and kindness, and now accepted as providential his offer to do all in his power to serve me in promoting the trial of the signals. In making my acknowledgments I asked him to kindly save me a few signals should they prove good, for models, as I had no recipe to make others from.

4*

CHAPTER VI.

A STRUGGLE AND SUCCESS.

JUST at this time of suspense and anxiety my second child, a beautiful boy, strikingly like his father and named after him, was taken ill, and after a long and painful illness expired. I was roused from my grief by a letter that came from Admiral Paulding, telling me that the trial had taken place, and that the signals proved utterly *good for nothing !*

This bitter blow was dealt in kinder language, but all the same the hard fact stared me in the face, and I hardly comprehended the close of the letter in which the admiral said he had told the Secretary of the Navy that the idea was an excellent one, and that I ought to be encouraged to carry it out; pleasantly concluding that he would not be the one to put my lights out.

Shortly after this the Secretary of the Navy wrote me himself, enclosing a copy of the adverse report, and warmly encouraging me to try and perfect my husband's invention, for which purpose he offered to place the laboratory of the Washington Navy-Yard, and its talent, at my service. I need not say how deeply I felt this generous treatment.

The man whom Admiral Dahlgren had caused to be made the successor of Mr. Coston as master of the navy-yard laboratory the more to mortify him, was much alarmed when bidden to perfect the signal invention, and after six months of worry and work he produced something less effective than his model, and another adverse report was made.

I have reason to think that this man was afraid of succeeding, as his success would have incurred the displeasure of Admiral Dahlgren, who preferred that I should not be brought in contact with the men who were engaged in manufacturing the primer.

Shortly afterwards, the master of the laboratory died, and it was said that his fatal illness had been accelerated by worry over the signal experiments, his mortification at not being able to perfect the invention, ending in fear of his being considered incompetent to fill his position, and the dread that if he did succeed in doing so Admiral Dahlgren would secure his dismissal was more than he could endure.

Again the Secretary of the Navy wrote me most kindly, and bade me not despair, adding that if I could find some one to aid me in perfecting the signals, he would pay the expenses from the contingent fund, as he felt satisfied that the invention if properly carried out would be of incalculable service to the government.

It would consume too much space, and weary my readers, for me to go into all the particulars of my efforts to perfect my husband's idea. The men I employed and dismissed, the experiments I made myself, the frauds that were practised upon me, almost disheartened me; but despair I would not, and eagerly I treasured up each little step that was made in the right direction, the hints of naval officers, and the opinions of the different boards that gave the signals a trial.

I had finally succeeded in getting a pure white and a vivid red light, but a third color was essential in order to make the necessary transpositions for the figures whereby to talk with the signals from the signal-book, which contains questions and answers with numbers and letters attached.

Blue I had set my heart on, in order to use the national colors, but I could not obtain it of equal intensity and strength with the other colors, and, considering the long distances at which these signals needed to be seen, this was a primary consideration.

The honorable Secretary of the Navy, Mr. Isaac Toucey, again sent me a kind note with the last adverse report, and bade me to "try again" to work out the invention, and whenever I thought I had succeeded, he would grant me a board to give them a trial.

As the months rolled on I grew desperate. I had eked out my little means as well as I could, and now I stood face to face with penury. My children, lovely and good, were growing fast, and had other needs than those of clothes and food, and my determination to succeed grew with the obstacles that arose.

At this time the whole country was in a ferment over the successful laying of the Atlantic cable, and tremendous was the excitement on the day when the first cable despatch flashed under the sea from Queen Victoria to President Buchanan.

Cyrus W. Field received a great ovation in New York City, and at night there was a grand display of fireworks, which took place from the City Hall. Fiery portraits of the Queen and the President, wreaths, rockets, Roman candles, banners, eagles, wheels, showers of colored stars, and finally ships of fire were represented paying out cables of highly-tinted lights.

This display suggested to me that among the New York pyrotechnists I might find some one capable of helping me. I opened communication with several of them, under a man's name, fearing they would not give heed to a woman, asking for a strong, clear, blue or green light, but not saying for what purpose I wished to make use of it. One man in an intelligent reply said he had several years before invented a pure blue, but threw it on one side on account of its being too expensive for ordinary use. I replied urging him to recover the color if possible; if not, to try green.

In ten days I received a package at my country home near Philadelphia, containing the desired colors, and I persuaded a friend to drive to a mountain some five miles distant, and burn them to show me the color. The trial was a success: the green fire brilliant and intense. I at once entered into negotiations with the pyrotechnist, and having received satisfactory references took him into my confidence, and engaged him to make further experiments.

It was necessary not only that each color should be

powerful and clear, but of uniform goodness when
manufactured in large quantities, and also that the
colors should be made to change one from the other
with the rapidity of lightning, each change being absolutely clean and distinct, there being, for convenience,
two or three colors in one case.

After weeks of work and experimenting, which I
spent at the house of the manufacturer, to whom I had
made myself known, in order to give him the results
of my own labors, his brother-in-law, a much more
skilful chemist, came to assist us, and we at last succeeded in producing such satisfactory results that I at
once wrote to the honorable Secretary of the Navy that
if he would be as good as his word and order me a
trial by board, I would be glad once more to present
my signals.

The Secretary was as good as his word, and at once
appointed a board, consisting of the then Commodore
John Rodgers, Commodore McCauley, and Lieutenant
Charles Henry Lewis. The board notified me of its
readiness with such promptness that, to tell the truth,
I was a little taken aback and obliged to ask for a few
days' delay, while I made my own preparations. At
last all was in readiness; the board was supplied with
signals, and I was politely invited to be present at the
trial with a number of my personal friends.

I was still in deep mourning, and possibly my
sombre apparel increased my pallor, for when the
preparations were made to fire the first signal, my
friends were looking at me with anxiety. The mo-

ment was indeed a momentous one for me, but all at once, clear, brilliant, and beautiful, burned against the dark sky the first Coston Night Signal. The exclamation of joy from those with me, and of pleasure from the officers on deck, assured me that I was not dreaming. Success at last! My heart was too full of emotion for me to speak.

I was then informed by the officers that a month's trial was necessary before any official report could be made, as it was imperative that the signals should be tested in different states of the atmosphere and at different distances. During this month, which was one of trial to me as well as for the signals, I remained with my friends, anxious but hopeful as to the result, upon which the whole future of my boys and self depended.

Four weeks dragged their slow length away; at the close of the last, my friends took me to a fashionable concert one evening, and among the audience I recognized one of the officers of the board. During the first interim, this gentleman came up smiling, took my hand, and said, " Let me congratulate you." I was so nervous that I did not dare to ask him any questions, but remarked, as I fluttered my fan,—

" The prima donna has surpassed herself this evening."

" The prima donna is nothing to you; you are a success," replied the officer, gallantly, and then he told me, under seal of confidence, that that day a favorable report had been sent in to the Secretary of the Navy, and to-morrow I would receive a formal notice and invitation to meet the board.

" You will not betray me," my informer concluded ; " but really I could not resist the temptation to tell you myself."

That evening my host insisted on celebrating my good fortune by a champagne supper, and I went to rest that night a very happy woman.

Early in the morning I received several notes from the different members of the board, and each told me *entre nous* of my success, which they desired me to hear of through them for the first time, and each writer in concluding begged I would not betray him to the other members of the board, as this mode of intimation was contrary to all official etiquette.

Later in the day I met the board formally, but not without a sense of the ludicrous, for each officer flattered himself on the innocent pleasure he had given me, and each feared I might inadvertently betray him, and was correspondingly pleased with the air of uncertainty I felt obliged to assume.

The president of the board, afterwards Admiral John Rodgers, saluted me with the remark, " Madam, your husband's mantle has fallen upon your fair shoulders."

The report, most favorable to the signals, was then read.

" WASHINGTON, DISTRICT OF COLUMBIA,
" February, 1859.
" TO THE HON. ISAAC TOUCEY, *Secretary of the Navy :*
" SIR : In obedience to your order of the 31st ultimo, the board

of officers ordered to examine and test the Coston Signals have the honor unanimously to report—

" 1. That the Coston Signals are better than any others known to them.

" 2. That the board strongly recommend them for use in the navy.

" 3. In stating ' their reasons for the conclusions or recommendations' to which they have arrived, it may not be out of place to say that signals being the means whereby orders are given or wants made known at sea, a good code of them, plainly intelligible to the persons addressed, is absolutely necessary to the efficient conduct of a fleet.

" In the navy two signal-books are used : one called simply the 'Signal-Book,' the other the 'Telegraphic Dictionary.' A peculiar flag designates when the Telegraphic Dictionary is to be employed ; without this flag, the meaning is to be sought in the signal-book.

" The signal-book consists of all the sentences, arranged alphabetically, which would occur in ordinary service, numbered consecutively from 1 to about 1300. The Telegraphic Dictionary has an alphabet, and the words of the language numbered from 1 to the end of the book, whereby an unusual name may be spelled by the alphabet, or any ordinary word designated by its proper number in the dictionary. By means of the numerical values attached to the signal flags the ship makes the number attached to the sentences or words in the signal-books ; and thus communications of any nature are mutually made between vessels.

" But in practice at night it has been found so difficult to make clear and distinct combinations of lights that the books in use by day were thrown aside, and a set of night signals were arranged in a separate code, of little extent and of uncertain determination.

" The Coston Signals consist of a colored firework, or a combination of not more than three colors, contained in a small metal case, and they designate by the order of the colors burnt the number to be understood.

" The application of the ' Coston Night Signals' to the navy

c   d   5

day signal-books gives a perfect code of night signals. They offer precision, fulness, and plainness, at a less cost for fireworks than it is thought we now pay for confusion and uncertainty.

" Very respectfully, your obedient servants,

" C. S. McCauley, *Captain and Senior Officer.*

" John Rodgers, *Commander U.S.N.*

" Henry H. Lewis, *Lieutenant U.S.N.*"

I received the congratulations of the other gentlemen and then, with a light heart, took the admiral's advice and went at once to the Navy Department. The Secretary of the Navy received me most cordially, saying, " Mrs. Coston, I knew I had not overrated you. Now, what is the next step, and what can I do for you? But first, what are these signals worth ?"

CHAPTER VII.

THE FIRST FRUITS.

It may seem strange to my readers, but so intently had my mind been concentrated on the one object of perfecting the signals, that I had never given their pecuniary value a thought, and for a moment I was overcome by this prompt and practical recognition of their worth. I stammered out that I could not tell. Mr. Toucey replied, with a smile, " There you show the woman; but after this long period of labor you should begin to reap some reward. Consult with your friends, fix on a price, not forgetting you deserve a fair one, and call here to-morrow."

I went home. Never had the sky struck me as so blue, the sunshine so radiant, the little parks so green and smiling, and the songs of the birds so melodious. I trod on air, and felt myself to be the most fortunate woman in the world, all the while blessing in my heart that good man, Mr. Isaac Toucey, who had been so real a friend, and whose goodness was now to be reflected in the happiness of my children.

I hastily consulted with my friends in regard to the price I should fix upon the signals, deciding on what seemed a fair rate, and then, not waiting to consult with my manufacturer, called on the Secretary with my decision.

Mr. Toucey at once sent for the Chief of the Bureau of Ordnance, a Captain Ingraham, told him briefly of the board's report on the signals, and that as the patent could only be bought by Congress, and the adoption of the signals for the use of the navy was desirable, he wanted an estimate of the amount needed to supply all our fleets in different parts of the world with sufficient quantities for trials on long cruises and in different climates.

Without knowing why, I felt intuitively that I had in Captain Ingraham an opponent, and I was hardly surprised, though visibly disappointed, when, a few moments later, he handed in an estimate for a very small amount. Mr. Toucey looked at it in astonishment, and then, with a twinkle in his kindly eye, said, "Mrs. Coston, are there not two sizes of the signals?"

I took the hint and responded at once, "There are to be, sir; the large size being double the price of the ordinary one."

"Then," said the Secretary to Captain Ingraham, "just add to your estimate an equal amount of the large signals;" and, evidently much against his inclination, the captain had to do it.

The signals were ordered to be divided between the North and South Atlantic, the North and South Pacific, and the African fleets, with orders for the commanding officer on the vessels to report on their trial from time to time, and I at once prepared the following letter to accompany the signals:

"COSTON'S TELEGRAPHIC NIGHT SIGNALS.

" *To the officers authorized to test the Coston Night Signals at sea on a long cruise:*

"GENTLEMEN: The honorable Secretary of the United States Navy having ordered three hundred sets of Coston Telegraphic Signals for distribution to vessels of the United States Navy (after several very satisfactory trials at Washington, by boards of officers convened for this purpose), as officers of *such* vessels you should be acquainted with the merits and objects of the said signals. I would beg leave to state that my late husband, Benjamin Franklin Coston, aware of the importance of a reliable system of signals for the purposes of communication between distant points at night, in cases of distress or in times of war, as well as for other purposes, conceived the idea of combining certain different-colored pyrotechnical fires in a case, to represent certain numbers or figures, according to a prearranged chart, *so long ago as in the year* 1840, and made one trial of his plan the following year at Hampton

Roads, off Norfolk, Virginia, by order of the honorable Secretary of the Navy. But before he had fully perfected it, it being incomplete for practical purposes, *my husband died*, leaving me in possession of merely a rough chart of his idea, without good recipes for the perfect combination of chemicals necessary for its perfection, which, together with the adverse circumstances arising from the difficulty of having the signals properly made, as I had to employ many chemists before succeeding, occupying a term of years, having tried all the different plans which the intellect could suggest, among which was the rocket-pistol, holder, with trigger, etc., the result of the experiments of each different chemist and pyrotechnist being presented for trial to the different boards which the honorable Secretary of the United States Navy was always so amiable as to grant me, thereby aiding me in a work which has finally succeeded, I hope, for the good of mankind, and which I am at last enabled to bring before you.

" The importance of being able to communicate between distant points at night under almost any circumstances can hardly be estimated, and in the Coston Signal, I think, you will find all that can be desired. These signals have already been tested in various ways and under different states of atmosphere, and, as the annexed report to the Secretary of the Navy will show, were pronounced superior to any heretofore seen or used. A set of the Coston Signals consists of twelve pieces, and are marked 1, 2, 3, 4, 5, 6, 7, 8, 9, 0, P, A, respectively. The P (or preparatory) signal is used to give notice to the point you wish to communicate with, and the A (answering) signal signifies that the preparatory was seen; the numerals are to be used as the day flag signals, with the exception that only one night signal can be burnt at a time, but at an interval of only the time required to put another on the holder. It is highly important to keep the signals in a perfect state, and in a dry place on deck. They are not subject to spontaneous combustion, being decidedly more safe to use at sea than any other pyrotechnic fire. From the small number of signals necessarily at your disposal for trial, it will, of course, be impossible by any previously devised system to communicate full sentences of any considerable length; your attention ought, therefore, be directed to establish the fact whether the system is practical, and advisable to adopt in the place of what is now used by you for the same purpose. The small size signals can be well seen at a distance of from four to six miles and the large size from six to ten or fifteen miles, with perfect distinctness.

" I am, gentlemen, most respectfully, your obedient servant,

" MARTHA J. COSTON,

" *Widow of the late B. Franklin Coston.*

" WASHINGTON, D. C., June 1, 1859."*

The day after receiving the orders, I left for New York to consult with my manufacturer, having an order for six thousand dollars, the first fruit of my perseverance, in my possession. A copartnership was agreed upon between the manufacturer and myself, he looking well to his own interests, as seems to be the custom in the business world. *Still juded by ruthlessness*

It was decided that he should pay for the patents, two being taken out; one for the original idea, that is, the application of numbers and letters to colored fires for signals; the other, under his own name, for the mode of manufacturing, and this notwithstanding that without my aid and experience he could not have perfected the invention. Half of my United States patent was made over to him, half of his to me, with the understanding that if Congress purchased the

---

* The most favorable reports were received, after a period of from one to two years, from all the United States squadrons in different parts of the world to which the above-named three hundred sets of Coston's signals had been distributed, and upon which reports Congress based its action in purchasing the right to use the patent for the navy of the United States.

invention for the use of the navy, he should receive one-quarter of the money, but for all mercantile or government orders he was to receive one-half.

I remained some time in Washington to take out patents for foreign countries ordered.

The Fourth of July dawned hot and sultry. My home was on Capitol Hill, and I rose almost with the sun, and strolled out to get a breath of fresh air, take a look at the Goddess of Liberty not yet elevated to the dome, and enjoy the unrivalled view from the brow of the hill.

You who have been there know what a magnificent spectacle greets the eye. The fairest city in the country, stretching its long arms of avenues as far as the eye can reach; avenues brilliant with foliage and flowers, artistic in fine architecture and statuary,—clasped by the mighty arm of the silvery Potomac, overarched by a sky of soft and matchless blue, and crowned with the splendid Capitol, its marble glittering and white in the clear sunshine, which touches almost into life the groups of peaceful sculptured figures that adorn it. I even began to indulge in sentiment, when I was startled by a voice saying, "You take early morning walks, madam."

I turned in surprise, and saw Admiral Dahlgren.

"Permit me to share your stroll," he continued, with an amiable smile. It was less embarrassing to consent than to refuse, and we walked on; I, quiet, and wondering what purpose this pleasant overture concealed. Presently the admiral congratulated me on

my success, and said, "Why did you not come to me
to help you?"

Knowing he had been on the spot the six months
during which they were trying to perfect the signals in
the navy-yard laboratory, I could ill conceal my feelings at this; but the thought of my success helped me
to answer him with complacency, which I did, and we
remained friends.

"You ought to go to Europe now and push your
invention. Why don't you?" he continued. Instinct
told me that the admiral had some reason for wishing
me away, but I replied, "I am only waiting for the
reports from all the squadrons to come in."

"Why do that? It is simply waste of time," he
persisted, with an offer to give me letters of introduction abroad. This offer I of course did not accept, and
after a few commonplaces we separated.

I went on slowly maturing my plans, and finally,
summoning my two boys from school, took passage on
a Cunarder for England in the month of August.

My children, Harry and Will, it is needless to say,
were delighted at the prospect of a voyage, and not
altogether indifferent to the new wardrobes it was
necessary to provide for them.

CHAPTER VIII.

STRANGE COUNTRIES FOR TO SEE.

WE started in fine spirits on the good ship "Africa," and made an uneventful and pleasant voyage. Most conspicuous among the passengers was Mrs. Harriet Beecher Stowe, with her husband and daughter. The celebrated writer was short, plain looking, dressed with absolute simplicity, and was only redeemed from phys-ical ugliness by the strength of character displayed in her brow and expression. She was certainly a woman of moods, though perhaps it is hardly fair to judge of any one's disposition on shipboard; at times affable and entertaining, and again disagreeably reserved, and almost morose.

I knew, however, that at this time Mrs. Stowe was preoccupied with a new book, shortly afterwards pub-lished in England, and meeting with great success, under the title of "The Minister's Wooing," and accordingly made due allowances for her variable behavior.

The Rev. Mr. Stowe was short, stout, most benevo-lent in countenance and agreeable in manner. The daughter was an extremely pretty brunette, bright, vivacious, and a universal favorite.

It was nearly midnight on Saturday when we steamed

up the murky Mersey and landed in Liverpool, the
city it is said that symbolizes England's commercial
greatness; and, it might be added, the one that also
prejudices the traveller against the whole country, its
climate, institutions, and honesty in particular.

It was too late to go on to London that night, and
we were obliged to go to a hotel, leaving our baggage
at the docks. The next morning Mr. Sampson Low,
Mrs. Stowe's English publisher, who had come to meet
her, very kindly offered to claim my baggage and get
it through the custom-house for me.

As the day was very English, rainy, foggy, and de-
pressing, I was glad to accept the offer and remain
within-doors. Mr. Low easily recognized my baggage
by the description I had given him, but was rather
disconcerted by finding with it a box of my signals,
which had been placed in the care of the purser of
the steamer to be stowed with the ship's fireworks.
Through some mistake, perhaps because my name was
marked plainly upon it, it had been put with the passengers' baggage.

This was a dreadful violation of British law, and
poor Mr. Low had to exert all his eloquent influence
and bribery to get me out of the scrape. In these
days, when a hand-bag is supposed to be stuffed full of
dynamite and a box of bonbons to conceal nothing less
than bombs, the dilemma would have been still more
embarrassing. These signals I had brought over for
trial by the English navy.

Remaining in Liverpool over Sunday, the hotel proprietor proceeded to give me my first insight into the principles of his guild by charging me sixteen shillings (four dollars) for a ladle of soup that my little son asked for at lunch. I remonstrated at this item, whereupon the smiling Boniface assured me that the soup was "real turtle,"—a soup, by the way, that they say is reserved for aldermen, Americans, and fools. The fact that I had not asked for it was not allowed to make any difference. On this scale my bill was made out and rendered on Monday, and it struck me as being simply enormous. However, I paid it, and was alarmed to find what inroads had been made upon the ready money I had with me, to last, I had expected, until I could get a draft on Rothschilds' cashed in London.

Monday noon we started for the station to take the train for London. I went to the booking-office and asked for the tickets, when to my intense mortification and embarrassment I found I had not enough cash with me to pay for them. I put down the tickets and stammered out the truth, adding that I had no idea they would cost so much, and could not go on until I could go to a bank and get a draft cashed.

That booking clerk had a heart; he glanced at the dismayed faces of the boys, at my own cheeks flushed with embarrassment, at my black dress, and said, "Madam, how much have you?" I quickly emptied my purse; he counted the money and said, "That is all right; I will give you my private card with the amount still due written on its back, and when you reach London you can send it on in stamps." As he spoke he put back some change in my purse; "for the comforts," he added, "that you will be sure to need on your way."

It was, to be sure, only a matter of a few shillings, but if it had been of a thousand pounds I should not have felt more grateful. That one act wiped out all my prejudices against the English; I even forgave my landlord, and shook hands at parting with the gentleman,—a title, perhaps, his countrymen would not grant him,—and my first act in London was to write him a grateful note enclosing the stamps.

As soon as we were settled in cosey lodgings, I bent all my energies to achieve success in the enterprise which had brought me over: namely, that of introducing to the British government the invention now well known and established in the United States as the Coston Telegraphic Night Signals. I should add that before sailing I had obtained patents in England, France, Holland, Austria, Denmark, Italy, and Sweden. My next step was to present the letters of introduction given me by distinguished officers of our navy and government officials of high standing, the most valuable of which was from Captain Matt Maury, of the National Observatory, to Rear-Admiral Fitz Roy, of her Majesty's navy, soliciting for me that gentleman's courtesy and service.

The rear-admiral, a man of elegant manners and energetic character, called at once, and, obtaining the proper papers from me, proceeded to the admiralty, and, being granted an audience, presented them to the Duke of Somerset, then the First Lord of the Admiralty, taking care to place my affairs in a proper light before his Grace.

Just at this time I was taken seriously ill, and curiously enough, my illness culminated in a severe attack of the whooping-cough. Confined to my room, I was greatly disappointed at not being able to take advantage of the audience the Duke of Somerset offered me by letter, and was obliged to content myself with his assurance that the invention should be thoroughly tested, and in the event of its proving valuable would as a matter of course be employed in her Majesty's service.

The case of signals was immediately forwarded to the admiralty, and Commodore Drummond, then in command of the Woolwich dock-yards, was ordered to make the first trial. The commodore experimented with them on board the " Vivid," near the dock-yards, and afterwards sent in a favorable report, recommending that a more thorough trial at sea should be made by the channel fleet, then commanded by Rear-Admiral Sir Charles Freemantle.

The Duke of Somerset acted at once on the recommendation, and ordered Sir Charles Freemantle to make the proposed trial and report thereon. Though convalescent when this order was given, I was unable to leave my bed and still under the care of a physician, who was not only of eminence in his profession, but a man of shrewdness and kind heart.

6

I had just received the notification of the trial from the admiralty one morning, when my doctor came to make his daily call, and at once demanded what I had been doing to so flush my cheeks. It must be remembered that at this time I was far away from my friends and kinsmen, and, devoted to my business, had not had the opportunity to form new ties and intimacies in England. It was therefore a relief to me to unburden my mind to the good doctor, and to finally ask his advice on the subject of sending some one to Sir Charles to interest him personally in the signals, and to instruct him with regard to their use, that the trial might be successfully carried out.

"Have you no friend who would run down to Weymouth or Portland, where the fleet is anchored, and see the admiral for you?" asked the doctor.

"No," I replied, sadly; and then in an agony of impatience and despair, adding, "If I were in America I should know what to do; I would go myself."

"If you could," said the doctor, smiling; and, with a flattering nod, "You would secure a thorough and perfect trial, and no doubt interest the admiral in your case. But the first question is, could you stand the journey in your present state of health?"

"If you think such a step would not outrage English conventionalities, I will go, and take my little son Harry with me."

"You are perfectly justified in doing so," replied the doctor, "and Master Harry will make an excellent chaperon."

Before going, the doctor ordered a powerful tonic for me, and, returning home, sent his wife to my lodgings.

Mrs. Rutherford was a very motherly woman, of warm impulses, and greatly interested in my project. She nursed me up to my task, both physically and mentally, and the next morning started me off for Weymouth with my little son, who was greatly elated at the honor of going as my protector.

When we arrived, late in the afternoon, I found myself very much exhausted, but did not dare to think of repose yet. On inquiry at the station I learned that the fleet was lying off Portland, a town on the English Channel, where the convicts are kept, and some five miles distant. I lost no time in securing a carriage, and away we rumbled.

CHAPTER IX.

SIR CHARLES FREEMANTLE.

THE day was bleak and desolate, and the drive through a sandy and barren country, and when we finally pulled up at a dreary-looking little inn at Portland I felt depressed and discouraged.

Not knowing it would be impossible to get another, I paid the driver his fare and dismissed the carriage.

We then entered the bare and forlorn little box of an office, half filled with common sailors and working-men. Not a woman was to be seen, and I greeted with relief the vision of a buxom chambermaid who suddenly appeared to show me to a small cold bedroom; a strip of carpet, an iron bedstead, and two rickety chairs constituted the furniture. Here the maid informed me I should be obliged to take my meals, as there was no accommodation for "women folk."

At the word meals Harry's eyes lit up, for he was at the chronically hungry age, and I too welcomed the idea of a cup of tea. We gave our orders, and in a few moments rosy-faced Nancy returned with a fossilized repast; the bread was so hard that I verily believe if fired from a cannon's mouth it would have knocked a hole in a stone wall; the ham might have been contemporary with Noah's eldest hopeful; and the tea was a hollow mockery, merely an infusion of willow-leaves.

This was Saturday. I pushed the tray from me in dismay at the thought of having to remain here over Sunday, realizing the importance of my having nourishing food in my weak state, and seeing that to get it here was out of the question. The possibility of the admiral having gone up to London to spend Sunday also occurred to me, and when Harry had finished nicking his teeth upon the hard fare I sent him down to inquire from any of the seamen or officers of the fleet he might meet on shore.

He soon returned to tell me that the admiral had just gone out to the " Royal Albert," the flag-ship of the fleet, and called my attention to the band playing the national air to announce his return. Opening the windows, I could hear the music coming faintly and softly over the water, and it seemed to breathe in my ear hope and courage. I made up my mind to make the best of circumstances and wait patiently until the next day, which, though Sunday, I hoped might not pass without my getting some communication to the admiral.

The following morning, after another stony repast, I made bold to write a letter to Sir Charles Freemantle, apologizing for trespassing upon his Sabbath hours, but begging him to consider the embarrassment of a lady being detained in such a place, and asking him on that account to name the time when I might have the pleasure of an audience.

I concluded by saying that, being aware that he had received instructions from the admiralty to test my invention, I felt the extreme importance of its being properly presented to his consideration; and knowing that my sex prevented my presence at the trial, I was the more anxious for him to take a personal interest in the affair, and to give me the full benefit of all or any merit the invention might possess to recommend it to Her Majesty's government for adoption.

This letter I gave to my son, who, though very young, was intelligent and had natural tact and discretion. Dressed in his best, and looking, as the good-natured maid said, "smart as a little lord," he started off to engage a waterman to row him to the "Royal Albert."

An hour passed; I sat watching at the window, when I saw Harry come running along, his fair curls blowing in the breeze, his cheeks rosy with excitement, and under his arm something that looked like a board. As he drew nearer I recognized it to be a letter, which, *à l'Anglaise*, was more than a foot long. When he entered, I tore open the huge envelope and found within a small card saying the admiral would be pleased to give me an audience on the "Royal Albert" the next day (Monday), at eleven o'clock in the morning. This prompt and courteous reply sweetened my board and softened my bed that night.

In the morning I made the best toilet I could under the circumstances. The excitement brought back the color to my lips and face, and I was glad to find myself not unpresentable. As the time appointed drew near, I proceeded with my son to get on board a small boat and row out to the flag-ship. We had proceeded some distance when we met a large naval barge, containing two officers and several oarsmen. They all saluted me, and one of the officers said that Sir Charles had sent the boat for my accommodation.

To tell the truth, I doubted my own capacity to change from one boat to the other on this deep, rough water, gracefully or even successfully, so I excused myself, and the barge escorted our little boat to the "Royal Albert," lying some four miles out.

As we pulled up alongside of the stately old ship with its ponderous armaments, I was very much impressed. It was one of the old three-decker line-of-battle ships, with one hundred and thirty powerful guns, and eleven hundred souls all told on board. Evidently extra preparation had been made for the reception of a lady, for beside the exquisite cleanliness and polish of the woodwork and brass mountings, the steps were enveloped in flags, and gay-colored bunting fluttering from every mast gave the old vessel a holiday appearance.

I was received with pleasing ceremony, an officer in full uniform assisting me to alight; and as they were at the moment testing the guns, I could have fancied that I read in the deafening noise a prolonged salute. The officer who had received me escorted me to the deck, and there we were met by another officer, also in full dress, who in turn passed me on until I reached the upper deck, where I saw standing in the door-way of the saloon, which was draped with the brilliant union jack, a splendid-looking old man, clad in a handsome uniform, his breast glittering with decorations.

As he advanced to meet me, his snow-white hair stirred with the breeze was turned to silver by the sun, and his eyes, beaming with benevolence, were matched by the smile that lit up his bronzed countenance. I guessed at once that this personification of a grand old warrior of the sea was none other than the rear-admiral. As I approached him I said, " This is Sir Charles Freemantle, I presume?"

"Madam, it gives me much pleasure to receive you,"
he responded, and then in a manner most cordial and
dignified led me into the saloon and placed me in a
large easy-chair.

Frankly speaking, I was greatly relieved at this
reception, which, though ceremonious, was without
stiffness, and I felt that I had not unpleasantly impressed my host. But, dreadful to relate, no sooner
had I seated myself than long fasting and nervousness
made itself known in a violent fit of whooping, and
for a few moments no Indian on the plains could have
surpassed me.

Mortification and pain brought the tears to my eyes,
but every attempt I made to apologize only started
me off afresh. There sat the nobleman stately and
serene, slightly anxious, yet too polite to interrupt me,
and apparently without that sense of the ludicrous
which was the last straw with me. His extreme kindness and delicacy I shall never forget, and after waiting for me to quite get over my attack, he rang for
wine, and would not allow me to speak until I had
swallowed a glass of amber and perfumed madeira.
Afterwards he ordered a delicious lunch, which in my
half-famished condition meant more than an empty
courtesy, and while we discussed it he chatted to me
most agreeably of the many distinguished Americans he
had met and known, inquiring after them, and quite
delighted at finding that we had so many friends in
common. By the time we had finished, I was much
refreshed, and, feeling that I knew Sir Charles better,

was more at my ease, and able to explain to him how I had fallen heir to such a mission.

Sir Charles told me that with the orders sent from the admiralty in regard to the signals he had also received the letters of introduction I had brought from eminent Americans to English government officials, so that he was quite aware that he was about to receive a lady. I found Sir Charles was much impressed with the merits of the invention, and the great need of such means of communication in the service.

He then proposed to order the commanding officers of the different vessels comprising the squadron on board to meet me and hold some consultations in my presence, adding that they had already received the instructions to test the signals, but that this interview would be of use to them and probably a satisfaction to me. I consented, and the good admiral at once had his orders conveyed to the officers by means of the flag signals. There were some fifteen large vessels in the fleet, though I can now only recall the names of a few, such as the " Mersey," " Trafalgar," " Blenheim," " Mars," etc.

In a very short time a number of fine-looking officers presented themselves ; of superb physique, their healthy skins, clear eyes, and sound teeth were emphasized by their fine and becoming uniforms; and as they came in two by two, erect and almost courtly in bearing, I thought that in the five years I had passed at a naval station I had never seen a group of naval officers their equal in appearance.

The admiral presented them to me in turn, and then invited them to be seated around a long mahogany table covered with green cloth; he himself sat in a carved-oak chair at the head, with me on his right. The scene would no doubt have struck the stranger as a curious one: the circle of splendid officers in dazzling costume, and the grave old admiral with his white hair and blending of authority and paternal interest might have been taken for their father; and beside him, the only woman in the English Channel that day,—an American, young, delicate, and clad in the sombre hue of mourning. Over all the soft, misty light of an English day.

To save me from the embarrassment of making a formal statement, the admiral with much tact began questioning me, the officers listening to my replies with intelligent and polite attention. I made my explanation of the origin and proper use of the signals as clear as possible, referring to my inability to be present at the trial, and expressing the hope that they would give the signals the advantage of a thorough test.

I then learned for the first time that another invention, purporting to be for the same purpose, had been offered the British government. However, when I had concluded, each of the gentlemen approached me to shake hands, and express his sincere interest in the invention, promising to do it every justice.

On their departure the admiral gallantly proposed to escort me ashore himself. My boatman was dismissed, and with kindly forethought a bright young midshipman, a little older than my son, invited as a companion for him. The admiral's boat was then ordered, and a few minutes later Sir Charles gave me his arm, and we descended the long staircase and passed through two lines of marines at the foot, who "presented arms" at our appearance, while the band played that soul-stirring air, "God save the Queen."

The admiral remained bare-headed until we reached the boat reserved for his personal use, which was distinguished from the others by its length, handsome finish, and coat of pure white paint, and was manned by fourteen oarsmen. It was provided with luxurious cushions, and Turkish rugs to keep the wind off, for this was in December.

I was comfortably seated in the stern, the admiral taking his place beside me. The word was given, the oars flashed through the air, and amidst the continued firing of guns and the inspiring strains of the national air, we pushed off.

Just at this time the sun emerged from its bed of clouds with that mild splendor peculiar to England, illuminating the sombre waters and disclosing the bold beauty of the stately fleet, even to the graceful etching of sail and spar against the sky, the billowy edges of the union jacks fluttering in the wind, and the outlines of the manly figures pacing the different decks, the rays of the sun burnishing gold epaulets and lacings.

Hundreds of small boats were darting hither and thither carrying supplies and sailors. Every one, as it

only 60+ years since
(revolutionary war

met us, saluted the admiral's boat, the men raising
their oars and remaining caps off until we passed. As
we swept by the different vessels of the fleet, in each of
them the commanding officer appeared to salute us, at
the same time giving a signal to the band on his ship,
immediately followed by a burst of the national air,
caught up in turn by the other vessels, until the atmosphere was filled with the sweet refrain.

There was something more than pleasurable in this
experience, a unique one for any woman, especially an
American; indeed, it was not a little thrilling, and I
said as much to the admiral, who was exceedingly pleased
at my appreciation of the scene, and of the fleet of which
he was justly proud to be the commander.

Reaching the shore, Sir Charles gave me his arm,
and followed by my little son and the young midshipman, we walked to the hotel, where he took leave of
me with many kind expressions, and the desire that if
anything should occur to me later that I had omitted
to say, I would not hesitate to communicate with him.
The natives of the town had congregated on the streets
to see the admiral pass, and from their audible remarks
I judged they pronounced me to be none other than
"the queen of America," which greatly amused my
little son, who for some time afterwards insisted on
designating himself as the crown prince.

CHAPTER X.

JOHN BULL AND YANKEE INVENTORS.

DURING the winter which I spent in London I received several very encouraging letters (two dated from Lisbon) from Sir Charles Freemantle on the progress of the experiments at sea, and I was most hopeful for the results.

In the spring the report of the Channel Fleet was sent in to the admiralty, of which Sir Charles was good enough to advise me *entre nous*, though contrary to official etiquette, intimating at the close of his letter that if I happened by accident to call in person at the admiralty I might hear of my fate and get a copy of the report.

Of course I followed the suggestion, and accidentally called on Captain Charles Eden, chief of the bureau, and he kindly read a copy of the report, covering fifteen pages of closely-written foolscap, to me, on the grounds that it was against the rules to give copies of government reports on inventions to any one, including the inventor.

When he had finished, it was impossible for me to refrain from saying, " You do me great compliment in assuming that I am capable of retaining in my mind the details of the lengthy report you have read to me.

D   7

It is impossible, I assure you, notwithstanding how deeply I am interested. I regret exceedingly that you should deny me a single copy."

At this the captain relaxed a little, and saying, "Well, considering that a lady asks the favor, I will inform the Duke of Somerset; possibly on that account His Grace will make an exception." The captain then excused himself, to return a few minutes later with the desired concession; and on his promise that a copy should be made and sent to my residence, I retired. In a few days I received the copy of the report, or rather, a brief summary of it, though quite sufficient to show it to be of a most favorable nature, and delighted I felt.

The London spring developed in all its loveliness of swelling bud, soft blue sky, and tender mist, and still I waited more decided action on the part of the admiralty. I was loath to leave for other countries without the grand precedent of success in England, but I began to get not a little heart-sick over the long-continued delay. Oh, the circumlocution! oh, the red tape of official business! I began to have a grim appreciation of the humor of Dickens's drawing of the Barnacle family.

One evening about this time I was sitting in my little parlor, the rain pattering on the window-glass, the wind softly soughing among the trees in the park opposite, when Mr. Jacob Snyder was announced, and a moment after the inventor of the greatest rifle that had ever been brought to the attention of the British government entered the room. An American, he stood before me, thin to emaciation, haggard, worn, and almost wild in expression. His clothes, past the stage of shabby gentility, were fairly in holes and rents. He had come, he said, because he had heard that I was successful with the British government, and he wanted to know by what magic I had gained my ends.

I listened appalled, for my efforts in England had been puny in comparison with his. For several years he had worked and written, and appealed, and brought to bear most powerful influence from his own country, in vain. He had even expatriated himself, thinking to gain favor as an Englishman, in vain; but in taking this last step I must confess, as a loyal American, he greatly impaired my sympathy. The government played with him as a cat does with a mouse, never really relinquishing their hold upon him, nor yet actually accepting his invention; and after a long period of this torment, poverty-stricken and despairing, he died literally of a heart broken by disappointment, and his rifle became the principal one used by the British government, and surpasses all others to this day.

His was only one of the many cases that came to my notice while living in London, and I began to seriously consider if I was not being beguiled in the same way, to possibly meet with the same fate. Ah, could I speak with a thousand tongues, it would be to warn American inventors never to go before the British government, until, at least, the rest of the civilized world had done him justice.

What an example was furnished in the treatment of Professor Samuel F. B. Morse, whom the British government refused to acknowledge as the inventor of the telegraph! From his own lips I heard his experience, while dining at his house in New York City, the day before the uncovering of his statue in Central Park. Personally I had reason to be grateful to Professor Morse; for when he was Commissioner of the Paris Exposition of 1867, on telegraphy, in his report to Congress, which was not confined to the use of electricity, he took occasion not only to substantiate his claim to the first transmission of messages by electricity, but also mine to the Coston Semaphore Night Signals for telegraphing, naming me " The accomplished inventress." Professor Morse was inspired to do this kind act for me by an article that appeared in the London *Times* claiming my invention for an Englishman, the statement remaining uncontradicted in spite of an appeal for justice that I sent to the *Times*, corroborating my claims by proofs, including printed reports of the actual trial of the signals by the Unite States navy, and their final adoption; and showin that, though unsuccessful at first, the original conceptio remained unchanged, and was made public twenty-fiv years before the Englishman claimed to even hav thought of it.

To return to my story. While waiting for new from the admiralty, I decided to lose no more tim before taking steps to introduce my invention to the French government. I took my eldest son Harry with me, and went direct to Paris. I need not say how I was enchanted with the change from smoky and foggy London to the exhilarating atmosphere of *La Belle France.*

Even poverty in blue blouse and snowy cap became picturesque here; though one noticed few signs of want, for in the palmy days of the Empire such an air of *bonhomie* and gayety pervaded the city that the very fountains seemed to play more merrily, and the flowers to bloom in more vivid colors, than elsewhere. Splendid were the toilets and equipages that made the Boulevards and the Champs Elysées sparkle with life, and the air of animation about the parks and palaces, in the Palais Royal and the Garden of the Tuileries, nay, even in the hotels and cafés, was such that one could scarcely realize the suffering that must dwell there, as it dwells in every great city.

On my arrival in Paris, I drove at once to the Hôtel de Louvre, and after a little rest and refreshment proceeded to the legation to present my letters of introduction to Mr. John Y. Mason, our minister to France.

Most fortunately, Mr. Mason had formerly been Secretary of the Navy, and, while holding that office, a warm personal friend and admirer of Mr. Coston.

It was most agreeable to me, after so much intercourse with strangers, to meet any one who had known and appreciated my husband, and the tears rose to my eyes. After a most cordial greeting, and hearing what had brought me to Paris, he said, "My dear Mrs. Coston, your mission interests me greatly; don't you know I consider myself as the father of those signals?—for by my order the first were made by Mr. Coston, the same as were afterwards tried by Admiral Paulding."

Mr. Mason at once selected a gentleman to act as my agent with the government of France, taking care that he was competent to present the invention in a proper manner. During our brief stay in Paris we were elegantly entertained by different members of the American colony; and the minister himself gave a most delightful dinner for me.

While we were at the table, Mr. Mason said to my young son, "You have only to emulate your father if you wish for a career;" then turning to a gentleman near him, added, "Sir, this lady's late husband, B. Franklin Coston, was the handsomest young man I ever met in my life; his countenance was brilliant with intellect, and in his splendid eyes burned the fire of genius."

Two weeks later, feeling that things were put in the right train, I returned to England, and passed the remainder of the year, and the long spring following, still anxiously waiting for some decided answer from the British government. None came, but one morning I saw in the *Times* an announcement to the effect that the Channel Fleet had returned to England, and that Sir Charles Freemantle was in London and had attended the Queen's levée. Hoping that at any rate I might now discover why the admiralty had refused to act upon his favorable report, I ordered a carriage and drove to the stately residence of Sir Charles, in Grosvenor Square.

When the footman answered my ring, he ushered me into the drawing-room, which, like the lofty hall, was darkened, and, with the servant's solemn demeanor, gave me something like a chill. In a few moments the answer came that the admiral would see me directly. I spent the interval in looking at the fine family portraits, the faces of which seemed to peer curiously at me through the semi-darkness.

When Sir Charles entered, so slow was his step and so sad his mien that I was dismayed; but I could scarcely believe that any displeasure at my calling would so affect his demeanor, the real cause of which I understood when he told me that his brother, to whom he was devoted, had been taken suddenly ill during the night, and was now lying dead in the room above us. I felt very much embarrassed at having intruded at such a time, and instantly rose to withdraw, but Sir Charles kindly added, " Of course I knew when your card was brought up that you were in ignorance of our bereavement, but I wish to ask you myself if anything has been done in your business by the admiralty?"

" No, not a thing," I responded, rather drearily.

" I feared as much, madam," said the courtly old gentleman. " Of course you will understand that at present I am unable to attend to any business, but when this sad affair is over, and I have arranged the affairs of my poor brother's widow, I shall make it my first duty to go to the admiralty and urge them to relieve you of this suspense." After expressing my appreciation of this kindness, I departed, and, in spite

of my better judgment, returned to my lodgings, once
more a hopeful woman.

A few days passed without event, and then one
morning when my white-capped little maid tripped in
with a dainty breakfast-tray, a livelier rose than usual
in her cheeks, I saw on the familiar willow plate a
huge letter, officially sealed and stamped. In that
letter I knew lay the English fate of my signals, and
turning from the round eyes of the little waitress, I
tore open the envelope, unfolded the letter within,
found it to be from the admiralty; brief, formal, but
courteous, to the effect that from the press of important
business of the Department it was impossible for them
to proceed with my affairs; but as they were aware
that they had officially encouraged me to remain in
England for so long a time, would I be good enough
to forward them a bill of my expenses?

The disappointment conveyed to me so delicately
was great, but at the same time I keenly appreciated
the justice of the offer to defray my expenses, and
which I felt intuitively was due to the kindly intercession of Sir Charles Freemantle. I hesitated at first,
fearing that an acceptance would interfere with the
final adoption of the signals by the British government; but being assured by my legal advisers that it
would not, I complied with the courteous request of
the admiralty, and in return at once received a check
for several hundred guineas.

CHAPTER XI.

FRENCH PROCRASTINATION.

JUST at this time came solace in the shape of a communication from the French government, telling me of the successful trials of the Coston Signals by their fleets, and their wish to enter into negotiations for the purchase of the patent for the use of the French navy. The same post brought me a letter from my agent in Paris, urging me to come on at once. Heartily glad to enter the field of action, I sent for my two boys to go with me, as I wished them to have the advantage of a visit to France.

They had both been at school in Wimbledon, Surrey, and my summons proved providential. It seemed that for a long time they had been the victims of the abominable English system of " fagging," and both ashamed and afraid to complain to me in their letters, which were overlooked, and in dread of their overbearing master, they had suffered in silence until they were both thrown out of health. When Willie reached me his torments had culminated in Saint Vitus' dance, and he then lost his speech for six months, while Harry suffered from violent and dangerous attacks of bleeding at the nose. Any mother can imagine what suffering this meant for me, and to this day when I hear a woman speak of putting her boys in an English school, it makes me shudder.

We arrived in France in the month of June. Paris was in her most charming toilet, and after securing comfortable rooms and good medical attendance for my children, whose health caused me the greatest anxiety, I divided my time between them and the endeavor to make a satisfactory contract with the French government.

Soon after my arrival, the Minister of Marine, L'Amiral Hamlin, convened a board of officers, twelve in number, with General Preuilly as president, and I was invited, through my agent, to be present at their meetings. I confess, this to me was the greatest ordeal I had been called upon to go through. I was not insensible to the fact that according to the French standard my position was a peculiar one, and that, properly speaking, to fill it reputably I ought to be both old and ugly.

Nothing is so difficult for the Parisian to understand as the independence of the well born and bred American. However, I assumed that they knew me to be a woman in polite life, and I took care to make my appearance in an exceedingly quiet toilet, wearing a long black veil, concealing for the most part my hair, which would remain both golden and curly, and maintaining to the utmost my dignity. When I entered the salon I was pleased to see all the officers at once rise to their feet and salute me profoundly.

General Preuilly gave me a seat at his side, and after a few preliminary remarks, not finding myself sufficiently at ease to continue the conversation in French, I called upon my agent to act as interpreter.. For two hours it was one continual " *Demandez* Madame Coston! *demandez* Madame Coston!" until the words reverberated through my brain. Once a week for the next month these councils were repe   d, and, though extremely dry and fatiguing to a d   ate and refined woman, I consoled myself, must ha e some valuable results.

Instead, however, of resulting in the purchase of the patent, as I so ardently desired, the board contented itself with merely ordering a large quantity of signals for further experiments at sea on long cruises, to prove their durability in different climates, and their power to retain color. Fortunately, I was able to show an analysis satisfactory to them, from Professor Doremus, of New York, proving the signals to be neither combustible nor dangerous. I was almost disheartened by this second disappointment, but remained in France in a true " Micawber" spirit until the order for the signals had been sent on to America and filled.

In the mean time I was not a little cheered by the favorable reports I received from the United States squadrons in different parts of the world on the Coston Signals furnished them by the Navy Department. This was during the winter of 1860–61, and when the air was full of the mutterings of war. Our flag had been fired upon at Charleston, and my anxiety became

signals used & tested in Civil War

intense to be on the same side as my friends, and with
them watch the great struggle that now seemed immi-
nent.

The thought also occurred to me that in case of war,
what a valuable auxiliary my signals would prove for
the navy! The night would lose half its terrors at sea,
when in the darkness and through the storm ships
could talk to each other as though gifted with the
tongue of man, and victories won largely through the
common understanding, that could never have been

achieved by the Fresnel lanterns, which up to this
time had been the only means of naval communication
at night, and consisting merely of three colored lanterns
run up on a pole, and in a mist undiscernible; while
the Coston Signals could easily be seen at a distance of
fifteen or twenty miles, and in the fiercest gales of wind
and rain at a distance of several miles.

Without further delay I sailed at once for home, and
proceeded directly to Washington with the intention of
bringing a bill before Congress for the sale of my patent
to the United States government, for the use of the navy.
On arriving at the capital I found it in a state of ferment, and Congress agitated by the resignations taking
place in both the House of Representatives and Senate,
by those in sympathy with the South.

During a business call at the Navy Department one
day, I said to Mr. Toucey, "What a dreadful state of
affairs this is! Why does not President Buchanan take
active steps to settle matters?"

"The Republican party have brought things to this

crisis, and I think we will leave it to them to settle," coolly replied the Secretary.

" Surely you will not wait until Lincoln is inaugurated in March?" I asked.

" We certainly shall," replied Mr. Toucey, with a meaning smile.

With a woman's impulse, I could not refrain from urging upon him that the South would certainly avail itself of this interval of inaction to strengthen itself, and that President Buchanan was showing unpardonable weakness, or something worse, not to nip the rebellion in the bud. It seems ridiculous to me to say that President Buchanan was a loyal Union man, as some of his biographers have since tried to make him out to be.

Shortly after my interview with the Secretary, I met old General Cass on the street. The tears stood in his eyes and his voice shook with emotion as he told me he had just resigned, as it was more than painful to him to remain in Buchanan's disloyal cabinet. I was at Willard's Hotel when Lincoln arrived after his perilous trip through Baltimore in disguise, and was present at his memorable inauguration.

I had scarcely returned to Philadelphia to see my children, when the war broke out in earnest. Soon I received a letter from Mr. Gideon Welles, the new Secretary of the Navy, saying that as President Lincoln had ordered a blockade of all the ports, the fleets needed fresh and large supplies of the Coston Signals.

I resolved at once to return to Washington, but found

I could not without a pass. Senator Zach. Chandler, who happened to be in the city, with another gentleman whom I knew well, kindly consented to take me on their passes.

CHAPTER XII.

BEFORE "THE WAR CONGRESS."

AT this time the Sixth Massachusetts Regiment had been attacked in Baltimore, and the most bitter feeling existed there. No one went through the city, travellers going round by boat to Annapolis, where General B. F. Butler was in command. We had an unlooked-for escort of honor in the Seventh Regiment of New York, which was on its way to protect Washington. Many of the soldiers in this famous regiment had excellent voices, and as we steamed along they, standing on deck, indulged in a burst of patriotic song that must have been wafted to the shores of Maryland. The weather was beautiful, the water glittering and blue in the sun, the soldiers so gay, and the uniforms so bright and new, that it was hard for me to realize that we were in the cruel season of War, until I found that I was the only lady on board.

My arrival greatly surprised the Secretary of the Navy, who told me the ladies were all running in the other direction as fast as they could, and he had supposed as a matter of course I would send down my manufacturer to represent me.

"When my country called, 'twas mine to obey," I replied; and smilingly adding, "My manufacturer is in command of a company raised by himself, now serving in the Second New Jersey Regiment with the army, and unless I can get him back to the factory I don't see how the signals are to be made and furnished to the navy." The Secretary at once sent for Admiral Paulding, who had been made Chief of the Bureau of Navigation, and on his arrival bade him escort me to the War Department to see General Scott.

We found the general gallant and gracious as ever, and Admiral Paulding at once told him that we called to procure the release of a man from the United States army to serve the navy.

"Who is the man?" said the general, promptly; and no sooner had I given him the particulars than he wrote out the required order. We then found that the Second New Jersey Regiment was encamped on Meridian Hill, in the suburbs of Washington. The admiral called a carriage, and away we sped.

On arriving at the camp, we were told by the colonel of the regiment that the very company including the man we were in search of had been left on the Baltimore road to protect the route to Washington. All we could do then was to despatch him General Scott's order to report to his factory in New Jersey, and inform him that he was released from army duty to serve the navy. We afterwards heard that the manufacturer's company

became insubordinate on learning that he was about to
return home, as they had enlisted through his persuasion
and on the understanding that they were to serve under
him. However, he pacified them and started for New
Jersey, where I had preceded him, and found his young
wife very sad and fearful lest the fortunes of war should
prevent their reunion in this world again. I bade her
be of good cheer, and prophesied she would see him
shortly.

Sure enough, at ten o'clock at night the door-bell
rang. "That is your husband!" I exclaimed. She
looked at me half in dread. A moment later he entered the room, and I felt the joy of their meeting was
a happy omen of the success of the signals.

"What brings you here?" I asked, gayly. Out
came the order from General Scott. "Bless me! and
who are you, that you should be honored by a special
order from the commander-in-chief of the United States
army?"

"Ah! Mrs. Coston, I see you in this magical order,"
he responded, and I had to confess my part of the
transaction.

The factory was at once opened, and in a short time
the six hundred vessels that the government had got
together were furnished with the Coston Signals, to
what effect will be shown later. As soon as the orders
had been filled I returned to Washington, where the
times were stirring indeed, and the Navy Department
in a constant state of bustle and excitement, the Secretary and his officials frequently doing business all night

by the aid of tallow candles and lamps, there being at that time no gas used in the Department.

I now prepared to make a determined effort to have a bill pass Congress for the purchase of my patent, and I was spurred on by the knowledge that other parties were forming companies to manufacture signals for army and navy use, with the bold purpose of infringing on my patent. Word came to me that a company recently formed for this purpose was about to hold a business meeting in a public office.

On the appointed day, accompanied by a prominent member of the Senate, I presented myself before them, and, apologizing for the intrusion, said, "I came to warn you that I am aware of your intention, and shall not interfere unless I find that you are infringing on my patent, which I shall defend to the utmost extent of the law, unless I receive full recompense for the use of it." I then read them a copy of the patent, which I had brought with me.

That visit broke up the company, and at the same time stimulated the Secretary of the Navy to recommend Congress to purchase my patent and allow the government to manufacture the signals for its own use. Acting on the advice of Admiral Paulding, Admiral Joseph Smith, and other officers of the navy, the Secretary also recommended that Congress should pay me the sum of forty thousand dollars for the patent.

President Lincoln, it will be remembered, called that year an extra session, known as the "War Congress," before which the widow of Senator Douglas and myself were the only ladies to appear; and to it my bill was presented. The discussion over it occupied an entire day; in the House of Representatives it was cut down to thirty thousand dollars, and passed with small difficulty, but when it was brought before the Senate by the Naval Committee, of which John P. Hale was Chairman,* a desperate fight ensued. The most bitter opponent of the bill was Senator Sherman, who on general principles was opposed to the purchase of patents by the government, and denounced this bill as a "job," while Senator Grimes showed his animus by proposing an amendment cutting the bill down to twenty thousand dollars.

Senator Thompson, of New Jersey, in the course of his remarks said he had been given to understand that rather than lose the bill Mrs. Coston had expressed her willingness to accept the twenty thousand dollars, and to this effect the bill was amended. I had never made such a declaration, and sitting silent in the gallery, unable to speak for myself, and filled with a turmoil of hope and fear, resentment and gratitude, which none but those who have been in the same position can understand, I followed the progress of the debate.

---

* It is worth while to remark here that Senator Hale would not present my bill until he was thoroughly satisfied of the worth of the signals. To satisfy him, I invited a number of friends to be present at a trial to be viewed from the balcony of the Library of Congress at the Capitol. Thanks to the energy of Admiral Paulding in procuring the signals for this purpose, which were burned on Arlington Heights, and the trial was a perfect success.

A bitterness of feeling was shown that astonished me, and when Senator Fessenden, whose opinion on the subject I did not even know, arose from his seat, I feared another enemy of the bill was about to declare himself. Imagine, then, my surprise and delight when he made a most eloquent appeal for me, full of facts, and directly to the point.

A few minutes before the bill was presented, I had seen Senator McDougall, of California, and found that he knew nothing of its merits. Aware that Senator Sherman intended to oppose its passage, I felt the need of friends, and giving my papers to Mr. McDougall, begged him to inform himself from them, and if he felt justified, to let me have the benefit of his support. No sooner was the Senator from California seated than the bill came up, and the contest began. Late in the day, and after much hot feeling had been displayed and many speeches made, the bill was brought to a vote.

It stood twenty to twenty.

I held my breath, and a wild prayer rose in my heart. In an instant Senator McDougall called on Mr. Breckenridge to stand up in a hurry, and his vote passed the bill. Strangely enough, this was the last vote that Senator Breckenridge ever gave in the United States Senate, and little did he dream that his vote was cast in favor of such a powerful auxiliary to the army and navy which he was to fight under the "bonny blue flag."

I dare say the sum of twenty thousand dollars will seem to many of my readers a liberal one for the government to pay me for my patent, notwithstanding that a board of officers had recommended the payment of forty thousand dollars as just recompense, even before the war had proved its full value ; but it must be borne in mind that out of this sum I was obliged to pay not only the enormous expenses consequent to presenting my bill to Congress, but also eight thousand dollars in cash to my manufacturer, and had devoted years of work and much money to perfecting the invention. In consideration of this I hesitated for some time to accept the twenty thousand dollars, though urged to by my friends, and especially by my business partner. At last I consented to, and so notified the Navy Department. The Secretary at once referred me to the Assistant Secretary, Mr. Faxon, who told me I should have to draw up a bill of sale.

Knowing little of legal formalities, I went to Admiral Joseph Smith, and asked him what steps I ought to take. He replied, " You will not need a lawyer," and taking up a pen he dashed off a bill of sale, bade me make a copy of it there and then, and return to Mr. Faxon with it. The Assistant Secretary read it over, pronounced it all that was necessary, and immediately arranged for me to draw the money.

Much relieved at the brevity of the transaction, I went over to the Treasury Department. There happened to be several people there on business when the money was handed to me, in five-hundred-dollar packages, and it created quite a sensation, as one by one I received and placed them in my hand-satchel.

CHAPTER XIII.

EXPENSIVE PATRIOTISM—AN ENEMY.

BEFORE I left Washington, at the request of the Navy Department I agreed to continue the manufacture of the signals for the use of the navy, as at that time the government had neither skilled hands nor necessary machinery to produce them, and in those troublesome times they were needed promptly, and, imperfectly made, would have proved disastrous instead of useful.

We continued, according to agreement, to manufacture the signals, but soon at a very small profit, as I had fixed upon a price when gold was at par, and my manufacturer was with his regiment in the army. I had named at the time a figure which I thought would enable me to realize something above my expenses from this useful invention. But it was not long before gold was at a high premium, and my price was paid me always in paper or government vouchers, which had to be disposed of at a discount to obtain ready money.

We imported all the chemicals, which required ready money and payment in gold, and the duties, which were high, had also to be paid in gold. Rates of exchange were payable in gold, even when gold at one time demanded over two dollars for one dollar. We were also obliged to pay several war taxes, notwithstanding a bill passed by Congress relieving those whose prices were fixed at the beginning of the war from the said taxes. Increase in the price of labor added to our other burdens and combined to make the price fixed at the commencement of the war a losing one.

The pressure upon us became so great that at last I summoned up my resolution and applied to the Secretary of the Navy for a rise in the price of the signals, on the ground that as the price of labor and all things had gone up twenty-five per cent., I was entitled to the same, or payment in gold. The Secretary thereupon convened a board of officers, comprised of Admirals Paulding, Charles Henry Davis, and Joseph Smith. This board agreed to grant me twenty-five per cent. on the price named when gold was at par, for which decision I was exceedingly thankful.

The Secretary endorsed the opinion, and sent it to the Bureau of Ordnance. When my bills were rendered they were made out on the new understanding, but to my surprise, Captain Henry A. Wise, Chief of the Bureau of Ordnance, refused to pay them. I went on to Washington at once to see what his refusal was based upon, and on what grounds he had the courage to refuse to recognize the decision of the Board of Admirals and the orders of the Secretary of the Navy.

Presenting myself at the Department, Captain Wise greeted me very brusquely, and, while I explained the object of my visit, walked up and down the room as though struggling to suppress his temper. When I had finished, he burst out with,—

" Mrs. Coston, you are making altogether too much money on those signals. I have nothing but my pay, and my wife is obliged to make her own dresses and bonnets."

For a moment I was too confounded to speak, but recovering myself replied, " I can hardly see the connection between the Coston Signals and Mrs. Wise's millinery ; but if you wish to discuss the matter on so personal a basis, I am aware that as Chief of the Bureau of Ordnance you receive at least four thousand dollars per annum, and with such an income, were I in your place, I should consider myself rich,—rich enough at least to insist upon my wife having her bonnets and dresses made for her."

At this Captain Wise grew exceedingly red and rude, and as he positively refused to pay me the advance price, I left his office and called upon the Secretary of the Navy, to report him. The Secretary sent for him immediately, and in my presence reprimanded him.

It is needless to say that from that moment Captain Wise became a most bitter enemy, and I was hardly surprised when a second time he refused to pay me the advance prices. Again I appealed to the Secretary, who urged me in his reply " not to stop the supply of signals to the navy, as it was of the greatest importance to have them at this, the darkest time the country has ever known."

Feeling confident that eventually he would vindicate his authority, and see that I had what was due me, as he had promised, I acceded to his request. I have never been able to understand why the Secretary did not at the time force Captain Wise to obey his orders, but I was told afterwards that it was a question of political influence, as Mrs. Wise was a daughter of Edward Everett, a niece of Charles Francis Adams, and a connection of the Blairs. Admiral Charles Henry Davis and Admiral Joseph Smith expostulated with Captain Wise on his course; in return he insulted them both.

Shortly afterwards he brought up the fact that the government had paid me twenty thousand dollars for the patent, and he openly charged me with an attempt to defraud, in withholding the recipes for the manufacture of the signals. It then transpired that the Navy Department should have been put in possession of the recipes when the patent was purchased, but this I was not aware of, nor was mention made of it in the bill of sale, and I could not consider myself responsible for the omission, as I had followed to the letter the instructions I had received at the time (see page 92); but when it was explained to me I recognized the justice of it, and that when I paid my partner his share of the twenty thousand dollars I should have demanded from him the recipes.

Now Captain Wise demanded certified recipes, and I had none. I wrote immediately to my manufacturer for them, in order to be at once relieved from even a shadow of suspicion. At first, to my intense mortification, he refused to yield them, and not until he was threatened with the law did he give them up, with specimens of the chemicals used, for the instruction of the Navy Department. Shortly afterwards Captain Wise's health failed him, and he was obliged to resign his position.

Meantime, I continued to furnish the signals at ruinous rates, until the close of the war, when a new Chief of the Bureau of Ordnance readily agreed to pay the advance price; but, unfortunately, by this time there was little use for them.

Before proceeding with my story, it will, I think, be of interest to my readers to know exactly what part the Coston Telegraphic Night Signals played during that terrible civil convulsion of our country. In the first place, nearly all the blockade-runners were caught by their use, as they generally made their runs by night, and the United States navy vessels gave chase after communicating with each other by means of the signals. Numerous battles and bombardments were successfully conducted through this ready means of communication.

Perhaps the most important historical occasion in which they figured was during the bombardment and capture of Fort Fisher, the following account of which was despatched to the *Baltimore American* by that brilliant journalist, C. C. Fulton:

"FRIDAY, January 13, 1865.

"At eight bells (four o'clock) this morning we were roused from slumber by a gun from the flag-ship, and the burning of Coston's preparatory signals, red and green, as an indication to the fleet that it is time to be up and stirring, preparing breakfast, getting through with the morning routine of duty, so as to be in readiness at dawn to commence the serious work of the day. . . .

"At five o'clock a second signal was given by the flag-ship, 'Get under way,' when the work of raising anchor commenced. At half-past five the signals of divisional commanders to move forward were given and responded to, causing a brilliant pyrotechnic display. The gunboat 'Tacony' having been sent ahead last night, to anchor off the Flag Pond battery, and the day not having yet dawned, her lights can be seen as the steering point of the fleet, in-shore, about three miles ahead of us.

"The three frigates 'Wabash,' 'Minnesota,' and 'Colorado' moved off first, led by Admiral Porter's flag-ship, followed by the 'New Ironsides' and the monitor fleet. The army transport signals also added to the scenic attractions.

"At the first dawn of day the whole armada was in motion. The wind has changed due east during the night, and being offshore tends to make the landing of the troops comparatively easy. At a quarter of seven o'clock the admiral signalled 'Form line of battle,' when the 'Brooklyn,' with her line of vessels, moved along close to the beach."

The correspondent of the *New York Times* sent the following despatch :

"UNITED STATES STEAMER 'SANTIAGO DE CUBA,'
"HAMPTON ROADS, Tuesday, Dec. 27, 1864.

"On the 20th the entire fleet were made jubilant at the news received of the capture of Savannah. The intelligence was telegraphed from the 'Malvern' by means of flag signals. While on the subject of signals, it will perhaps be instructive to many to know that the system of communication between ships is so perfect that a vessel experiences no difficulty in receiving an order or message, even if she is miles away from the vessel giving the signals. At night colored lights [meaning the Coston Signals] are used in the place of flags.

" This is decidedly a remarkable and valuable invention, and the parties who originated and perfected the code are entitled to something more substantial than thanks. I have noticed that the rebels use rockets and flash-fires when communicating with · blockade-runners at night. In the daytime they display flags like ourselves."

While this book was in preparation I received the following kind and graceful letter from Admiral Porter, which, as it bears directly on the subject in hand, I insert here :

"OFFICE OF THE ADMIRAL,
"WASHINGTON, D. C.,
"March 10, 1886.

"MY DEAR MRS. COSTON :

" In answer to your several questions regarding the use and benefit of the ' Coston' Signals, you know very well that I have always been a strenuous advocate for their use. Having had the benefit of them when I commanded on the Mississippi, and also at the attack and capture of Fort Fisher, I am able to speak understandingly.

" My first experience of the value of the Coston Signals was on the Mississippi, where the numerous gunboats were passing up and down the river and using them to exchange signals with each other. When your husband invented the signals which bear his name, he conferred a benefit on the navy for which you could hardly have been repaid.

" The signals by night are very much more useful than the signals by day made with flags, for at night the signals can be so plainly read that mistakes are impossible, and a commander-in-chief can keep up a conversation with one of his vessels distant several miles, and say what is required almost as well as if he were talking to the captain in his cabin. This was the case in the Mississippi and also in the North Atlantic Squadron during the war, where we read hundreds of these signals (nay, thousands), which were frequently kept going all night long.

"One can easily judge of the perfection of the Coston Signals when they were made from a hundred vessels with rarely a mistake.

"I shall never forget the beautiful sight presented at ten o'clock at night when Fort Fisher fell. I was determined to be a little extravagant on that occasion, and telegraphed by the signals to all creation that the great fort had fallen and the last entrance to the Southern coast was closed. The order was given to send up rockets without stint and to burn the Coston Signals at all the yard-arms, mast-heads, along the bulwarks, and wherever on shipboard a light could show. The sea and shore were illuminated with a splendor seldom equalled, and no doubt the dazed inmates of Fort Fisher were for a moment under the impression that the heavens had opened with all their glory to honor the good work that the soldiers and sailors had accomplished.

"What could there be more beautiful than the Coston Signals on that occasion, and what more could I say of them?

"Yours truly and respectfully,
"DAVID D. PORTER,
"*Admiral U. S. Navy.*

"To MRS. MARTHA J. COSTON,
"*Washington, D. C.*"

It also gives me pleasure to append the following letter, lately received from an officer on the staff of Admiral Porter during the war:

"NEW YORK,
"January 29, 1886.

"DEAR MADAM:

"In response to your request, it affords me much pleasure to convey some words of the faithful part played by the signal lights bearing your name, so well known to the mariner. It was my privilege to take an humble part in the suppression of the great rebellion, as a naval officer. As such I experienced the efficiency of this method of signalling in communicating and responding to orders. In the darkness of night, in storm of ocean, in battle and quiet; at all distances limited by the horizon the Coston Signal ever efficiently did its work. I particularly recall its services during the winter of 1864 and '65, when an aide and signal officer on the staff of Rear-Admiral David D. Porter, commanding the North Atlantic Squadron. He had assembled at Hampton Roads the largest squadron of American history, if not of modern history, preparing for the conflict destined to close forever to the Confederacy the mouth of the Cape Fear River, through which was fed its nourishment from abroad.

"While at the rendezvous, at departure, *en voyage*, during the battles of Fort Fisher and those of the Cape Fear River, at night this signal was ever its method of intercourse; at all times a prompt, efficient, and faithful messenger.

"With high regard, believe me, madam,

"Yours very truly,

"AARON VANDERBILT.

"To MRS. M. J. COSTON, Washington."

CHAPTER XIV.

THE SIGNALS IN WAR.

ON the darkest night, if the atmosphere was clear, it must be remembered that the signal could be discerned at a distance of from fifteen to twenty miles, and penetrating with a radiant glow of color the thickness of mist and fog to nearly the lesser distance. It will be seen not only by the extracts I have given, the important service these signals rendered in the long chill winter nights, but later, that Admiral Porter, Admirals Farragut, Rogers, Trenchard, Smith, Paulding, and

9*

others have testified to the grand usefulness of the signals, and gave me warm praise for persevering in my work.

I felt particularly thankful during the war that while the signals were made the means of capturing the enemy, they also played an important part in saving the lives of our own men. In one instance twenty-six lives were preserved through their medium.

It will be remembered that in 1862 the famous "Monitor" was lost off Cape Hatteras. The rest of the story shall be given in the words of Lieutenant Stoddart, who was on the "Monitor;" and whose statement was afterwards verified by Admiral Trenchard in command of the "Rhode Island."

"On the night of December 30, 1862, while we were on our way from Fortress Monroe to Charleston, South Carolina, in company of the steamer 'Rhode Island,' a fearful tempest arose. The sky became black as ink, the wind swelled into a tornado and lashed the water into huge waves that at one moment raised us to a mountain's height, and the next plunged us down into the valley of the shadow of death, with a shock that made the mighty boat tremble like a leaf in the breeze.

"So frightfully did the storm rage, that finally the water rolled completely over the turret, nearly drowning us, and our peril was so great that it seemed as if no human power could save us. The 'Rhode Island,' under Admiral Trenchard, ploughed on, but it was entirely obscured to us by the storm, and in utter ignorance of our frightful danger. Our only chance of

communication with her was through the Coston Signals.
It seemed now that at any moment we might founder.

"We tried in vain to ignite a signal, but again and
again the water rolled over us, and again and again
cigar-light, match-rope, and port-fire were extinguished.* Finally, in the ingenuity of desperation

THE SINKING MONITOR.

some one got a shovelful of live coals from the engine-
room, ignited the signal inside the turret, and passed
it up to the men on top.

"The next instant the vessel swept the side of a
mountain of water, and our silent cry of distress blazed
forth. The 'Rhode Island' recognized our appeal and

---

* The Coston Signals were not, as now, self-igniting by means
of a percussion-cap.

answered, though it seemed an eternity before help was started.

"We guessed at the truth : the sea was so fearful that the men hesitated to make what seemed a suicidal attempt at rescue, and it finally transpired that a crew was forced at the point of the bayonet to man a boat and come to our help.

"It can be imagined with what feeling we twenty-six men, whose lives seemed worth as many straws, watched the approach of our rescuers, and our gratitude when we were taken from the top of the sinking turret into the boat, which, tempest-tossed as it was, proved a haven of safety."

In *Harper's Monthly Magazine* for October, 1863, was published an exciting narrative entitled "The First Cruise of the Monitor 'Passaic,'" from which I make the following extracts, to show to what practical use the Coston Signals were put during the war :

"... By noon the next day we were off Cape Hatteras, the wind all the time increasing and still ahead. Signals were made to the 'State of Georgia' to head more inshore. Toward dusk a steamer passed us with a clipper ship in tow loaded with troops, and the 'Monitor' was made out far ahead. We were a little mortified to think she had so far beaten us, and everything but blessed the pilot of the 'Georgia,' who was again heading out to sea. Once more signals were made as before, and at the some moment a leak was discovered in our bows, apparently from the straining of the projecting part. A stream was poured in like a tear out page

answered, though it seemed an eternity before help was ——

"We guessed at the truth; the sea was so fearful that the men hesitated to make what seemed a suicidal attempt at rescue, and it finally transpired that a crew was forced at the point of the bayonet to man a boat and come to our help.

"It can be imagined with what feeling we twenty-six men, whose lives seemed worth as many straws, watched the approach of our rescuers, and our gratitude when we were taken from the top of the sinking turret into the boat, which, tempest-tossed as it was, proved a haven of safety."

In *Harper's Monthly Magazine* for October, 1882, was published an exciting narrative entitled "The First Cruise of the Monitor 'Passaic,'" from which I make the following extracts, to show to what practical use the Coston Signals were put during the war:

". . . By noon the next day we were off Cape Hatteras, the wind all the time increasing and still ahead. Signals were made to the 'State of Georgia' to head more inshore. Toward dusk a steamer passed us with a clipper ship in tow loaded with troops, and the 'Monitor' was made out far ahead. We were a little mortified to think she had so far beaten us, and everything but blessed the pilot of the 'Passaic,' who was again heading out to sea. Once more signals were made as before, and at the same moment a leak was discovered in our bows, apparently from the straining of the projecting part. A stream was poured in like a

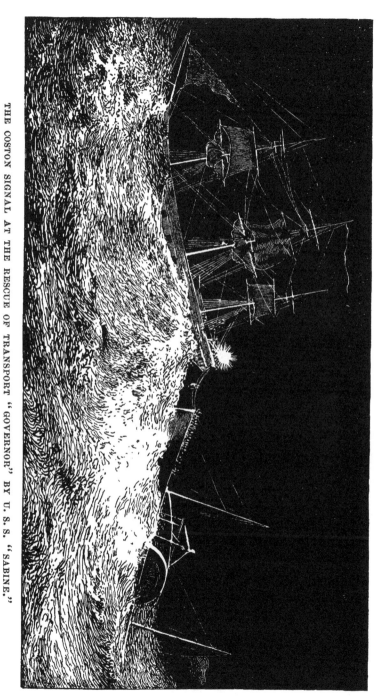

THE COSTON SIGNAL AT THE RESCUE OF TRANSPORT "GOVERNOR" BY U. S. S. "SABINE."

miniature cataract, but with the velocity of that of a steam-engine, and threatening to give serious trouble.

" About seven in the evening another leak was found in the after-part of the ship, that in the turret increasing, and both our main pumps (two Worthington's) just given out. Coston signal-lights were burned, ordering the 'State of Georgia' to turn back again for the nearest lee. Before midnight the gale blew so fearfully that we began really to fear for our safety; and especially when the wind was found to be changing and blowing again ahead. The leak gained rapidly, and we began to despair of ever seeing port. All hands were ordered to take out ballast to lighten the ship. It was done in vain. Shot were then ordered up to be thrown overboard; four hundred were thrown over without lessening or retarding the leak. Another pump gave out, and our last resort, the pumps known as the bilge injections, were the only ones at work. Coston's signal-lights were burned, and a rocket sent up indicating our distress, and informing the 'State of Georgia' that we were sinking.

" While the lights were burning a steamer was discovered through the darkness, on the port bow, also burning signals. All this time we were rolling fearfully. At intervals the gale would burst with redoubled fury, and we would rise high on a monstrous wave, and then plunge down completely out of sight of our convoy, or come crashing down on the succeeding wave, with a shock that made the ship tremble like an aspen. . . . .

" Just before the storm the 'Georgia' burned Coston signals informing us that a man was dead on board, and asked permission to stop and bury him. It was granted, in so far that we moved more slowly. The flag was lowered to half-mast, a short service was read, the plank on which he lay was raised, and he slid into the sea. A melancholy burial !"

Shortly after the events I have related in connection with the passage of my bill, and while feeling exhausted, and in fact ill from my experience in Washington, I received a letter from the French government, to the effect that it was now ready to close negotiations for the purchase of my patent. The communication was in French, and while I was puzzling over its technical phrases, my physician entered.

" I begin to think," I said to him, smilingly, " that my good angel usually appears in the shape of a doctor. Will you convince me by kindly translating these expressions for me ?"

I made this request because I knew that Dr. Gaburri was a fine linguist, and a foreigner by birth. He quickly interpreted the letter, and then I said, " Is it not too unfortunate that just at this time, when it is so much to my interest to go to France, I should be broken down and ill ?"

" My dear Mrs. Coston, I could not prescribe anything in the world that would do you so much good as a sea voyage. We must get you up, and you must sail with as little delay as possible. Besides," he continued, with some hesitation, a slight flush on his worn, sallow face, and a brightening of his earnest eyes under their long sweeping brows, " I am glad to say that I can do something to assist you. You, madame, have known me as the world here knows me,—a poor and struggling physician ; but I am noble by birth, and have powerful connections in the old world. I can give you a letter to my uncle, General of Division Bougenel, who won his title under Napoleon the Great, and is now Chevalier of Honor to the Princess Mathilde. Admiral Le Ronciere le Noury, now Chief of the Marine Department of France, was brought up under the care of my uncle, and he I am sure will be delighted to serve me in this matter."

This, indeed, was an agreeable surprise to me, and I appreciated both Dr. Gaburri's kindness, and the extreme modesty that had prevented him from trying to make capital of his family pretensions. It seemed to me also that Providence had brought him in my path, for I knew that the letter of introduction he brought me a few days later, and which was most flattering to me, would be of great benefit.

My kind friends in New York made my preparations quickly and quietly for me, and my passage was engaged on the " Great Eastern," which three months before had torn a huge hole in her bottom, and had been in dock ostensibly for repairs. My old friend Admiral Paulding called to bid me good-by, and with all the superstition of a thorough-bred sailor said, " Mrs. Coston, why in the world do you sail on that ill-fated ship, and, of all days, on Friday?"

I explained that I was too late in getting ready for any other steamer, and as I felt that I was really in the line of my duty I was not afraid to sail even on a Friday. I made this reply with a bold front but a sinking heart, for, to tell the truth, in the delicate state of my health, the uncertainty of the future, and above all, the parting with my dear boys, was a severe trial.

CHAPTER XV.

THE STARS AND STRIPES *vs.* THE UNION JACK.

On the 3d of January, 1863, I again set sail from New York, and a great lump rose in my throat as I stood on deck, waving a handkerchief to my children, until their little figures on the wharf were lost in the softly-falling snow. As soon as land was out of sight I hastened to my state-room, and was touched to find that the very best on board had been given me. I tried to recover my calmness while I busied myself in unpacking the necessary conveniences and preparing for the voyage. At dinner all the passengers met at table, and I was surprised to find they consisted of fifteen gentlemen and myself; if it had not been for the presence of the captain's wife, I should have really been embarrassed. She was seated at his right, and I next to her, but, much to my disappointment, I found her to be an under-bred Englishwoman, who, feeling herself to be in her own castle, as it were, was disposed to take advantage of it.

The war, it will be remembered, was then at its height, and I saw that Mrs. Paton, like most of her country-people, was in sympathy with the South; and as I myself was a loyal Union woman, it was to be regretted that on the second occasion of our meeting the conversation turned upon the rebellion. I was asked which side I was on, and of course declared myself to be a warm Unionist; when Mrs. Paton asked me in a high voice, "What are you going to do in England with such sentiments as those? You won't dare to utter them there."

"Madam," I replied, "I am sorry to hear that one cannot be free to utter any honest sentiment in England, especially about one's country; at all events I shall have my own apartment, and over its entrance I shall hang the Stars and Stripes, so that my visitors can have no doubt as to my patriotism."

"Your Stars and Stripes will soon be pulled down," she answered, with a sneer.

"Who will pull down the American flag? Surely not the English people," I asked.

"You think a great deal of your precious flag!"

"Do you not love the flag of England?" I inquired.

"Certainly I do; the union jack is something to love," she replied.

"Madam, I honor you for it, since it is the flag of your country; and I reserve to myself the right to love the stars and stripes of my country's flag."

10

"Your country!" she said, contemptuously; "you have no country. We will soon have to send over one of our English princes to take charge of you."

"You forget, Mrs. Paton, that when we were only three millions of people we snubbed English royalty pretty effectually; and now as thirty millions I scarcely think that any one of your German nobility would like to 'take charge' of us."

At this the gentlemen, who had been listening in quiet, applauded, and the poor captain, who had been on thorns, exclaimed, "Ladies, a truce is declared;" and ordering champagne, he sent it round to me, and drank to my health.

After we had left the table, Captain Paton approached me, and said, "Mrs. Coston, have you the American flag with you?"

"Yes, indeed; I always take it with me on my travels," I replied.

He then asked me to show it to him, and I went to my state-room and brought the flag forth. It was a new and handsome one of silk, over two yards in length, and I shook out its lustrous folds with pride.

The captain took it from my hands, and then, seizing a new union jack, skilfully and quickly draped them on either side of a large bust of Brunel, the illustrious engineer, bringing together a corner of each around the neck, and knotting them under the chin.

The clear red, white, and blue, and the brilliant scarlet and white of the American and English flags, mingled gracefully. Of course this tribute to our national colors seemed to me and the other Unionists a triumph in war times for the American flag; and notwithstanding the remonstrance of some Southern sympathizers, including the captain's wife, the two flags remained where the good captain had placed them until we sailed into port.

The weather continued calm and beautiful, and we steamed steadily ahead, in spite of the rather alarming fact that there was a hole eighty feet long in the bottom of the steamer, that had not been repaired as was supposed in New York. But the captain assured me that the rend affected only one of the air-tight compartments, that there was no real danger, and the insurance companies had pronounced it safe to make the trip, and wait to repair damages on the English side.

We had been out nearly a week, when one morning I awoke with the consciousness of a great commotion on board; presently, to my extreme consternation, guns were fired again and again, until the great ship trembled. I thought of the hole in the bottom of the ship, I thought of the corsair " Alabama," and then remembered that I was the only woman, indeed almost the only passenger, on that part of the steamer.

I called for the stewardess with an energy born of fright. She had entirely forgotten me, though I was her only care, but quickly responded to my call, to tell me that the firing of the guns meant neither distress nor war, but the advent into the world of " a little captain, a veritable little prince." The captain had a son. Mother and child were doing well, she concluded.

Hastily making my toilet, I went up on deck, and found the "Great Eastern" a floating island, almost hidden in flags that fluttered from stem to stern, and covered the rigging. Of course the union jack predominated. The sight was a very pretty one, but only a feature of the general rejoicing that followed. The gentlemen serenaded the captain, and told him they would furnish the wines if he would give a supper and a ball. This the captain readily agreed to do, and asked me to help him receive the guests, including the second-class passengers, a very nice set of people, and among them several pretty young girls.

I consented, on condition that he would have a trunk brought up for me out of the hold, that I might appear in proper toilet. This was done, and with the aid of the stewardess I donned a robe not unbecoming to the occasion, of sea-green silk, with a shell trimming, a quantity of foam-white lace, and coral ornaments. When I entered the grand saloon I found the tables had been removed, the walls decorated with bunting and colored lights, and the band, which was an excellent one, stationed in front of a large group of green palms.

Dancing was begun, and continued with great zest until two o'clock in the morning. The supper was very fine, the pastry cook exerting himself to produce wonders in confectionery and miracles in ornamental pieces. The wines were of the best. The sea was as smooth as a huge mill-pond, and the "Great Eastern" so steady that none of the passengers were prevented from being present by sea-sickness.

The festivities were closed by a grand display of the very Coston Signals that had been put on the "Great Eastern" three years previous to signal its first entrance into the port of New York, which, however, took place in the daytime, so that the signals were of no avail, and the captain unaware of their presence on board until I, who had presented them to the company, reminded him of them. He then stationed a man at each end of the great ship, and they signalled back and forth to each other, to the great amusement of those on board. The captain himself was delighted at the means of communication, and the deck was kept for some time in a brilliant glow of red, white, and green fire.

A few days after this gay celebration, another but sadly interesting incident of the voyage occurred. This was the funeral at sea of one of the passengers, who had been noticed all the way out for his extraordinary consumption of champagne and cocktails. It transpired that he was a young Englishman of noble birth, who had come out to "do America" in a fortnight, on the previous trip of the "Great Eastern," intending to go back on her return trip. The accident to the ship, however, to which I have alluded, had lengthened his stay, which he had spent in seeing New York City, with grievous consequences. Having squandered all his money, pawned all his jewelry, injured his appearance, and almost ruined his health, he had been hunted up by the captain, just in time to sail with us ; but, unfortunately, the sea air only sufficiently sobered him to make him so ashamed of his exploits that, in order to forget them, he took to drinking again, and finally wound up by tumbling down the hatchway and fracturing his skull.

The captain decided to bury him in the broad Atlantic. I was surprised to find that the great ship was brought to a dead stop, and the stillness that ensued, when all the mammoth machinery had ceased to work, was almost oppressive. We all assembled on deck; the chaplain, in his gown, read the service of the Church of England for the dead, and the body, weighted with lead and swathed in the union jack, was lowered over the side of the ship into the ocean. Thus we had within a few days a death and a birth, so that the "Great Eastern" went into port with the same number of passengers that she had started with.

On nearing Liverpool, the captain came to me and said, "Now, Mrs. Coston, we have had two of the great events in existence take place on board; will you not let us be indebted to you for the third and greatest of all? You have been such a belle that if you could now make up your mind to choose from among these gallant gentlemen some one to accompany you in the voyage of life, the wedding could take place, and I promise you in good style, on shipboard."

I laughingly replied to him that the gentlemen presented such equal attractions that a choice would be impossible, and that, as I could not marry them all, I should decide to cling to my widowed estate.

how polite of her

idictitare of people's unacceptance of her active life w/out a man?

CHAPTER XVI.

A PARISIAN BANQUET—FINE FEATHERS.

ON my arrival in Liverpool I learned that my old friend Captain Matt. Maury and a number of other Southerners were staying there, but I avoided seeing them, for at that time we were so divided in sympathy that our very affection would have made it painful for us to meet. I therefore hastened to London with pleasant anticipations of returning to my old lodgings and being once more under the care of my kind landlady, who had taken so genuine an interest in my affairs before.

The thought of the warm reception she would give me, and her gratified pride at finding I had taken care of the handsome shawl she gave me at parting, cheered me in my fatigue and roused me from the lassitude one always feels after first landing.

When the cab rattled up to the old familiar door, with its shining brass knocker, the same servants came out to greet me, and Betty, the same little maid, grown larger and rosier than ever, ushered me into my old rooms.

"Where is Miss Hubbard, Betty? Why is not she here to welcome me?" I asked.

"Please, mum, the missus has been dead a year come next Michaelmas; we have got a marster 'ere now," said Betty, mournfully.

This was such a disagreeable shock to me that I could not remain in London, and giving up all idea of a rest in that city, I speedily made my arrangements and started the next day for Paris, apprising my agent there by telegram of my departure.

Once more in the beautiful French capital, I lost no time in announcing my arrival, and immediately the government opened negotiations. I had hoped for a prompt settlement this time, but found their notion of negotiation meant a prolonged haggling over the price of my patent,—haggling which was continued until Paris burst forth in her spring attire again.

In the mean time I was glad to enliven the weary monotony of suspense by going into society, though I was still so delicate that I dared not enjoy too much of it. Perhaps the most delightful entertainment given for me was a dinner by General Bougenel, the uncle of my kind doctor, and Chevalier of Honor to the Princess Mathilde.

On my advent in Paris, I had of course, with my card, sent to the general the letter of introduction from his nephew, and he hastened to call upon me and place his services at my disposal. In due time I explained the business that had brought me to France, and he at once interested himself in it, taking pains to inform me almost daily. of the discussion going on. His notes—large, imposing missives in parchment envelopes, the seal stamped with the arms of the Princess Mathilde —were a source of great curiosity to the *concierge.*

This dinner was really my first introduction to court life in France, and was of great service to me, as the guests were noblemen of eminence. General Bougenel, a man of distinguished character, was equally distinguished in appearance; he had the eye of an eagle, under black arched brows; his hair was white, and his gray goatee as sharply pointed as the ends of his long, well-waxed mustachios. The general had the manner of a born courtier, and his conversation sparkled with wit,—that wit, without malice, so characteristic of his race.

His establishment, in the very heart of the Faubourg St. Germain, was elegant, and furnished with extreme taste; the walls hung with costly Gobelin tapestry and antique armor; oriental lamps, swung from the ceiling, yielded a soft and perfumed light, and on this occasion the chief salon and dining-room was beautifully decorated with orchids and rare roses from his own conservatory, in which he took great pride.

Madame d'Antin, his widowed daughter, presided over his establishment with that elegance and *savoir faire* that distinguishes a Frenchwoman, and she received me most cordially, and looked, I thought, a veritable picture in her Watteau costume of pale pink and blue, with a huge bunch of pink roses thrust inside her bodice.

Later, as we sat down to the table, I was struck by the magnificent service, which was of pure gold, beaten into the most exquisite shapes. The glass iridescent, and cut with a fineness that made it sparkle as if set with diamonds ; and the china of Sèvres, in a thousand beautiful designs suitable to the different courses as they were served ; over all fell a soft and becoming light from myriads of wax candles. The wines were old and perfumed, the *plats* choice and delicious, the company gay and congenial.

After dinner was over, gold finger-bowls studded with semi-precious stones, and filled with rose-water in which floated a few violets or a cluster of orange-blossoms, were placed before us by the lackeys in powder and embroidered livery, and while coffee was served we enjoyed listening to the bird-like *chansons* of a famous Italian artiste.

As I said, spring came, and the French government had not arrived at any decision, when I received a letter from our minister to England, Mr. Charles Francis Adams, in which he said it would give Mrs. Adams and himself great pleasure to present me at the queen's next Drawing-Room. Before I had decided what reply to make, a letter arrived from Miss Morse, daughter of our consul-general, Mr. Morse, telling me that with her sister she was to be presented at court by Mrs. Adams, and that they all hoped I would accompany them on that occasion. The letter closed with a most pressing invitation for me to pass the London season with them and their family.

The next mail brought me a second letter, earnestly repeating the invitation, and enclosing the address of a

French modiste who was making Mrs. Adams's court dresses, that I might engage her for myself, and to also make the dresses of the consul-general's daughters.

I finally decided to go, and gave the necessary orders, leaving much to the taste and discretion of Madame Fleury, who was noted for her beautiful court toilets.

When they were completed and carefully packed, I started for England in time to get thoroughly rested before the great occasion.

I found that the Drawing-Room was to be held in honor of the anniversary of the queen's accession to the throne, and this being shortly after the marriage of the Prince of Wales to the Princess Alexandra, was also considered a Bridal Drawing-Room, which made it somewhat incumbent upon the ladies to appear in white toilets.

Fortunately, a lady of the English aristocracy whom I knew in Paris had given me this hint, and Madame Fleury had devised a toilet in accordance for me, a description of which may interest my readers of my own sex.

According to the fashion of those times, the full trained skirt was of heavy white corded silk, with an entire overdress of white lace, delicately puffed, the puffings connected by tiny folds of white satin. The corsage *décolletté* was a bewildering combination of white silk, satin, and lace, fitting to perfection. The court train, the most important feature of the robe, was four yards in length and of rich white satin, lined with corded silk and bordered by a broad trimming of lace and waves of tulle, caught down by clusters of pure white water-lilies with very natural green leaves. This train was not fastened in the English style, from the shoulders, but in the mode Eugénie established, from the waist. A long spray of water-lilies fell from the shoulder over the back of the dress, and the same lovely flowers trailed over the front of the skirt, while a few were mingled with the Prince of Wales feathers which it was *de rigeur* to wear in the hair, with long lappets of point-lace falling down the back.

On the morning of the day, the court hair-dresser came early to arrange my *coiffure*, but he was good enough to think he could not improve on my own simple arrangement, which he pronounced in its curly blonde abundance *très distingué*. When I was dressed, the finishing touches were given by Mrs. Morse's maid, which included fastening on my jewels, a diamond and emerald parure, which harmonized with my costume.

I descended at ten o'clock to breakfast, to which, as was common on such occasions, I found a number of friends had been invited. The breakfast itself was elaborate, the guests animated, and the young ladies very charming in their dresses of white tulle and silk, showered with lilies of the valley and white roses, their ornaments and necklaces of pearls with diamond crosses, which were admirably suited to the dazzling black eyes and the dark locks of the wearers.

At eleven o'clock the court carriages were announced, —I say court because the equipages used on these occasions are differently constructed from the ordinary carriage, being made almost entirely of glass, so that the occupants are visible; much ornamented with gilt, and the servants wearing an extra livery trimmed with gold, and including plush knee-breeches and hose of silk; the whole having to my republican eyes as fairy-like an aspect as did the celebrated pumpkin coach to Cinderella, after her wise godmother touched it with her wand.

CHAPTER XVII.

QUEEN VICTORIA'S DRAWING-ROOM.

AMIDST a storm of pretty compliments, our trains were thrown over our left arms, and we passed down the stairs to our carriages, which we found surrounded by a mass of people, who surmised what was going on and were watching for our departure. The day was one of June's loveliest, soft, warm, and bright, and no wraps were required. I was seated in the first carriage alone, as my train and dress entirely filled it. In the second carriage, equally grand and glittering, rode the young ladies.

The palace grounds were crowded with the populace, the curiosity being great to see the Prince of Wales and his fair bride. It was not a little trying to me to sit in this glass case in full evening dress and listen to the comments of the crowd, who expressed themselves freely, and were good enough to put me down as a duchess.

In a measure I was prepared for this ordeal, as my friends had told me before we left the house that I must not on any account yield to the temptation to pull down the blinds, as the dear public considered it their right to witness this part of the Drawing-Room spectacle, and had not hesitated on more than one occasion to stone the carriage, the occupants of which had attempted to draw the shades to conceal themselves from the thousand " Peeping Toms."

The line of vehicles was so long that we could only progress a few steps at a time, as the preceding carriages were unloaded of their fair and haughty freight and drove off. The crowd meanwhile increased to such a degree that they pressed close up to the carriage, regardless of the wheels and the horses' feet; and look which way I could, I encountered a myriad of eyes, and finally was feign to fix my own steadfastly on the buttons of the coachman's greatcoat, while I tried to appear oblivious; but my dignity tottered for a moment when an exceedingly small and exceedingly dirty boy, crooking his bony little fingers into the shape of a binocular, exclaimed, " Oh, my h'eye !"

At length we arrived at the palace door. I alighted, and as soon as the young ladies could join me we entered, each of us handing to the Royal Chamberlain a card bearing the name and address of the person presenting it, as well as that of the United States minister, and reserving a similar one, not to be given up until we entered the Throne-Room.

We passed on through the broad and lofty corridors of the old palace, alternately panelled with huge mirrors and life-sized portraits of former kings and queens, in their robes of state, an arrangement that was curiously effective and almost bewildering ; for the eye glancing over the masterpieces of art, caught reflections in the glass of the slowly-surging crowd of courtiers and grand ladies in their rich attire, until one could hardly distinguish between the real and the painted figures, and I must confess I found myself looking at a tall lady in a dress of pure white and water-lilies for several seconds before I recognized myself.

When we entered the first of the suite of reception-rooms, which was as large as a ball-room, we found them filled with rows of gilded chairs, placed about three feet apart, that each lady might have room for her immense train. We were conducted to the farthest one, next to the Throne-Room, and comfortably seated.

In a very short time the great apartments were filled, and presented a really gorgeous spectacle; the ladies wearing every imaginable style of dress, only alike in their length of train and the magnificence of their jewels; while the gentlemen were mostly in uniform, and glittering with decorations, for this being the anniversary of the queen's accession, was a Collar day. The Knights of the Garter, the Thistle, and St.

Patrick, and the Knights Grand Cross of the Orders of the Bath and St. Michael and St. George, appeared in their collars of burnished gold and finely-colored enamel, which, added to their other decorations, made of them a dazzling wall and background for the ladies' toilets.

Presently we heard the band strike up "God save the Queen," and knew this signalled the arrival of the royal family. In a few moments the doors of the Throne-Room were thrown open, and the Prince and Princess of Wales, who had been escorted by a detachment of the Life Guards, were received with much ceremony by the Mistress of the Robes.

They were accompanied by the Princess Helena and Prince Alfred, his Royal Highness the Duke of Cambridge, and the Duke de Montpensier, the hereditary Prince of Reuss Schleiz, Prince Edward of Saxe-Weimar, and Prince Frederick of Holstein, with their titled attendants.

The prince was at that time young and good-looking, and his general's uniform was becoming, and made more gorgeous by the collars of the Garter and the Golden Fleece, and the stars of the Orders of the Garter and India.

The princess appeared so charming that a low murmur of admiration rose from every side at her beauty. Slender and almost delicate in figure, innocent and childlike in face, with a singularly interesting expression, she was more attractive in appearance than even the professional beauties of that day; and still more remarkable for the modest dignity and perfect breeding that distinguished her—a princess from the little Court of Denmark—among the haughty dames of the English aristocracy.

The princess wore a mauve petticoat, and a long train of white moire antique, both trimmed with the superb Brussels lace that was a part of her bridal present from the King of the Belgians. A great many lovely white roses were scattered on the dress and around the low corsage, which exposed a swan-like neck and sloping shoulders, and were fastened with diamond and emerald ornaments ; and the same precious stones were mingled with the white feathers and long tulle veil worn on her graceful head.

I had scarce opportunity to notice this before the brilliant procession of ambassadors, ministers plenipotentiary, and envoys formed and passed slowly through. The men were in court dress, very rich, and glittering with gems and various insignia of rank, and the women vied with each other in their costliness of attire, many of their costumes having a national significance.

The most striking of all was the beautiful Baroness Brunnow, wife of the Russian ambassador, in a dark red velvet that seemed to radiate a crimson light, an enormous train covered with exquisite gold embroidery, depicting with marvellous fidelity the birds and flowers of her native country ; and on her head the national head-dress studded with rubies, diamonds, sapphires, and emeralds, some of enormous size. This head-dress

11*

was at once so unique and becoming that it became the fashion that season.

When these distinguished personages had paid their respects to the Throne, and the persons of the heir-apparent and his bride, it was announced that the presentations would take place, and the first row of ladies rose, and one by one approached the entrance of the Throne-Room, where pages in powder and livery deftly removed the train held by the left arm and spread it out full length before they passed in.

Every move was made slowly and with dignity; there was no haste, and each lady had ample time to be announced, identified by name, make her courtesy, and retire before another approached.

When my turn came, I gave my card to the gentleman in waiting, and he handed it to the queen's Master of the Ceremonies, Lieutenant-General Sir Edward Cust, who announced, in what seemed to me a very loud voice, "Miss Coston," and then hastily correcting himself, read, "Mrs. Coston, presented by United States Minister, Mr. and Mrs. Charles Francis Adams."

As I approached the Throne, in front of which stood the princess, a faint but very sweet smile lit up her face as she gracefully recognized my obeisance. In the group supporting the princess were a number of the royal princesses; most conspicuous among them was the Princess Mary of Cambridge, in a singular and striking toilet of white silk and flounces of black Brussels lace, and a lofty head-dress formed of feathers, tulle veil, and diamonds; her stomacher, necklace, and ear-rings were of large, pure blue turquoise set in diamonds.

According to court etiquette, which forbids one to turn their back to the Throne, I stepped sideways—a rather difficult thing to do—until I had courtesied again to these ladies; and once more when I came to the Prince of Wales, who, with the Duke of Cambridge at his side, returned my salute with gracious dignity.

My train was then carried by pages as I passed the Throne and joined Mr. and Mrs. Adams, who greeted me cordially, and congratulated me on the manner in which I passed through the ordeal. In a few moments, Miss Morse and her sister having gone through their presentation and joined us, we passed into the adjoining salon, where we found a large number of eminent people assembled.

Sir Edward Cust, having finished his duties as Master of the Ceremonies, requested Mr. Adams to present him to me, and then invited me to make a tour of the state apartments on his arm. As we slowly promenaded, he introduced me to many people whose names were familiar to the world.

There was the Duke of Argyll, in his Highland dress as the McCullum More, which he preferred to the official dress of a cabinet minister, and wearing his collar of the Order of the Thistle; near him, Gladstone, alert and dignified, in the gold-embroidered robe of the Chancellor of the Exchequer.

Under a crystal chandelier stood the fascinating Princess Giustiniani-Bandini, Viscountess Kinnaird in

England, in a wonderful dress of white moire antique, lace-trimmed, and ornamented with bouquets of flowers made of precious stones, while the lace sleeves were looped up with gorgeous jewels. Around her snow-white neck the princess wore a solitaire diamond necklace with long pendent rays, set on a broad band of scarlet velvet, and on her shining hair a mural crown studded with diamonds.

Not far from her stood Mr. Cobden, then in the height of his fame, and chatting familiarly with the charming Madame van de Weyer, the queen's most intimate friend, in a delicate robe of mauve velvet ornamented with lace and oriental pearls.

Lord John Russell and Lord Palmerston were two of a group that surrounded the young Marchioness of Northampton, who had just been presented, and was very beautiful in a white silk dress covered with white lace, embroidered in silver, and ornaments of luminous pink pearls.

On a Russian divan, making one of the prettiest pictures in the room, was a cluster of lovely young débutantes, dressed in beautiful combination of white and green ; and as they sat directly in front of a mass of palm ferns, they really looked like forest nymphs.

About three thousand persons were in the palace at the time, but out of them only two hundred and fifty were presented. Twenty years ago the Queen's Drawing-Room was more exclusive than since the Prince of Wales has had a voice in the presentations, and Mr. and Mrs. Adams, who then represented us at the Court of St. James, stood social sponsors for so few Americans that to be presented by them was a special distinction. *connections!*

The *Court Journal*, in its formal account of the Queen's Drawing-Room, was kind enough to mention me as one of the five belles of the affair, so that, as Mrs. Morse laughingly remarked, " I might consider myself sealed, stamped, and ready for delivery in the *crême de la crême* of London society."

Some of the people I met on that occasion afterwards developed into most agreeable acquaintances and friends ; among the latter were Mr. Cobden and his lovely wife, who invited me to visit them at their country home ; an invitation I was not able, most unfortunately, to accept, as for the few weeks that remained of the season I had many engagements, and, indeed, hardly stopped short of being a frivolous woman.

CHAPTER XVIII.

STRASBURG——BADEN-BADEN AND TRAGEDY.

HOWEVER, it must not be thought that I was so entirely absorbed in pleasure as to forget my little affair in France, and as soon as the London season closed I returned to Paris to see what my agent there had been able to accomplish in my business. To my surprise and chagrin, I found that no progress whatever had been made, and that the government wished to defer further negotiations until the fall.

While still undecided what step to take next, I received a warm invitation from General Hennequin, who with his family were in Baden-Baden, to join them there the next week ; and almost at the same time a letter came from friends in the neighborhood of Saxe-Gotha, urging me to spend some weeks with them at their country-seat.

As I was very desirous of seeing as much of Europe as possible, I determined to take this opportunity to dip into Germany, and to break the long period of waiting before the autumn. My preparations were soon made, and I started off by rail for Strasburg, my first stopping-point, for I could not pass through that grand old imperial city, of which since childhood I had read so much ; indeed, one of my favorite stories, as a little girl, was of the famous Strasburg clock, with its marvellous mechanism and poetical legends.

On arriving there, I only waited for some slight refreshment before starting, in the spirit of an explorer, through the narrow, crooked streets, lined with mediæval dwellings, grotesquely carved, in search of the ancient and imposing cathedral. Once there, I spent the greater part of the day examining its beautiful architecture, the delicate tracery and reliefs of the walls, the numerous statues and rich windows of stained glass, and—shall I confess it?—I stopped before the clock of my childhood's imaginings long enough to watch the angel strike the quarters with the bell in his hand, the symbolic deity of the day—this time Diana (for it was Monday)—step out of the niche, and the twelve apostles circle around the figure of the Saviour at noon ; and my amusement was quite undignified when the cock flapped its wings, stretched its neck, and crowed until the echoes of the remotest nooks of the cathedral were awakened.

Afterwards I took in the superb view from the tower,—a view which embraces not only the quaint city and the plains of the Rhine, but the mystical Black Forest, the Vosges Mountains, and blue in the far distance the range of Jura.

On leaving the cathedral I drove through the parks and about the various places of interest, and then returned to the hotel quite prepared to enjoy the *pâtes de foie gras* for which Strasburg is renowned.

It must be confessed that there is nothing very appetizing in the idea of eating the diseased liver of a German goose, and the fact that the dish before me was prepared from one weighing four pounds, as the waiter informed me with an air of professional pride, did not affect me as he intended it should. I must confess, however, that the pâtes were so delicious that I did my best to forget the horrid particulars.

The next morning I ordered a carriage to take me to the station, which I afterwards learned was just around the corner ; but, alas for the brave honesty for which the Strasburgians are said to be noted, I was driven four miles through the country to the next station at which the train I should have been on stopped ; the driver of course taking advantage of my ignorance, and I obliged to pay him twenty marks for the privilege of being imposed upon.

On my arrival in Baden-Baden, I was pleased to find General and Madame Hennequin waiting for me, and we were soon bowling along in a comfortable carriage to their hotel in the picturesque valley of the Oos, which is surrounded by the beautiful hills forming the entrance to the Black Forest.

In the evening we went to the Conversationshaus, in front of which a fine string band was playing, while streams of well-dressed people entered the broad doors of the elegant building, which contains ball-, reading-, and concert-rooms, gorgeously fitted up, as well as salons in the style of the Renaissance, decorated by the best of French masters, and devoted to gaming.

It was the first time in my life that I had ever seen ladies gambling, and at first it was difficult for me to realize that the beautiful women seated at the tables, their eyes outglittering their diamonds and their cheeks flushed redder than the roses in their hair, were respectable.

One of the most desperate gamesters of the evening was a handsome young Russian of refined and scholarly appearance, whom I recognized as the occupant of apartments next to mine at the hotel. His excitement was so intense that it had robbed his face, even his lips, of every tinge of color, and his pallor was increased by the blackness of his hair and long eyelashes.

He was still playing when we left the salon, and his air was that of a man who had staked his all on the last chance.

Passing into the grand salon, we met some very delightful people, among them the wife of Dr. J. Marion Sims, who with her family was spending the summer in the chateau of the Duchess of Hamilton, who had put her superb place at their disposal, as a mark of the esteem in which she held our eminent physician. Mrs. Sims I found most charming, her daughters lovely, intelligent girls; and that evening a friendship sprung up between us that has been a source of pleasure to me for a quarter of a century.

It was late when we returned to the hotel, and on our way we overtook the young Russian, who was slowly walking on with head bent and teeth clinched.

That night I had scarcely entered into my first sleep when I was aroused by a door being violently slammed, and presently I heard my neighbor ring his bell with a violence that broke the rope. When a servant answered it, he received an order that presently made him return with a jingling tray.

A moment afterwards a crash of glass, china, and bottles, told me they had been thrown in different parts of the room, and I heard the servant's footsteps as he fled past my door to escape from the frenzied young man, who paced up and down raving in his own language. Suddenly all became quiet, and judging that my unhappy young neighbor had exhausted himself, I fell asleep.

In the morning the chambermaid told me, with the perfect *aplomb* that results from custom and tried nerves, that the fine young gentleman in the adjoining room had cut his throat with a razor in the night.

The week in Baden-Baden passed agreeably and quickly away, and then, in company with some pleasant acquaintances from Java, I started on the way to visit my friends. Our first halt was made at the ancient town of Heidelberg, where we visited the venerable university and the historical castle, the latter the most magnificent ruin I have ever seen, its crumbling splendors clothed in a luxuriance of German ivy.

A pleasant feature of our day's travel was our sojourn at a pretty village, Forellen, for dinner ; where we selected the fish we wanted for our meal as they swam in a natural pool of clear water. It was a daintily served repast, and with the Affenthaler, or Vin du pays, was greatly enjoyed.

CHAPTER XIX.

A QUIET RETREAT AND COLOGNE.

At Frankfort-on-the-Main we were met by the son of my German friends, who had come to escort me to his home, where I was most cordially received, and everything in the world was done for my comfort and enjoyment.

Picnics were the order of the day during my stay, as the weather was fine and the country beautiful in the bloom and freshness of its foliage. We started early in the morning, usually mounted on plump little donkeys, and penetrating sometimes in one sometimes into another bridle-path in the green forests of Rheinhardsbrun, visiting different places of interest, including the castle of Duke Leopold, Prince Albert's brother; the servants accompanying us also riding on donkeys, laden with panniers filled with fine fruit, wines, cakes, and cold meats; and at noon we were quite ready to enjoy lunch *al fresco.*

The days we remained at home to receive visits we generally deserted the drawing-room in the afternoon for the lovely park near us, and which was a part of the family estate. Here, under the splendid lindens, we sipped coffee or chocolate, served with delicious little cakes, and listened to the music, for which the younger members of the household had the true German love and talent; and from their own ranks they formed a band that played with no mean amount of skill.

My friends were Moravians, and the place had been settled by their ancestors many generations back. In the little old church might be seen brasses and effigies of their predecessors, and on almost every stone in the garden-like graveyard was traced in script the family name.

When I left these hospitable people, I was laden with flowers, fruit, pretty souvenirs, the heartiest good wishes, and in the care of an escort who saw me safely on the Rhine steamboat at Frankfort-on-the-Main.

I intended to proceed directly to Cologne, but while gently steaming down between the beautiful banks of the Rhine, I determined to get off at Eltville, in order to visit Schlangenbad, a place famous for its beauty and its baths, and remain there until I gained the rest I was really in need of.

When the boat stopped and I was safely landed, it suddenly occurred to me that I had not a word of German at my command; but determined not to betray my ignorance, I beckoned to the coachman who had been summoned by one of the sailors, motioned him to take up my trunk, and making the most I could out of the one word said, " Schlangenbad."

" Ya, ya," he responded smilingly, and whipped up his horses.

The drive was most charming, and took us past many luxuriant vineyards, handsome country-seats on romantic heights, and an occasional shrine, before which bowed in simple devotion was some yellow-haired Gretchen or pious old peasant woman. We entered the town, enviably situated in a valley richly wooded and stirred by a cool wind. The driver turned to me for further directions; I made my second attempt in German and said, " Russifer Hof."

" Ya, ya," he responded cheerfully once more, and in a moment we dashed up to the hotel. The polite proprietor welcomed me with *empressement,* and put at my disposal the apartments just vacated by a *grande dame.* The driver was paid by the landlord, my baggage carried in, and after the landlord, who spoke admirable French, had given me full particulars regarding the customs of the place, and the baths, I was left in the quiet I rejoiced in.

Two weeks I passed at this hotel, and, except to give the necessary orders on my arrival, without once speaking to a living soul; which to those who have known me will seem a remarkable feat on my part. The days passed rapidly and pleasantly. I greatly enjoyed the baths and the old Curhaus, which was built in 1694 by Carl of Hesse-Cassel, then Lord of the Soil.

The water was delightful; free from odor, smooth and oily to the touch, and its effect most agreeable. The baths, with the usual promenades, reading-rooms, etc., and the variety of romantic walks in the neighborhood, furnished amusement enough, and I also made a pleasant excursion to Schwalbach, an ancient watering-place some five miles distant, famous even in the year 300, and in the seventeenth and eighteenth centuries the Saratoga of Germany.

Thoroughly refreshed by my rest, I left Schlangenbad and resumed travelling on the Rhine. On the boat I met an English gentleman with his friends, but we had hardly exchanged a few commonplaces on the beauty of the scenery when he said, "I believe this is Mrs. Coston, whom I met in Washington society several years ago, when I was secretary of the British Legation."

I was a little mortified at my own forgetfulness,

but indeed glad to meet any one whom I had known in my dear country. Mr. Fenton and his party were *en route* for Cologne, and on our arrival there we drove to the same hotel.

The next morning I rose early, and after breakfast ordered a carriage, intending to see as much as possible of the city,—the pride of Prussia. After waiting what seemed to me an interminable time, a magnificent equipage, emblazoned with a coat of arms and with servants in livery in waiting, appeared.

"Madame's carriage is announced," said the proprietor of the hotel, with an obsequious bow.

"You are under a mistake; that equipage is certainly not for me. I ordered a common cab," I replied, recognizing this as an attempt at extortion.

At this the landlord entreated, then insisted that I must make use of the turnout. I positively refused; he grew red and angry, when happily my old acquaintance in Washington appeared upon the scene, took in the situation at a glance, peremptorily dismissed landlord, carriage, and servants, and very kindly insisted upon doing the honors of Cologne himself.

A modest cab was ordered, and we visited the world-famed Cathedral or Dom, which was not yet completed, though forty years of labor and four million dollars had been spent upon it; the Museum, with its superb collection of antiquities, tapestries, carvings, pictures, and gems; and some of the oldest and most interesting of the churches, including that of St. Ursula, where are stored the bones of the eleven thousand virgins, attendants of the English princess who were murdered with her at Cologne; winding up with a drive through the gloomy and tortuous old streets and some of the new and fine business thoroughfares, not forgetting, by the way, to purchase a quantity of the famous and delicious eau de cologne.

The next day we made one party in a merry trip to Brussels, and there, after seeing together that interesting city, we separated, and I went on my way alone to Paris. This pleasant encounter with the ex-secretary of legation was but one of the many instances when I found that my long residence in Washington had provided me with friends and acquaintances in all parts of the old world.

[handwritten annotation: She was amazing connections]

CHAPTER XX.

A LETTER TO THE EMPEROR

On my return to France, I was grieved to hear of the death of my stanch friend, General Bougenel, for I knew that in him I had lost my strongest ally in dealing with the French government. I began to seriously ponder on some means of gaining the attention and prompt action of the Marine Department. Things had changed at the American legation, and I felt there was no use in my looking to it for assistance, as Mr.

Dayton, then the American minister, was occupied with other matters, and had so ignored my affairs that for some time I had absented myself from the legation receptions.

Finally I hit upon the expedient of addressing the emperor by letter; the only hindrance to which was my ignorance of the proper mode of procedure. The next morning, however, when my French professor came, I asked him to devote the lesson to teaching me how to address persons of rank, beginning with the emperor. M. Durand's eyes twinkled a bit with curiosity, but with the courtesy of his country he made no comment, and proceeded with due gravity to instruct me as to the proper style in which to address his august master.

As soon as the lesson was over, I put on my wraps and went out to get the necessary and superfine stationery. On my return I wrote the letter with all due form and ceremony, asking for an audience, and then placing it in a huge envelope,—for etiquette demanded that the sheet should not be folded,—addressed it with the proper flourishes, and with my own hands dropped it in the Post-Office.

I took no one into my confidence, and waited patiently through the next ten sultry August days, when I saw in the *Figaro* that the emperor had been away, and had just returned to the Tuileries for a day's sojourn. The same evening I was sitting in my little flower-lined balcony watching the water splashing in the fountain of the court-yard below, when a messenger, dressed in the Imperial livery and mounted on a fine horse covered with gold trappings, dashed up to the door and handed the *concierge* a large missive.

In a few moments the old woman entered, her white cap fairly quivering with excitement and curiosity and anticipation of the *pour boire* which I gave her, handed me the Imperial letter, which proved to be an extremely courteous reply to my own, saying that all court audiences were over for the summer, but that His Majesty would grant me an audience in the autumn, on his return to the Tuileries.

The failure of this *dernier ressort* was a dire disappointment. There was nothing left for me to do but accept the order for more signals and return to America, which I did in a sorely discouraged frame of mind.

The signals were quickly manufactured, but it was with great difficulty that I succeeded in getting them shipped, as, in spite of the favorable analysis, the different lines persisted in considering them as dangerous. Soon after this the factory was burned, including a large store of expensive chemicals, and my manufacturer obliged me to share the loss.* This misfortune, and the expenses of my disastrous trip abroad, nearly overwhelmed me.

In the mean time, as I mentioned before, we continued to furnish the signals to the Navy Department.

---

* The fire was not caused by any of the chemicals used in manufacturing the signals nor by the signals.

not a great
business
move

at literally cost price, hoping for remuneration in the future. In 1865, however, the signal business was transferred to the Bureau of Navigation, but too late to secure us proper compensation, as on the close of the war the Bureau of Ordnance took measures to manufacture the signals in the Washington Navy-Yard for their own use; but made, I am sorry to say, such poor work of it as to injure the reputation of the signals.

It was now very plain to me that instead of amassing a handsome competence, as I should have done from my husband's invention, I had only sold my patent for an insignificant sum and furnished the signals at a ruinously low rate during the war, in the expectation of justice being done me later. My only hope then was to introduce the signals into the navies of the European countries, and thus win a proper recognition of my husband's talent and my own labors, as well as the wherewithal to educate my children.

I am trenching on a delicate subject in mentioning the only other method of escape from my difficulties open to me, and which was urged upon me by my friends: that is, through the door of matrimony; but the marriage estate was to me too tender, too holy a relation to enter into with the sordid motive of gaining a home; and in consequence, opportunities that came, as they do come to all women, unless unnaturally repulsive, were no temptation to me, no matter in how glittering a disguise; and my children were saved from the pain of seeing a stranger put in the place of their dear father, whose memory to them was sainted.

very revealing of her personality & motives

CHAPTER XXI.

TESTIMONIALS FROM GREAT MEN.

EARLY in the year 1865 the French government, which had treated me much as the British government did poor Jacob Snyder, again opened communication for the express purpose of closing the negotiations. Resolved to try this last chance, I set sail that winter in the French steamer " Lafayette," taking with me my son, Will, now old enough to profit by foreign travel, and a very pretty niece of sixteen, whose parents were anxious for her to see a little of the other side.

Just before we left the wharf a messenger came to me and placed in my hands a packet of letters. I found them to be from my friends in Washington, who, knowing of my persistency and departure, were glad to help me with the following testimonials, of much value in appearing before foreign governments :

" NAVY DEPARTMENT,
" Dec. 5, 1865.

" MADAM :
" Forwarded herewith is a letter from the Chief of the Bureau of Navigation, who has immediate charge of the signals invented by your late husband and perfected by yourself, relative to their value and use in the navy. During the recent rebellion they were

of *incalculable service,* and I take pleasure in transmitting to you this testimonial of their worth.

" Very respectfully,

" GIDEON WELLES,

" *Secretary U. S. Navy.*

"'BUREAU OF NAVIGATION, NAVY DEPARTMENT,

"'WASHINGTON, December 5, 1865.

"'SIR: I have respectfully to report in reply to the communication of Mrs. Martha J. Coston (which has been referred to this bureau) that the lights known as "Coston Signal Lights,".invented by her late husband, Benjamin Franklin Coston, and the right to use which in the navy of the United States was authorized by act of Congress, approved August 5, 1861, have been used on board of all the vessels of the navy during the late rebellion, and are now the only signal symbols used in the navy for signalling at night.

"'Prior to the adoption of these lights of Mrs. Coston, they were subjected to the severest tests known to professional experts, and it was upon the favorable reports of these officers that the Department determined to introduce them into the navy.

"'No lights or other symbols for making night signals in fleets or squadrons have been found, so far as this bureau is aware, in any degree comparable to those known as Coston's Telegraphic Night Signals.

"'I have the honor to be, very respectfully, your obedient servant,

"'THORNTON A. JENKINS,* *Chief of Bureau.*

"'HON. GIDEON WELLES,

"' *Secretary of the Navy.*' "

The following letter speaks for itself:

" WASHINGTON, Dec. 20.

" MADAM:

" It is with great pleasure that I inform you that the signal lights

---

* Now Admiral.

prepared on your plans have been used with entire satisfaction in the Signal Corps of the U. S. Army.

" The lights burn with great brilliancy, intensity, and exactness, and are distinctly visible with the unaided eye at a distance of several miles. They have been of much service to the corps in establishing signal stations during the night. The intensity of the light caused it at once to attract attention, and to be easily distinguished from other lights or fires at any distance. I regard them as the most available and best prepared composition light known to the service.

(Signed) " ALBERT J. MYER,
"*Chief Signal Officer U. S. Army.*"

Again, I found kind words from Admiral Farragut :

" BROOKLYN NAVY-YARD,
" June 22, 1865.

" . . . I can now, however, say to you that during my late command of four years during the war your signals have been in constant use throughout the fleet, and I think have given general satisfaction ; and inasmuch as I know of none which possess any advantages over them, it gives me much pleasure to add my testimonial to their great utility, and I trust you may be fully rewarded for the genius of your late husband, and the zeal and perseverance with which you perfected and introduced them. . . .

" D. G. FARRAGUT,
" *Admiral U. S. Navy.*"

The extract below is taken from a letter from Admiral Porter :

" . . . As you know, I have always been a great advocate of your signals ; they are the very best ever invented, and although we have tried to get up something better, we have never yet succeeded. . . .

" D. D. PORTER,
" *Admiral U. S. Navy.*"

The last but not the least kind testimonial was from Rear-Admiral Smith, and is given in full:

" MADAM:

" It affords me pleasure to add my testimonial to others more potent than mine to the great value of your signals to your country, especially during the recent rebellion, when their great importance was fully tested. The service you have rendered in perfecting and bringing out what your late husband had labored long upon and left unfinished, reflects the highest praise upon your patriotism, ability, and perseverance in completing this valuable improvement.

(Signed) " JOS. SMITH, *Rear-Admiral.*"

These flattering and valuable letters put courage into my heart and nerved me to fresh effort.

Our voyage was rather monotonous, and we were glad to leave the steamer at Brest and take the train for Paris. After a few days at the Grand Hotel, I rented an *appartement* on the Champs Elysées and went to housekeeping; my friend Mrs. General Hennequin procuring for me an old Frenchwoman, Madame Girard, as housekeeper and cook.

Madame Girard was a character; a very marvel of economy and neatness. The most delicious dinners, yet never a scrap of waste, and cooked over a handful of charcoal; wine corks for kindling; potatoes peeled so lightly that they never knew how they had lost their jackets; and the daintiest of *entrées* created out of nothing, one might say. She was so faithful, and made my interests so entirely her own, that Madame Girard became more than a servant to me.

One morning she came to my bedroom, quite excited,

and asked permission to invite a priest, who had called to see her, into my little salon. After he had gone she told me that the good father was the confessor of the Empress Eugénie, and brought her every month a certain sum of money.

"Who sends it to you?" I asked.

"Mon Dieu, madame, I do not know what to make of it!" cried she; and then little by little, relying on my sympathy, she told me her story, remarkable enough to be worth relating.

It seemed that the madame's late husband had been, twenty years before, a prosperous merchant dwelling in a pretty villa in Neuilly, and happy in the possession of one son, Émile, who was handsome and unusually precocious. As soon as the boy was old enough he was placed as a midshipman in the navy, but had scarcely gone on his first voyage to Rio Janeiro when his father was taken suddenly ill and died, leaving his business very much involved.

On Émile's return, some time after, more mature and handsomer than ever, his mother became aware that some influence had been brought to bear not only to send him home, but to give him a fine education and the accomplishments of society. At whose instance this was done Madame Girard could not discover, and the son would not, if he could, reveal.

At twenty, Émile Girard was tall, robust, and elegant in appearance, that I could see from the handsome portrait taken at the time that his mother showed me, and which was her most sacred possession.

Suddenly the young officer was again sent to Rio Janeiro; and very soon after his arrival there, word was received by his mother that her adored son had died of the yellow fever. No satisfactory proofs, however, were sent her, and the stories of his death were conflicting.

A few months after this painful announcement, the priest who had just called began to visit her, and prompted, he said, by charity, brought her every few weeks a certain sum of money. Need I say that Madame Girard clung to the idea of her son's being still alive, and that she looked upon this monthly gift of gold as evidence of it.

Shortly after this confidence, my faithful housekeeper was sent for one evening by a lady of rank in the Faubourg St. Honoré, and on her return came to me, white with agitation. She had found the Countess X—— very ill, and, having partaken of the last sacrament, determined to tell with her expiring breath what she knew in regard to the son so lost to Madame Girard.

It then transpired that on Émile's first visit to Rio Janeiro, a titled woman had fallen desperately in love with him, and, notwithstanding his inferior age and station, made her preference known to him. This lady was the Duchess of ——, and an own cousin of Napoleon III. At her instigation Émile had returned to France to be educated, and on his second voyage to South America they were at once married, and he endowed with a title and exalted to an important position.

Pride, ambition, and flattery had induced the young officer to deny his mother, in compliance with the wishes of his *inamorita,* who was ashamed of his humble origin.

The countess, it seems, had been in the confidence of the Duchess ——, and helped to carry out her plan; but being herself a woman of warm heart and a mother, she had a deep sympathy for the unhappy widow, who knew not whether her son was living or with the dead, and she could not expire in peace until she had lifted a weight from the poor mother's heart.

Madame Girard, though humble by birth, was a proud and sensitive woman. She was cut to the quick by this revelation, and at once determined to make no further investigation, though she was greatly disappointed to find that Rio Janeiro was not in my America, for, like the French people of her class, she did not distinguish between the divisions of the continent. So it transpired that the mother-in-law of a truly *Grande Duchesse* cooked my dinners.

We spent the winter months quietly and not without pleasure, though I was much worried by the dilatoriness of the government, and my suspicions were aroused as to there being something behind this long-continued procrastination. When the spring came I gave up my *appartement,* and for the sake of greater economy put my niece in a *pension* and accompanied her as a parlor boarder.

13*

CHAPTER XXII.

FRANCE COMES FORWARD.

AT last the government, ignoring my price of one hundred and fifty thousand francs for the patent, offered me forty thousand francs (eight thousand dollars) as their final decision. I was loth to accept such a sum, but as it was that or nothing, and as the weather was growing hot, and the cholera threatening, I notified my acceptance to the Minister of Marine, and regarded the affair as settled.

Not so; the agreement was only the preliminary to a severe course of official circumlocution. Thirty times I had to sign my name, " Mme. Veuve Coston," and as many times did I have to explain to the curious officials how it came about that an *Americaine* was drawing so much money from the coffers of France. In fact, I was nearly talked to death, and delighted at the prospect of leaving Paris.

The Minister of Marine at once issued the following bulletin to the French navy:

" FRANCE:
" OFFICIAL BULLETIN OF THE FRENCH NAVY,
" 1867.

" Adoption of new signal lights for sea service, entitled ' Coston's Telegraphic Night Signals.'

" The Minister of the Navy and Colonies to the *Préfets Mari-*

times, Governeurs of Colonies, Generals, Superiors, and others, officers commanding at sea.

" 1. Administration—movements of the fleet and military oper-ations. 2. Bureau—movement of the fleet. 5. Administration—artillery. 1. Bureau. 2. Section material.

" PARIS, January 11, 1867.

" GENTLEMEN : For several years the Department of the Navy has caused experiments to be made, by the Squadron of Evolutions, of the Telegraphic Night Signals invented by the late Mr. Coston, and submitted by his widow, who has secured them by letters patent in France.

" The report upon these experiments proves as follows :

" *First.* That these lights are superior in brilliancy, rapidity, and above all in extent of range, to those heretofore in use.

" *Second.* They can always be determined with precision and without hesitation by the naked eye at a distance of five and a half miles. The largest can be perceived at a distance of eleven miles, the smallest at a distance of six miles only; while at a distance of three miles it is impossible to recognize the combina-tions of the regulation lights, and at five and a half miles the latter can no longer be distinguished with precision even with the aid of the telescope.

" *Third. The duration of the Coston Lights, during the existence of a northeast gale, experienced by the squadron on the* 21*st of August,* 1863, *was not sensibly altered;* and it has always been possible to make use of them by the simple assistance of two men.

" *Fourth. Their use, during the confusion of a battle, allowed the admiral to cause the firing to cease and be resumed instantane-ously at various intervals, notwithstanding the density of the smoke and the flashing of the exploding guns.*

" *Fifth.* And, finally, these signals form a night telegraph as simple, as certain, and as rapid as the day telegraph with aid of flags.

" On the other hand, complete sets of these signals have been shipped on board of vessels destined to make long voyages, and after having remained for *two years and a half* on several different ships their state of preservation was found to be satisfactory.

" The Board of Admiralty having indorsed the immediate adoption of the ' Coston Night Signals,' which the Committee of Marine Artillery moreover found to be in good condition as regards manufacture and serviceability, I have entered into an agreement with Madame Coston, which secures to the government the right to manufacture, *for its exclusive use*, either in public arsenals or private establishments, the Night Signals in question, the same to retain in their official title the name ' *Coston Telegraphic Night Signals.*'

" I am making arrangements for the manufacture of a certain quantity of these lights, and you will receive in due time instructions for their use.

" Accept, &c., &c., &c.

" P. ed Chasseloup Laubat,

" *Minister Secretary of the Government for the Navy and the Colonies.*"

In this connection I print a letter bearing on the subject received some time before :

" Flag-ship, 'Solferino,'

" Squadron of Evolutions,

" Office of Admiral, Com.-in-Chief,

" Jan. 25, 1865.

" Madame :

" I take pleasure in informing you that all the admirals, captains, officers, and sailors of the Squadron of Evolutions, for the last two years under my command, are equally astonished with myself at the results the signals have afforded us at sea, in all weathers and under all circumstances. The Admiral Rigault de Genouilly,* my predecessor, was not less satisfied than myself. All my reports, as well as his own, give evidence of this fact.

(Signed)   " Count Bouet Willaumez,

" *Vice-Admiral, Commander-in-Chief of the Squadron of Evolutions.*

" To Madame Coston, Hôtel d'Albe,

" Champs Elysées, Paris."

---

* Afterwards Minister of Marine.

In this connection I give the flattering extract, translated from a letter* written the 26th of April, 1860, by the Count, Admiral Lebarbier de Finan, to his Excellency the Minister of the Naval Marine of France,—Bade d'Hyeres :

"These signals, 'Feux Télégraphiques de Nuit Coston,' could also be employed with advantage in the army for the transmission of orders at night. If the French army had been furnished with signals of this kind before Sebastopol, the surprise which led to the premature attack of the command under General de Miran would have been an impossibility."

CHAPTER XXIII.

ROMA—A HANDSOME MARCHESE

As soon as the affair was settled, I sent my son home to America, and with my niece Eleanor started for warmer climes, on the recommendation of my physician. *En route* to Nice we stopped at Toulon, where I sent with my card a letter of introduction to the naval commander. He at once called and invited me to visit the island, where the signals were being manufactured, and see what perfection they had already attained.

---

* On file at the French Navy Department, Paris.

A government boat, with the French colors flying, and well manned, took us to the manufactory. A large room was then darkened, and the signals burned with success. During these experiments the commander excused himself to visit another part of the factory; and while he was gone one of the artisans, not knowing who I was, informed me with the greatest ingenuousness that they had been trying for five years to make these colors, but could not until the American recipes had been bought.

I was really shocked, for this at once explained to me not only why the purchase of the patent had been so long delayed, but the reason for the French government buying repeatedly quantities of the signals. It was almost incomprehensible to me that the government of a great nation could stoop to swindle a stranger, —that stranger a woman.

On arriving at Nice, I was entranced with the delicious climate, abundance of fruit, variety of lovely flowers, and the discovery that quite a number of my friends, both French and American, were here in their villas; and indeed during my stay here their kindness and hospitality was most unbounded. Only one blot marred my sojourn in Nice, and that I shall give as an evidence of what a few careless words may effect from the lips of a compatriot in foreign society.

At a dinner given by a wealthy lady, Admiral Goldsborough, who was in command of the United States squadron then stationed near Nice, was present, and so also were two friends of mine.

In the course of conversation at table one of these friends, Mrs. Depau, who knew that at the commencement of his career my young husband had been in the United States navy, asked the admiral if he knew me.

"Oh, no," replied the gallant sailor. "Mrs. Coston's husband was only a gunner, and we never associate with people of that rank, you know."

This reply extremely annoyed Mrs. Depan, who replied that while ignorant of Mr. Coston's rank, Mrs. Coston was her friend, and most certainly a lady; and she afterwards took occasion to say to him that she regretted that he should have made a remark in public so calculated to injure my standing in society.

Just before I left Nice, Mrs. Depau told me of this conversation, and asked me to frankly tell her the truth. I did so with indignation, and she was shocked, and at a loss, like myself, to understand the admiral's statement, which had resulted in coolness on the part of several society people who had heard him. She begged me to remain and openly contradict it, but this I felt it beneath me to do.

When we left, it was for Italy, and accompanied by a daughter of Dr. J. Marion Sims, who had been left in my care by her father, but had since accepted an invitation to visit our minister to Italy, Mr. and Mrs. George P. Marsh, and wished to make the journey with me.

We started, a cheerful little party composed of Miss Sims, my niece Eleanor, and myself, in a *vettura,*— *via* the Corniche Road so celebrated,—drawn by good stout horses. A more delightful drive one could not conceive. We took three days for the journey to Genoa, resting at night at the little inns on the way.

In Genoa we visited many of the private palaces, and bought some of the delicate filigree jewelry for which the city is famous, and then went on to Florence, where we were met by Dr. Sims and Mr. Fred. Frothingham, the young son of an old and true friend of mine who wished to make the tour of Italy with us. After a brief rest we parted with Dr. and Miss Sims, and, accompanied by Mr. Frothingham, pushed on to Rome that evening.

We found the train crowded to excess, and with difficulty obtained seats in an already well-filled compartment. Eight adults and two babies I counted as we rolled out of the depot, and though the night was warm, the windows remained tightly closed for fear the *bambini* would take cold.

The atmosphere soon became unendurable, producing nausea and headache. How should we bear it until morning? I wondered. We made several attempts at stations by the way to see the conductor, but in vain, and on we rushed nearly asphyxiated.

Fortunately for us, at about midnight the carriage took fire from the friction of the wheels underneath; the flames bursting forth just as we were starting off from a way station. Later, the consequences might have been serious; as it was, we were promptly bundled out by the guard, and with the firm determination not to get into that carriage again, we walked along the length of the platform, and at last discovered the door of a first-class carriage open.

Looking in, I saw it was occupied by only one gentleman. I asked him in French if the compartment was private, or fully occupied. He looked at me for a moment in silence, and then sprang out with the courteous remark,—

"I have taken this compartment for myself, but I am most happy to place it at your service."

We gratefully accepted his courtesy; indeed, there was no alternative, for the conductor gave the signal to start, and we had barely time to get in. The change was delightful; there was room for us to recline in comfortable positions and rest from the fatigue of sitting bolt upright, as we had been obliged to do for four hours.

I fell into a light slumber, occasionally waking to observe that my niece, who was very timid, was sitting erect, and with her big brown eyes wide open. From my own, half closed, I noticed that the gentleman opposite cast an occasional half-furtive, half-admiring glance at her.

When we stopped to have our passports examined,— for this was in 1867, during the reign of the Pope, —our fellow-passenger volunteered to show us the way, and with Mr. Frothingham preceded us. He was so apparently pleased at recognizing the spread eagle upon our papers that I felt sure he had entertained a high regard for some of our compatriots. In the light of early morning I had a better opportunity to judge of

14

his appearance and face ; I was struck with the beauty of his thoroughly Roman profile, and the elegance of his bearing when he threw off the greatcoat of fur that had enveloped him.   As we drew near Rome, our handsome Samaritan pointed out the various places of interest as we passed, and finally asked if we knew anything of the hotels in the Eternal City ; if not, he would take the liberty of recommending to us the Hôtel d'Angleterre as the best.

I thanked him and replied, " We have made our arrangements to go to the Hôtel de Rome, and prefer not to deviate from our plans."

As we steamed into the depot, the gentleman handed me his card and begged me to accept the use of his carriage, which would come to meet the train, and was quite at our disposal, while Mr. Frothingham remained with the keys to have our baggage examined.

I glanced at the card, and saw that it bore the name of the Marchese Celso Bargagli, Palazzo Torlonia. I hesitated embarrassed, when our impetuous young escort exclaimed, " Pray do, Mrs. Coston ; it will save you and Miss Eleanor from waiting in the uncomfortable station while I go through the customs catechism."

I made an evasive reply, the train came to a stop, and for a few moments we were busy gathering up our various wraps, umbrellas, etc., then we gladly alighted.

An imposing coachman, in drab livery braided with gold that made him look like a Quaker bandit (if one can imagine the combination), came forward to greet the marchese, whose carriage stood near at hand, and was, I noticed, emblazoned with the coronet of a duke and attended by outriders in drab and gold.

" Madame," said the marchese, with a profound bow, "will you not honor me by accepting this trifling courtesy from a Roman? I myself shall drive home in a *voiture.*"

I felt to refuse would offend, though I disliked incurring this fresh obligation, and accepted only on the stipulation that the marchese went with us. His black eyes sparkled with pleasure as he accepted the condition and assisted us into the satin-lined carriage.

It seemed as if fate had appointed the marchese to be our rescuer from difficulties, for when we reached the hotel we were told that every room was taken and we must look elsewhere. No sooner, however, did the marchese intercede for us than, as if by magic, comfortable apartments were found, and the profound attention paid to every suggestion he made showed that in Rome at least he was a person of importance.

By the time we had made our toilets and descended to breakfast, Mr. Frothingham joined us, and was delighted with our arrangements. Later in the day we went out to drive and pay some visits, in the course of which we learned through friends long resident in Rome that the Marchese Bargagli belonged to one of the most ancient and noble houses in Italy, and was heir to the fortune and title of the late ambassador from the Grand Duke of Tuscany, near to the Holy Father.

The elder Bargagli it seems was greatly attached to

the Grand Duke, and when the latter was dethroned, it so affected his mind and health that he succumbed easily to an attack of fever. The marchese himself was considered a man of brilliant parts and a leader in society. He lived in the same princely style as his late uncle, whose fortune he inherited, and used the family carriage and livery which I had already noticed.

CHAPTER XXIV.

AN AUDIENCE OF THE POPE.

THE next day Mr. Frothingham called in person upon the Marchese Bargagli to make his acknowledgment of that gentleman's courtesies to my niece and self, and returned delighted with his visit, the agreeable manner of his host, and his luxurious surroundings. After an exchange of compliments, the marchese asked permission to call, which Mr. Frothingham of course granted. The following morning the marchese appeared in grand toilet, to pay his respects and to tender the use of his box at the opera for " Traviata," the next evening; adding that as he was in mourning for his uncle, he could not have the pleasure of accompanying us.

My niece, who was passionately fond of music, turned her large eyes pleadingly towards me, and this, with the delicacy with which the invitation was extended, decided me to accept.

The next evening we made our toilets before dinner for the opera; but while we were still lingering in the dining-room over dessert, a black-bordered note was placed in my hand, which I found on opening was from the marchese, and a graceful request that we should make use of his carriage for that evening, as his servants were familiar with the route, box, etc.

In a few moments we had donned our opera-cloaks, descended to the carriage, and were whirled away to the opera; Mr. Frothingham of course acting as our escort.

The audience was fashionable and brilliant, the boxes well filled, and our own of course, as that of the marchese, attracted no little attention, which might have been attributed to the fact that we were foreigners, and that my niece in her dress of white silk, swans-down, and camellias, was really charming, and my own severely simple toilet of black velvet and jet showed hers off to even greater advantage.

We enjoyed the evening thoroughly, and were sorry when the divine music came to a close; but the drive through the moonlit, romantic streets seemed a fitting finale.

Every day that followed was of pleasure, and time fled with dazzling wings. Sight-seeing, society, the opera, and delightful drives in the country were enjoyed, often in the society of the marchese, who was always entertaining and considerate. His devotion, however, to my niece was becoming so apparent that it would have caused me anxiety had I not seen that to her the gallant marchese was but one feature of her visit to Rome.

One enchanting afternoon we drove to the Pincian Hill, where all the fashionable world assembles to listen to the dreamy music, enjoy the cool air, fragrant with flowers, and gossip. Among the gentlemen who came up to our carriage was the marchese, who asked permission to present Count Piccolomini, his cousin, and for many years First Chamberlain to the Grand Duke of Tuscany, the marchese himself having been Second Chamberlain.

The count, a descendant of the famous family of Piccolomini, which had given Italy a pope, four cardinals, and a number of great warriors and literati, was a man of about fifty years, of majestic appearance, a scholar and a finished linguist, and also gifted with extreme felicity of expression. His society was most agreeable, and later we passed many pleasant hours, listening to his delightful discourse on the history of Rome, with which he was thoroughly familiar, on the church, of which he was a devout adherent, and on Pope Pius IX., with whom he was on intimate terms.

The count himself occupied a suite of apartments at the Hôtel de Rome, so that we naturally saw much of each other.

About this time, in company with a number of other American ladies, including my niece, I was presented to His Holiness the Pope. We of course wore the plain black dress and long black veil, without gloves, that Papal etiquette with good sense prescribes; and on driving to the Vatican at the appointed hour, found a large number of people assembled in the grand logia; and as all were clad in the same simplicity of sable, one could have imagined the occasion to be of the funereal order.

After some time the doors were thrown open and the white sheep separated from the black; that is to say, the Roman Catholics were gathered together and ushered into the audience-chamber, where they had a special reception and were dismissed. The rest of us, all Protestants, were then allowed to enter; but it did not seem to me that this distinction was truly catholic, or a very happy one. However, we entered the large chamber, at one end of which, on a raised dais, stood the Pope.

His Holiness was clothed in flowing white, with a broad girdle, from which was suspended a carved crucifix; on his head was a small, close-fitting cap. This garb became him, and I was impressed by the paternal, nay, almost maternal expression of his benevolent countenance and fine black eyes.

We were required to stand in two rows, one on either side of the chamber, and running its entire length,— of course facing each other. His Holiness then briefly addressed us in French, and with some indifference of manner, though his words were well chosen, congratulated us that the terrible war in our country was over, concluding with, "I suppose you are all travelling for pleasure, and will go from here to Naples; may you have a pleasant journey, and welcome back to Rome for Lent;" adding, "I see many of you have beads and rosaries in your hands, which I suppose you would like blessed" (in a matter-of-fact tone, and extending his hands); "I hereby bless them (*ensemble*) all together."

This wholesale way of doing things was not impressive, but I suppose for convenience' sake was necessary.

As His Holiness descended from the dais and passed down between the lines, a Boston lady who had her little child with her, dressed in pure white,—as if *voue au blanc*,—rushed forward and threw herself at the Pope's feet, exclaiming, theatrically, "Holy Father, bless my child!"

The Pope naturally asked, "Are you a Catholic?"

"No," murmured the lady, blushing; and the kind-hearted old man, with a look of gentle reproof, blessed the little maid and passed quietly on. The rest of us were mortified at the bad taste of a countrywoman who wished to gain for her child the privileges of a faith that she did not profess.

One evening, not long after this event, we were at the dinner-table, when the conversation, which was general,—for most of those present had been in the hotel for some months and had become acquainted,—turned on the holy staircase.

It happened that on my right sat a good-natured Irish priest from Cork, Father Scannel, and just opposite us an American lady, a recent convert to the Romish faith, and, like all converts, more bitter and bigoted than those born in the belief, and delighting to give a thrust whenever occasion offered to any one differing from her; feeling, I suppose, that she would also be supported by other Catholics, a number of whom were present.

When the subject of the holy staircase came up, she asked me if I had seen it. I replied that I had been up the holy staircase that day.

"Do you mean to say that you, a Protestant, have ascended the staircase on your knees and recited a prayer for each step?" she queried.

"No," I replied, calmly; "for I do not believe in the custom and could not conform to it."

"Pray, how did you get up, then?" she asked.

I then proved that I had been up to the altar by describing the interesting things to be seen there, and concluded by saying that I had ascended the side staircase.

"Ah!" she said, ironically. "I suppose that is the way you expect to get to heaven?"

I was mortified and surprised that a countrywoman should so far forget herself, when Father Scannel, in dignified and measured words, said, "Madame Coston will go there upon Jacob's ladder of faith, hope, and *charity*," emphasizing the last word.

This utterly silenced my Catholic countrywoman, and I was given to understand that afterwards this kind-hearted man reprimanded her in private, admonishing her that it was a poor way to make people respect her church. I myself was aware that her ill-bred and sarcastic thrusts—for this was one out of many—emanated from jealousy of the devotion of the gentlemen present to myself and niece. Little did I realize that through this trifling incident I had made a bitter enemy.

About the same time I was reminded of the unpleasant occurrence in Nice, by a lady with whom I was intimate telling me that a fashionable woman of New York had refused to be introduced to me, because she had been given to understand at Nice "that Mr. Coston was a common gunner in the United States navy."

I told my friend how the story originated. She was shocked, and at once insisted on my writing to Admiral Goldsborough and demanding to know on what grounds he had made his assertions in regard to my late husband. This I at first refused to do, but was finally overruled by Mrs. L——, herself a woman of the world, who declared I owed it to my friends as well as to myself to put an end to this rumor.

I addressed my letter to the admiral's flag-captain, whom I bade read and present it to his chief. I did this to prevent the admiral ignoring the letter, which he could not do when another officer was aware of its existence.

In reply the admiral admitted that he had made the remark attributed to him, but without the intention of doing me any harm, and closing with an humble apology. I at once sent the letter to my friends in Nice, who were astonished that Admiral Goldsborough should have placed himself in a position requiring such an apology.

They were satisfied, but I was not, for I knew that no one realized better than a naval officer what rank meant abroad; and if it had been true that my husband was but a common gunner, the admiral should have been pleased to see me holding such a position abroad, and have tried rather to sustain than to crush me.

CHAPTER XXV.

COUNT PICCOLOMINI.

In spite of the revival of this unpleasant incident, our days in Rome passed by like a beautiful dream. That much of my happiness was due to the devotion of Count Piccolomini I could not deny to myself, and the evident pleasure he took in my society, his intelligent delight in listening to my descriptions of America, its politics, its laws and people, naturally flattered me, for the count was a man accustomed to being listened to.

I knew that I was idealized, and the profound reverence with which he not only treated, but talked about me I was made aware of by the marked courtesy paid me by the different members of his titled and illustrious family. I was warmly urged by his niece, a duchess by marriage, to visit the Piccolomini palace near Sienna with her.

My respect and admiration for the count's character and ability was great. I felt, too, the sweetness of being beloved, nor was I insensible to the fact that as the Countess Piccolomini I could hold my own in the proudest courts of Europe. To be brief, our delightful friendship terminated in a betrothal, and we received the congratulations of our friends.

One calm, perfect evening, a few days after our engagement had been announced, I found myself unaccountably depressed, and filled with a thousand doubts and fears. Unable to eat, I excused myself and retired from the dinner-table. Almost immediately the count followed in alarm, for I was not a woman of whims, and insisted on ordering for me some rare old cordial.

I sipped a tiny glass of this to please him, but could not shake off my depression, though he tried to divert me by planning all sorts of pleasures for our future and the happiness of those we loved.

It had happened that afternoon that the Marchese Bargagli had formally demanded of me the hand of my niece in marriage, and I found was basing his hopes not a little on the belief that as the Countess Piccolomini I would remain in Italy, which in itself would be an inducement to Eleanor to listen to his suit. He added that by his uncle's will he could only marry a Roman Catholic, and live on the family estates. Did I think there was any chance for him?

I replied to the marchese that I could not listen to him, and, as he must have been aware, had endeavored to discourage his attentions to my niece, who was not only too young to think of marriage, but I myself was responsible for her return to her parents free from any entanglement, and he must address himself to them, though it seemed to me wiser for him to defer his suit altogether until she was more mature.

At this the marchese, naturally so gay and witty, became quiet and almost morose; his handsome face so tinged with melancholy that it increased my low state of spirits. However, he with the others soon joined us in the salon, which rapidly filled, as the Marchese Ferdinand Lotoringa della Stufa, a very high-bred Tuscan, who spoke English with perfection, and some other Italian friends came to pay their respects, also Captain Beaumont, of the United States navy, who commanded the monitor "Miantonomah," then lying at Civita Vecchia.

The captain called to invite us to make up a party to visit his ship, which it was agreed we should do the next day. Our visitors stayed an hour or more, and with great difficulty I exerted myself to conceal the unaccountable depression that had seized upon me, while I thought I had never seen the count so charming and considerate in his endeavors to save me from ex-ertion in entertaining our callers.

Scarcely had they gone when I rose to retire to my apartments. The count begged me to give him a few moments. He was anxious, fearing that my low spirits

H   15

indicated some unhappiness or trouble, and in the most eloquent and impassioned language he pictured my life as it should be, and the care and devotion it would be his delight to surround me with.

When I bade him good-night his fine face was aglow with feeling; love had brought out every tender and refining sentiment, softening the lineaments of his rather severe countenance, and I thought that I had never realized before how perfect a type of noble Italian beauty and manhood he was.

Through the night I slumbered uneasily, and rose early in the morning, irritated at finding the same heavy weight upon my spirits. While I was dressing, just at seven, as I noticed by my travelling clock, came a rap at the door. It was the count's valet asking me to give him the address of Dr. Tausey, the eminent German physician, as his master wanted to see him.

My niece, who was already dressed, went to our parlor, found the doctor's visiting-card, and gave it to the man. Dr. Tausey was the physician and friend of Miss Charlotte Cushman, at whose artistic and lovely villa I had often met him. I idly wondered for a moment why the count wished to see the doctor, and then remembering his fondness for early morning walks on these fine days, and his expressed intention of calling on the doctor, I concluded he had merely gone to make the call. That Count Piccolomini was ill did not for a moment occur to me.

It was nearly nine o'clock when Mr. Frothingham came up to see if we were ready for breakfast. I told

Eleanor to go down with him, and I would follow a few moments later. Before I left the room, however, she rushed in with a pale, excited face to say that the landlord had met her on his way to my room with the words, "Count Piccolomini is most dangerously ill; does not Madame Coston know it?"

I was extremely startled, and went at once with Mr. Frothingham to the count's apartments. The door was ajar. I walked quickly in, and then stood rooted to the spot at the spectacle of the man whom the night before I had parted from in robust health and full of hope and *gaieté de cœur*, now stretched out on his bed, white and rigid, his eyes fixed under their purple lids, and his breath coming and going in short gasps.

At the foot of the bed stood his body-servant, weeping bitterly. The Marchese Bargagli, pale and troubled, stood with folded arms by his side. Dr. Tausey was feeling the sick man's pulse. He let go of his hand and, coming forward, led me from the room with gentle force. Once in the corridor, I implored him to tell me if the count was in great danger.

"Mrs. Coston, I cannot deceive you; Count Piccolomini is dying!" he answered, gravely.

The blow made me reel, but I felt I must know the cause of this terrible calamity, and begged the doctor to tell me the cause of this sudden and fatal attack.

"I do not know," said he, in a strange voice. "I have only been here ten minutes, and I came too late."

"What do you mean, Dr. Tausey?" I cried, with a suspicion too dreadful to put into words.

"I mean—nothing!" answered the physician, in a cold, hard voice; but I noticed his expression was strained, and the lines of his face deepened as he spoke.

He returned to the room where the unfortunate count lay, still unconscious, and deaf to the voice even of the woman he adored. In this heavy sleep he passed into death.

The next few days were a bitter trial, culminating in ceremonious funeral obsequies, in which the Piccolomini family insisted on my taking part as the *fiancée* of the late head of their house, for the count had announced our betrothal to them. The funeral took place in the ancient and stately church, where a grand high mass was celebrated.

Robed in deep mourning, we drove in the family carriage, which was sent for us, to the church, where we were met at the doors by the Marchese Bargagli, who led us to the seats reserved for the mourners, placing me at the head of the coffin as chief mourner. The ordeal was so painful to me that in order to maintain my self-possession I tried neither to think nor to feel, and mechanically began observing all the details of the arrangements.

I saw that over the coffin, which was placed in the nave before the great altar, was thrown a huge pall of rich red cloth quite twenty feet square, heavily embroidered in gold and gems with the Piccolomini coat of arms, a deep fringe of gold forming the border that lay upon the marble floor.

The count's court uniform of écru, lined with crimson and worked in gold, his jewelled sword, *chapeau de bras*, and glittering decorations were laid on the coffin, around which were grouped the ladies of the family, the Monseigneurs of the Pope, Prince Corsini, Prince Rospiliosi, and various other titled dignitaries.

The mass was long, and the music impressive and soul-stirring. Only the strangeness of my surroundings, and the extreme dignity and hauteur of those about me, enabled my pride to overcome my emotion. . . .

To my surprise, though I supposed it incumbent upon me to make the first formal visit of consolation, I was forestalled by the noble ladies of the Piccolomini family, who came to see me and were profuse in their expressions of sympathy.

CHAPTER XXVI.

THE MYSTERY—THE ITALIAN MARINE.

As I began to recover from the sharpness of the blow, over and over again, like an irritating phantom, rose the question, " What did the count die of?" For no one as yet had given the cause of his death a name, although heart-disease and apoplexy had been hinted at. The thought so haunted me that I determined to see Dr. Tausey, but failed so repeatedly in my endeavors that I began to think he avoided me.

At last I met him one day in the Corso, and in spite of our surroundings I seized the opportunity to ask him the cause of Count Piccolomini's decease.

"Do not ask me," he said, brusquely. "I was called in too late."

"At what time were you called in?" I inquired.

"The count's valet called for me at a few minutes before nine; I came at once, and had not been in the room ten minutes before you entered."

I knew that I gave Tito, the valet, the doctor's address at seven that fatal morning, and I paused a moment in surprise at this revelation, but roused myself to ask,—

"Was there no post-mortem or inquest held, such as we have in America?"

"No," said the doctor, starting off hurriedly.

"Stop, Dr. Tausey," I cried. "Do they do these things in Rome?" my voice rather than my words revealing my meaning.

"Mrs. Coston," said he, with averted eyes, "they do all sorts of things in Rome." And with that he hastened away, leaving me more than dismayed.

Any one can imagine the horrid conjectures that after this preyed upon my mind, rendered the more dreadful when I discovered that others beside myself entertained them, especially the count's friend, Marchese Lotoringa della Stufa. The Count Piccolomini, I may not have mentioned, was a very wealthy man, and the last lineal heir of the Piccolomini family. Dying unmarried, his immense fortune would have gone to his relatives in Rome and Sienna, or, it is said, the Pope thought would revert to the church. Married, it was in his power to will it to me,—a foreigner and a Protestant.

Indirectly I was led to suspect that the American lady with whom I had had the absurd little tilt about the holy staircase had taken pains to attract attention to the count's devotion to me, and inadvertently brought a dreadful influence to bear upon his fate. At all events, a hateful mystery surrounded the affair, and was not lessened when the Marchese Bargagli placed all the papers of his cousin, the late count, in my hands, to deliver to his relatives in Florence and Sienna, which struck me as especially strange, as the marchese intended going shortly to Florence himself.

Some few weeks after the count's death we moved quietly on to Florence, where we took apartments, and I acquitted myself of my painful mission.

At that time the American legation was stationed in that city, instead of at Rome as it is at present. I had before had the good fortune to meet our minister, the Hon. George P. Marsh, who for twenty-four years has so ably represented us abroad, as well as Mrs. Marsh, a highly cultivated and charming woman.

They now took this opportunity to show me every kindness, and Mr. Marsh presented me to the Minister of the Marine as a woman not only of business capacity, but a lady of high social position in her own country, asking for me every consideration. As both Mr. and Mrs. Marsh were on intimate terms with King

Victor Emmanuel and the Princess Marguerite, whose English education Mrs. Marsh was superintending, their introduction was of great weight, and instead of my being obliged to petition the Marine Department for a trial of my signals, the Minister of the Marine at once called upon me and asked me to send him some signals for trial by the Italian government.

Unfortunately, I had brought none with me, and was obliged to say so. Signor Rachia then asked me if I could not obtain some from the United States Mediterranean Squadron. I did not like to refuse this request, so much to my own interest to fulfil, though it necessitated my writing to Admiral Goldsborough.

Still, I thought after the unpleasant experience with him he might be glad to do me a service by way of reparation; so I sacrificed my dignity and wrote for them, not as a favor to me, but one he might extend to the Italian government. I felt I deserved the humiliation, when the post brought the reply that " Admiral Goldsborough did not feel himself at liberty to give away the government goods."

I was forced to admit my defeat to the Minister of the Marine, who stroked his long beard thoughtfully as he asked, "How can we get some signals for trial, madame? We have been anxious to do so ever since we learned that France had adopted them for use in her navy."

I was more than puzzled, for after the United States government had taken to making the signals my manufacturer had closed his factory and joined a whaling expedition to Iceland. Finally a happy thought struck me.

"Do not," I asked, "governments do each other favors? and if so, cannot you, Signor Rachia, write to the Italian minister at Washington, asking him to obtain through the Secretary of the Navy a sufficient supply for trial?"

The minister thought this a good idea, and asked me if I would at the same time indite a letter to the Secretary of the Navy, saying that the request had been authorized by me.

Of course I complied, and by return post received an exceedingly kind letter from the Navy Department, to the effect that Mr. Welles was happy to render me such a slight service, and had ordered a box of signals to be sent to New York and shipped on the " Franklin," which was to sail in a few days under command of Admiral Farragut.

Mr. Faxon, the Assistant Secretary of the Navy, also wrote that Admiral Farragut would leave the box of signals at Cherbourg in care of the United States consul there, and suggested that I should address him by letter at that place, in care of the consul, reminding him to leave the signals, as the admiral was on his way up the Baltic, and, with the press of other matters on his mind, might forget this mission.

I at once followed Mr. Faxon's suggestion, and in due season received in reply a very pleasant letter from Admiral Farragut, saying that the box of signals had been forgotten and left in the navy-yard at Brooklyn;

m

but that my letter was so explicit that he understood the purpose for which I wanted the signals, and had at once given orders to have all the signals on the " Colorado," Admiral Goldsborough's vessel, collected, boxed, and, accompanied with the directions for use, forwarded to the Italian Minister of the Marine.

This letter also explained to me that the " Franklin" was hereafter to be the flag-ship of the Mediterranean Squadron, and accordingly Admiral Goldsborough had been obliged to take the "Colorado" home and turn over his flag to Admiral Farragut.

By this strange turn of the wheel of fortune Admiral Goldsborough was forced to give up the signals he so churlishly refused to grant the Italian government ; and at the same time a mere accident saved me from an utter failure with the government of Italy ; for it afterwards transpired that the box of signals left in the Brooklyn Navy-Yard were made by the government, of inferior material, and eventually proved utterly worthless, while those on the " Colorado" were some left of the war supply made by my own manufacturer, every one of which was perfect.

When the signals were delivered to the Marine Department, Mr. Marsh kindly selected for me an able agent to carry on the negotiations with the government, as it was so contrary to the Italian code of official etiquette to negotiate with a lady. Mr. Jacob Brown, the agent, was not only a shrewd man, but had a thorough knowledge of the Italian language.

CHAPTER XXVII.

THE GUEST OF THE GOVERNMENT.

DURING our stay in Florence we took occasion to visit the Piccolomini palaces, under the escort of the Marchese Bargagli. I was enchanted with the beauty of the drive to Sienna; the mountains that rose before us, one after another, some gray, barren, and forbidding, others refulgent in splendid russets and vivid greens. Now and then we passed vineyards, purple with their glory of fruit and gay with the voices of women and children wearing the big Siennese hats, and singing in their clear high voices the joyous songs of the people.

The green of the roadside was dotted with yellow and crimson flowers and a beautiful dark-blue daisy, which I had never seen before. As we left the country and drove through the rough and crooked streets of the old city, lined with tall dark palaces, the church-bells rang out with a sweet volume of sound, and the mellow sunshine lit up the red walls and brought out the odor of the golden and crimson roses that were trying with success to climb over the old stony ramparts. St. Catherine's City seemed filled with light, music, and vivid color.

We roamed through the grounds of the Piccolomini palace, under the yellow chestnuts, through clumps of

broad-leafed fig-trees, thickets of red and white camellias, and groves of the pale gray-green olive;
gathered handfuls of double roses, dark wall-flowers,
scarlet sage, fiery geraniums, gorgeous cacti, and the
brilliant blossoms of the pomegranate.᾽

With some reluctance I followed the others through
the portals of the palace, and hurriedly passed through
the different apartments, desolate and forlorn to me in
their treasures of art lavishly scattered about, the heirlooms and relics on every side, and the magnificent
picture-gallery of departed Piccolomini.

To me, far more interesting was the little crumbling
chapel attached to the grand cathedral, where for five
hundred years the count's ancestors, including the Popes
who had made the name historic, had been laid to rest.
Here, too, had been interred the body of the count, the
bold Roman script that recorded his titles and age painfully clear and fresh in comparison with the almost
indecipherable inscriptions of the antique stones about
him.

Later in the day we dined at the palace of the Marchese Bargagli, but I was unable to eat, and, partly
from emotion and over-fatigue, was taken suddenly ill
and obliged to retire to one of the vast and uninhabited
chambers of the palace, attended by an old Italian
woman, the care-taker of the place.

I could not, as I lay upon a bed of state, huge, high,
and hung with ancient tapestry, divest myself of the
idea that I was in a church, so lofty was the vaulted
ceiling, so plainly did the marble floor resound at the

footsteps of the old woman; while the carved stone pillars and the frescoed walls added to the illusion.

Neither my niece nor self could speak in the Provincial dialect, and we had to express our wants in pantomime to the willing attendant. Towards morning I fell into a sound sleep, waking from it feeling much better and refreshed.

A delicious little breakfast of fruits, wine, coffee, and the daintiest of rolls, arranged on an exquisite little service of ancient silver-gilt and Venetian glass, was sent up to us, and soon afterwards we took our departure, escorted by a brother of the Marchese (Mario), and returned to beautiful Florence.

Shortly after this we decided to visit Venice, and were started off on our journey by many kind friends, who, laden with lovely flowers, came to see us off at the station. Among them were the Marchese Bargagli, his brother, the Marquis della Stufa, and Captain Racchia, the Assistant Minister of the Italian Marine Department.

A private car had been placed at our service, adding much to the comfort of the journey, while the Minister of the Marine telegraphed to Venice to an Italian naval officer stationed there, "relieving him from duty to meet Madame Coston, and show her Venice."

The next morning we arrived at the famous city, for we had travelled steadily all night. When we left the train, a fine-looking young officer, dressed in full uniform, presented himself, and, after asking if I was Madame Coston, made a profound bow, introducing himself as Lieutenant St. Ambroise, and stating that his government had placed him at my service as long as I should remain in Venice, and that he had already there a government gondola waiting for us, and another for our baggage, which he said the gondoliers would take charge of and bring to the Hôtel Danielli, where we had arranged to stay.

The lieutenant insisted on seeing that we had pleasant rooms, and then took leave of us, with the understanding that he should call the following morning and take us on our first sight-seeing expedition in the city.

There seemed to be an unusual commotion in the hotel; a great many flags were flying, the rooms were lavishly decorated with flowers, and every now and then strains of music floated through the windows. On asking the occasion of this, we were informed that Prince Napoleon, "Plon-Plon," the husband of the Princess Clotilde and son-in-law of the king, was stopping at the hotel.

The next morning a beautiful gondola, with the government flags flying, arrived with the young officer, and at the same time looking from our balcony we saw another gondola equally handsome, and evidently intended for the prince, as servants wearing his livery at once entered it. It seems the prince, too, was a guest of the government, and as he also had the Italian colors flying from his gondola, we attracted a great deal of attention, the people in the house and vicinity being greatly exercised to know who the ladies were that were receiving such flattering attention from the country.

We spent the day and the following week in visiting various places of interest, including the venerable churches, the curious glass-works and interesting picture-galleries, and many private palaces and art collections never opened to the ordinary traveller, under the care of Lieutenant St. Ambroise, who, familiar with the history and literature of both his country and our own, was a very intelligent cicerone, and we were pleased to have him dine with us on our return, when the day's pleasures were over.

One evening a grand serenade was given to Prince Napoleon. A large and magnificent barge had been stationed at the upper end of the Grand Canal, and was so decorated that it appeared to be formed from a luxuriance of growing plants, vines, and flowers, mingled with silk flags and illuminated by thousands of tiny colored lanterns.

Under canopies of roses, camellias, and lilies were different noted *prime donne,* and at one end of the gondola, behind a thicket of tall lilies, oleanders in bloom, pelargoniums, and Roman hyacinths, was concealed the band, which played, with superlative skill, selections from the favorite operas.

It had happened that the young lieutenant, knowing what was to transpire, came that evening with his gondola to take us out. According to the programme the prince's barge was to move from the upper end of the Grand Canal, escorted by the brilliantly decorated gondolas of those who wished to pay him honor, including the wealth, rank, and beauty of the city.

We found on getting into our own, that so great was the number of gondolas that we could without fear of an accident step from one to another for a distance of nearly a mile.

In the mean time, programmes printed in gold on white satin were distributed from the royal barge, passed by hand from the gondoliers of one boat to the other. When the prince's barge started, the band burst forth into a triumphal march, and the gondolas moved along in unison, the oars falling quietly, but keeping perfect time with the music, to which the faint splashing of the water seemed a pleasant accompaniment. We glided on like a huge floating garden; the effect, not only novel but most beautiful, was produced by the lavish floral arrangements, colored lights, and transparencies which each gondola boasted.

When we again arrived opposite the hotel, Prince Napoleon stepped forth on his balcony, standing literally in a frame of superb flowers. The entire flotilla now came to a stand-still, and upon the air rose the divine voices of the young Italian artistes; the entertainment concluding with tremendous cheers for the prince.

CHAPTER XXVIII.

COFFIN AND BONES.

THIS for the time being was our last and most pleasant experience of Italy. The next week we took the steamer to cross the Adriatic for Trieste, where we made a brief stay, principally for the purpose of seeing the historic palace of Miramar, the home of Maximilian, the unfortunate brother of the emperor of Austria.

Maximilian, young, brave, and handsome, was the idol of the people; and I was told whenever he made his appearance in public with the beautiful Carlotta there was more enthusiasm shown than the emperor and empress ever invoked. This it is said roused a bitter jealousy on the part of the emperor, who was glad to make an instrument of Napoleon III. to get him out of the country.

We journeyed on to Vienna, and shortly after our arrival there seemed to be a great excitement in the dining-room of the hotel, numbers of people leaving hurriedly. Motioning to the head waiter, we inquired the cause of this commotion. He replied that " news has just been received that Prince Maximilian has been shot in Mexico through the influence of your Minister of State, Mr. Seward." I replied, "Not so; you are

16*

indebted to Napoleon III. for his death." I was very much shocked at this, and more than shocked as I noticed the bitter looks of the people, who as they passed recognized us as Americans.

Among the letters I had brought with me to Vienna, the most important was one to the Grand Admiral Tegethoff, who on the following morning called in person; a courtly and handsome Austrian in full uniform. The admiral informed me that he had just come from the emperor, who had commissioned him to leave at once for Mexico and bring home the body of poor Maximilian. He politely expressed his regret at being obliged to leave before rendering me any assistance, and added that he had a great desire to test the signals, having heard much of them through French naval officers.

I felt that to push the subject of the signals just now before the government would be impolitic and lacking in good taste, and therefore abandoned the project for the present.

While we were in Vienna we made the acquaintance of one of the most eccentric beings I ever met,—Baron Henickstein, a leading banker, to whom we had a letter of introduction and credit.

The first time we went to the bank on business we were received by the baron, who at a casual glance would readily have been taken for a dapper little Englishman of fifty, as the reader may judge from the copy of his photograph, in which the English peculiarities are emphasized.

It soon transpired, however, that not only was the baron a born and bred Viennese, but one who had never stepped outside of his native city, and who had apparently been satisfied with all things Austrian until he had reached the allotted age of man,—threescore years and ten,—when he celebrated his birthday by

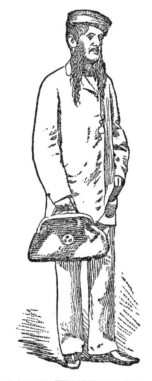

BARON HENICKSTEIN.

donning English apparel, and, portmanteau in hand, going to a photographer to have his picture taken. His friends of course took this as a joke; but joke or no, the baron was so charmed with his appearance, his drooping side-whiskers and travelling costume *à l'An-*

glais, that he stuck to it, and was never so flattered as when taken for a son of "John Bull" on his travels.

The baron received us cordially, and with great politeness. While attending to our wants he chatted pleasantly about the city, giving us much valuable information, and was pleased in his turn when he found that we had met his brother, an Austrian general, in Italy. When our business was completed, the baron invited us to visit his private museum, which filled an upper floor of the bank building.

It had taken the noble banker some fifty years to form this collection of rare and valuable antiques, each piece having a history, which he related to us with much interest and vivacity. After making the tour of the long hall, the baron drew from his pocket a massive iron key, and, unlocking a door at one end, beckoned us to follow him into a dimly-lighted room. On entering we saw ranged about it a series of tall and narrow mahogany wardrobes, the doors of which our host rapidly threw open, disclosing to our astonished gaze a grim and ghastly human skeleton in each.

Was this a Bluebeard?

"Ladies," said this extraordinary man, "let me introduce you to this select circle of my intimate friends, —friends, ladies, in whom I confide all, and who reveal nothing. Here is my beautiful Etalka, the love of my youth, who cast aside her flesh half a century ago and is still true to me. This is all that remains to me of old Heinrich, the faithful cashier of forty years of my father and myself. This lofty frame once supported my comrade Winklemann; many a bout we have had together, and even now, ladies, he rattles his bones at a good joke."

Eleanor and I might have passed for fossils ourselves while this strange presentation was going on, for we were both numb and dumb with horror; but recovering myself by a violent effort, I made a motion to go.

"Wait, wait, madame!" cried the baron. "You have not yet seen the gem of my collection;" unlocking as he spoke the door of another room, which was partly blocked up by a huge music-box. This the gentleman stopped to wind, and it started off in sharp, rasping notes, a quick military *galop*.

"Enter, and fear nothing!" cried the baron; and as much afraid of refusing as to obey, we passed the box, and found ourselves standing in a close, cell-like apartment, hung with heavy black draperies and lavishly ornamented with armorial bearings and numerous deaths'-heads and cross-bones. Nearly filling the place was a huge casket or coffin of ebony, lined with black velvet and arranged to receive a body; and on the silver plate attached to the lid was inscribed the baron's name and title, with a blank space left for his age and date of death; above it the family coat of arms were engraved.

To the foot of the coffin was attached a parchment scroll, containing instructions for the baron's funeral; in which, among other stipulations, he directed that the horses attached to the hearse should be driven on a fast trot,—"no slow pace,"—to the tune the music-box was then playing, the name of which has slipped my mind.

Whether this grotesque fantasy was suggested by the sepulchral whims of Frederick William, or have served as a precedent for those of Madame Bernhardt, I do not know.

Notwithstanding this curious conceit of Baron Henickstein, he proved to be on further acquaintance most agreeable, and introduced to us a number of distinguished people, among them his cousin Baron Scholl, chief engineer of the Austrian army, and M. Dué, the Swedish minister.

The baron was very proud of his beautiful Vienna, and delighted to escort us to the Volksgarten to hear the celebrated Strauss band, and enjoy the delicious beer and famous Vienna bread, and was flattered at our admiration of the lovely women, attractive shops, the gay gardens, pleasant streets, and lovely opera-house, where his box was constantly at our service.

Several years later, while again visiting Vienna, I was sorry to find a great change had taken place in the baron's position. It seems that he gradually became so absorbed in preparing for his departure for another world that he neglected his affairs in this; the bank failed; his brother-in-law, who was his partner in the bank, went mad; the extraordinary collection was sold; and—oh, the vanity of human wishes!—even the sacred coffin was sold under the vulgar hammer of the auctioneer to meet the demands of the baron's creditors.

Baron Henickstein only was unchanged ; the same dapper little English-looking man, still nearly as thin as his former skeleton friends, and feeling himself to be quite the gay bachelor about town.

CHAPTER XXIX.

THE RUSSIAN HEEL.

I LEFT Vienna with the most pleasant impressions, and, accompanied by my niece, started for Warsaw. We had not travelled far when I discovered that, stupidly enough, I had neglected in changing my money to get any small coin, which we were constantly in need of for fees and to supply our little wants. Apparently this sort of stupidity was common, for at the first station a Jew came to the carriage-door offering change for sale. His face was so repulsive, his eyes so full of greed, and his greasy corkscrew ringlets so set off his hook nose, that I shrank back, afraid to take the opportunity ; but a gentleman in the carriage told me in excellent English that the man was honest and I need not fear being cheated. With this encouragement I made the exchange, getting for a gold piece a quantity of roubles and small coin.

This little incident resulted in our making the acquaintance of the gentleman, who proved to be a Russian naval officer, who with his sister was returning home. Both were highly educated and refined, and they added much to the pleasure of our journey, which was so devoid of interest that we were glad to arrive at the venerable city of Warsaw.

As we stepped upon the platform, I thought of the sorrows of Thaddeus, which as a romantic girl I used to weep over, little dreaming I should ever see the city which Miss Porter pictured so graphically.

This was in 1867, a sad time for Poland, fairly ground down under the Russian heel. All the shop and street signs had been changed into the Russian language, which the oppressed people were also ordered to speak; their ignorance of the tongue not being given the least consideration. If two men stopped in the street to speak to each other, an officer would immediately approach to prevent them. The gloom of the city was so great, the faces of the Poles so dark and unhappy, that one could have imagined the place given over to some dreadful pestilence.

In the hotel where we were stopping were several Russian officers, at the very sight of whom the poor Poles shuddered.

On one occasion while my niece and I were at dinner, the waiter had just removed our fish-plates, and placed before us the roast, when ten or twelve officers entered and seated themselves at another table. Immediately our waiter flew to assist in serving them, entirely ignoring us.

We had neither knives, forks, plates, nor vegetables,

and for some time waited patiently, until we saw that the waiter was actually serving their dinner, and expected us to wait for the remainder of our own until the officers had finished theirs. This was intolerable, and we rose and left the room. The landlord hastened after us, and in a low voice began to apologize, and begged me to return.

I told him that we came from a country where it was the custom to serve ladies first, and that in no civilized country where I had been were they left with their dinners partially served. He then insisted on sending the meal up to our apartments, which offer I accepted with a little twinge of remorse for my severity ; for, after all, fear of the Russians, not intended neglect, was at the bottom of it.

It seems after we left the room the officers, who saw the cause of our going, spoke to the landlord, who under threats told them what I had said. The consequence was, when we entered the dining-room for breakfast in the morning, these same Russians rose and remained standing until we were seated. This was, I suppose, to show us that they could be polite to ladies. The afternoon of the same day we left to take the train to Saint Petersburg.

On our way to the depot I was amazed to see a Russian soldier draw his sword from the scabbard, and with the flat of it beat most unmercifully about the head a Polish peasant, who was seated in his wagon driving peacefully along. There was no apparent cause for this abuse, but not once did the man try to ward off the blows, and took the savage onslaught with perfect meekness.

A lady in the coach, who also saw the incident, told me with flashing eyes that if the peasant had offered the least resistance he would have been immediately arrested and thrown into prison, his horse and wagon confiscated, and perhaps months elapsing before he would again regain his liberty.

I was glad to step into the comfortable railway carriage and be whirled away from this ill-fated city.

We travelled through a thousand miles of the most uninteresting country I have ever seen. Now and then we passed a small mound of earth, but no hill or mountain relieved the dreary, treeless waste. At intervals we saw groups of serfs' huts, undiscernible until just as we came upon them, as they were the color of mud, and the eaves of the thatched roofs rested nearly on the earth, the huts being built for warmth half underground.

Not a vestige of paint or color was about these forlorn habitations,—a dreary monotony in brown; and touching this color, I may remark *en passant* that the hue of the national uniform of Russia is also of a dull brown, that enables the troops to steal upon the enemy nearly unobserved.

As we steamed over these steppes, I recalled meeting a Russian count in Nice, who told me he had never ridden over his estates in Russia. I was much impressed at the time, imagining the speaker to be enormously rich; but after travelling over these barren plains, of which his lands were a part, I could easily understand how he could deny himself the pleasure.

This same count, by the way, cut quite a figure in Philadelphia society at the time when Mrs. Rush was its leader, and delighted not only to entertain distinguished foreigners, but the most eminent and talented of her own country people.

At a dinner given by Mrs. Rush, at which I was present, the count met a lovely girl whom he at once admired, and understanding that she was not only of good birth, but heiress to considerable property, made haste to pay his addresses, and she, delighted at the thought of being a countess, promptly accepted him. After her marriage the countess realized the force of the old proverb, " Scratch a Russian and find a Tartar," for in truth, beneath the calm and polite exterior of the count dwelt the Tartar.

He married principally for the money he might get ; she was desirous of wearing his title ; and their marriage proved just what might have been anticipated. The fact that the lady's parents were shrewd enough to settle their daughter's money upon her was the final irritant to the Russian husband.

During my long sojourn abroad I met many American women bearing the titles of baroness, countess, my lady, and occasionally duchess and princess. As a rule their marriages had been made on the usual basis of exchange,—gold for a name ; and as a rule, naturally enough, the marriages differed only in degrees of misery.

Laying quite aside the *motif* of these alliances, what can be expected of a life-long partnership where each party has not only distinctly different habits of life, tastes, and standards of morality, but fixed opinions as to the relative positions of the sexes?

It has been said truly enough that in America every woman is queen; and while at home we are inclined to smile at the saying as a pretty exaggeration, abroad it strikes us as a plain statement of fact; so different, even among the highly-educated classes of Europe, is the position accorded woman.

CHAPTER XXX.

IN ST. PETERSBURG.

WHILE I was meditating on the subject which has beguiled me into a digression, we arrived in the city of St. Petersburg, drove at once to the Hôtel Clay, and found not only pleasant apartments, but luxurious baths, called there Pompeiian, but which under the name of marble pools have been recently introduced into the houses of the rich in this country, notably the Garrett residences of Baltimore.

The bath consists of a marble room, the walls of which are beautifully inlaid with mosaics of enamel, and lighted from above by stained-glass windows.

Around the room are ranged luxurious-growing plants, and in the centre is the bath proper, of huge dimensions, into which one descends by five marble steps.

We appreciated this comfort after our long and dusty journey; and, making our toilets, descended to dine, with excellent appetite. At the table we met Dr. Cottman, a native of New York City, and a gentleman of fine as well as benevolent appearance, who spoke the Russian language perfectly, and had served for many years in the Imperial Guard.

The next morning we started in a drosky to look for Miss Benson's boarding-house, which at that time was a famous resort for English and American travellers. The landlord gave the coachman his directions in Russian, bidding him wait for us while we made our call, and bring us back to the hotel.

The driver cracked his long whip, and off we went. For some time I was so diverted by the beauty of the broad avenues, the novel architecture, and the quaint costume of the people of the city founded by Peter the Great and barbaric, that time passed unheeded, when suddenly it occurred to me that the man must be taking us by some roundabout route, as Dr. Cottman had remarked the distance to Miss Benson's was very short, not more than a ten-minutes' drive. Doubtless we should find the item of a long drive in our hotel bill.

This was very irritating, as, unable to speak a word of Russian, we could not remonstrate, and were completely in the power of the driver, who continued to drive us first in one direction and then another. At last I became alarmed, fearing that his motive might be of an even more sinister nature.

Finally we approached the confines of the city, when we passed in front of a large building which I recognized as the army barracks. Just leaving the entrance was an officer. It flashed upon me that all officers spoke French. Here was help at last.

I pulled the coachman's cape to make him stop, and beckoned the officer to approach our drosky. He at once responded, politely raising his cap. In a few words I explained our dilemma. Instantly the officer turned and addressed the coachman. His words I could not understand, but his voice and manner were terrible. The man trembled and fell on his knees, but the officer simply emphasized his threat; then, turning to us, he became once more the elegant and suave Russian, assuring us that it was all right now: the driver would take us direct to our destination, which it ought not to have taken us ten minutes to reach; adding that he had taken the man's number.

This proved to be but one instance out of many of the dishonesty of the lower classes of Russia, who at the same time have a passion for crossing themselves before every street-corner shrine; another and much more trying proof of this same dishonesty was not discovered until after my return to America, when I found that though all my letters to my boys at school were prepaid in Russia, they had invariably been robbed of their stamps by the Russian postmen,—my children having to pay double postage on their receipt;

which being valued in gold at that time one dollar or more, was a serious item in the pocket-money of school-boys. It was also mortifying to me, as not only my children but probably my friends had found correspondence with me decidedly expensive, though they were too delicate to tell me so at the time.

Our drives in St. Petersburg were generally eventful. On the second we took, supplied with a more honest coachman, we were jogging quietly down the pleasant esplanade, when we were passed by a drosky in which were two well-dressed men, holding down on the seat a young and fresh-looking girl of about sixteen, who, without hat or shawl, was struggling frantically to escape or to cry out. One of the men put his hand forcibly over her mouth, while the other forced her back on the seat. This was certainly an abduction in broad daylight.

My niece was terribly excited, but on calling the coachman's attention to it he merely shrugged his shoulders, and with an impassive face drove on. A few moments afterwards, a couple of mounted police dashed by us at a gallop, and the driver nodded to me expressively, intimating that they were in pursuit, and urging on his own horses. We came up just in time to see the girl, white and insensible, rescued and the men arrested.

As I found out afterwards, Russia is a country where it is never safe to act upon an impulse, no matter how praiseworthy the impulse be in itself; and it is certainly the most unsafe of all the European countries for any one of either sex to travel in alone. If a person faints or falls in a fit upon the street, the passers-by will run away instead of volunteering assistance, as nine times out of ten while playing the part of the good Samaritan a man will be arrested and, on suspicion of foul play, thrown into prison, where he may linger for months, to the ruin of his business, health, and the welfare of his family, before the cumbrous machinery of the Russian law will effect his release.

While I have been idly gossiping about Russian ways, my readers may have been wondering what brought me to the land of the samovar at all. My answer is, the same object that has induced me to brave the terrors of the deep and endure frequent separations from my children and long sojourns in strange lands, —the introduction of the Coston Signals to all the maritime nations of the old world.

I had chosen this time to visit Russia, because I knew that Admiral Farragut was on his way there, and hoped to have the assistance of this great, warm-hearted man and personal friend in presenting my invention to the Imperial government.

We had been in St. Petersburg but a few days when the fleet arrived at Cronstadt. Dr. Cottman offering to be my escort, I decided to go out to Cronstadt and meet the admiral. Accordingly, we went by steamer to that island which figured in the old legend as the one place so dear to Satan that in the Temptation on the Mount he reserved it for himself.

On leaving the Neva, we took a drosky and crossed

the island, then got in a small boat and were rowed out to the " Franklin," which, with the fleet, was not only a picturesque but very welcome sight to me.

Admiral Farragut gave me a most hearty welcome, and informed me that my son Will was the last person aboard his ship before leaving America, and had lunched with the French admiral, whose squadron was then in the United States, and himself. He seemed pleased that I should be the first American to greet him on his arrival in the Baltic.

I was disappointed to find that Mrs. Farragut had remained in Germany, and would not for several days rejoin her husband; the admiral urging me to visit them when she did so on the " Franklin." I took this opportunity to thank my host for his kindness to me in forwarding the Coston Signals to the Italian government, and he was much pleased to find that this service had been so opportune.

A few days after this I addressed a letter to the admiral, explaining that I had chosen this opportunity to come to Russia, thinking that his high appreciation of the value of the signals during our late war would aid me greatly in introducing them to the Russian government, and asking him to present me by letter to the Minister of the Marine.

I should have hesitated to ask this favor of Admiral Farragut, but I knew that his greatest happiness was found in promoting the welfare of others, and that his offers of assistance were genuine.

I sent my letter to the office of the American legation, where, I understood, all letters for the officers were forwarded, and waited a whole week for a reply, each day of which seemed a month to me, when I remembered the length and expense of the journey I had made. I heard that the admiral was constantly in the society of the Grand Duke, the nominal head of the navy, and of the Grand Admiral Lesofsky; and numerous brilliant entertainments were being given for him. I prayed that he might take advantage of some of these opportunities to say a word for me, but I heard nothing, and I could not again appeal to the admiral.

Finally the news came that Mrs. Farragut had arrived, and that the entire party were to visit Moscow and the grand fair at Nijni Novgorod. I felt my last opportunity was through Mrs. Farragut, whom I knew well, and I determined to precede the party to Moscow, a city my niece was also desirous to visit, on the possibility of meeting the admiral's wife.

Accordingly, we went off quietly to Moscow, spent a few days there sight-seeing, and then took the train on which the naval party returned from the fair, laden with curious wares, both Russian and Oriental. Mrs. Farragut welcomed me warmly, and insisted on joining us in our carriage, as their own was full. After we had chatted pleasantly for some time, I took courage and told her my object in coming to Russia, and of my unanswered letter to the admiral.

Mrs. Farragut replied promptly that she was positive her husband had not received the letter, and they had both wondered why I did not come to see them in St.

Petersburg. At the next station she sent for him to join us, and he assured me that he had received no communication from me whatever, and was extremely sorry, as he had been constantly with the Grand Duke the preceding week, and he feared now the golden chance was lost.

On returning to St. Petersburg I told Dr. Cottman of this, and he at once called at the American legation, where sure enough lay my neglected letter, which with a number of others had never been delivered to the admiral.

During the remainder of our stay in St. Petersburg we were invited to all the elegant entertainments given to and by the admiral; and though we went to many of them, it was with little heart on my part, for I felt that my visit to Russia had been a failure as far as my main object was concerned. I was glad, at the suggestion of Mrs. Farragut, to escape from the everlasting twilight of Russia and seek the brighter skies of Sweden.

CHAPTER XXXI.

THE KING AND QUEEN OF SWEDEN.

WE made our journey in a trim little steamer, the "Dagmar," hugging the shores of Finland and stopping overnight at the quaint little villages; occasionally during the day visiting the pleasure-gardens of the towns bordering on the shore. In three days we arrived at Stockholm, the Venice of the North, and found there one of the best hostleries in Northern Europe, the Hôtel Rydberg.

The day after our arrival, the admiral, who had been descending the Baltic with his fleet, arrived, and, with Mrs. Farragut and the officers and ladies accompanying him, came to the hotel, as the water was too shallow to permit a near approach of the "Franklin." Here the admiral informed me he had not lost sight of my interests, and had made a display of the Coston Signals to the Russian fleet before leaving there.

Admiral Farragut was received with the most distinguished attention in Stockholm, the king placing the royal barge and one of his *aides-de-camp* at his disposal.

A great fête was given on board the "Franklin" one beautiful day, to which the foreign ministers, the officers of the army and navy, and many eminent persons were invited; the guests leaving Stockholm by steamers provided for them. The "Franklin" was dressed superbly, as only naval officers know how to dress a ship, with flags, flowers, and banners ; and the military band rendered fine music.

Admiral Farragut, who was a charming host and a very graceful dancer, led out the Countess Platen, the wife of the Minister of the Marine, in the opening cotillion ; and Count Platen was given as a partner to Mrs. Admiral Pennock, as Mrs. Farragut did not dance. The scene was exceedingly gay, the ladies being handsomely costumed, and the guests in court dress or full uniform.

I was pleased to see that none of the young ladies had more attention than my young niece, who, becomingly attired and beautifully booted, danced with a grace and vivacity that was much admired. Admiral and Mrs. Farragut exerted themselves to secure our pleasure in every possible way, and thoughtfully ordered our carriage to accompany theirs in going to and from the hotel.

The next day the king and queen invited Admiral and Mrs. Farragut, with their staff, to dine at the summer palace, Rosendal, some four miles from the city. Mrs. Farragut was in mourning for her mother, and had only black satins, crapes, etc., with her ; but having, with her usual good sense, inquired as to the etiquette of dress at the Swedish court, was informed by the Countess Platen that neither black, white, nor pink was admissible.

Fortunately, Mrs. Farragut had on board the

"Franklin" a handsome blue silk, made for the grand entertainment in New York given to General Grant and the admiral just before their departure for Europe. This was sent for, and I assisted at her toilet. We both thought the dress needed a little more ornamentation, so I arranged about her fair shoulders an exquisite shawl of point-lace, fastening it in place with diamond pins. It was very effective, as Mrs. Farragut's delicate figure admitted of this style of drapery.

As she stepped from her own room into the main saloon, where the admiral and his officers in their gay uniforms were waiting to receive her, she really looked *a peindre*,—one might have fancied her to be a queen surrounded by her courtiers, and the admiral gazed at her radiant with admiration. Let me remark *en passant* that I have never seen a more beautiful example of what the marriage relation should be than Admiral and Mrs. Farragut afforded; their pride in and love for each other was unbounded.

Mrs. Pennock spent the evening with me in talking of old and new friends, and at nine the admiral and his party returned, when Mrs. Farragut gave us a very graphic description of the entertainment, which they had greatly enjoyed.

It seems that on being conducted to the dressing-room to remove her wraps, Mrs. Farragut found several of the queen's ladies in waiting assembled to receive her, and the chief of them at once informed her as delicately as possible that it would be *mauvaise goût* for her to appear in a lace shawl, as the queen was not wearing one, and etiquette forbade the guests to be dressed more than Her Majesty ; so poor Mrs. Farragut was compelled to unfasten the graceful folds of her lace drapery and leave the shawl in the dressing-room.

Charles XV. of Sweden was a great admirer of women, and I expect he found Mrs. Farragut very fascinating. At all events he insisted on showing her through the palace himself; and as they both spoke French with fluency, the conversation was interesting.

The Queen Louisa, a sensible and kind-hearted woman, but exceedingly plain in appearance, was a daughter of the king of the Netherlands, and one of the richest princesses in Europe. It is said when she landed,—a bride,—it took a procession of men nearly half a mile in length to carry the great chests containing her enormous trousseau from the wharf to the palace.

Her royal father had shrewdly secured her dowry upon the queen, so that her royal husband had no chance to squander it, as he doubtless would have done if opportunity had offered, for he was a spendthrift and most extravagant in his tastes; the country having more than once been called upon to pay his debts. The only daughter of this ill-mated pair was married to the crown prince of Denmark, and she inherited her mother's fortune.

Perhaps the only woman that Charles XV. was not interested in was his wife, and his indifference and open neglect caused her much pain and bitter mortification. While we were in Stockholm a *bonne bouche* concerning the royal couple was given to the gossips. Since then

I have heard the story tacked on to various other royal couples; rather, by the way, a sad commentary on the morality of the European monarchs.

It seems that one day, the queen having occasion to visit the king's apartments, at the opposite side of the palace from her own, entered his boudoir without being announced, but just in time to see a lady vanish through the opposite entrance, who in her hurry to escape closed the door after her so quickly that she shut in a portion of her silk dress.

What a situation! Of course the fleeing beauty did not dare to free herself by opening the door, for fear of being revealed. The face of Charles kindled with wrath as the queen moved quietly and swiftly across the room; before he could interfere she had opened the door, but only far enough to release the treacherous flounces; then shut it again, without knowing who the fair one was, and quietly seating herself on a fauteuil, talked on as if nothing had happened.

The king was so transported by the generosity of his wife that he embraced her, saying that she was the best woman God ever made. Unfortunately, however, her magnanimity did not seem to make a lasting impression.

We were treated with the greatest kindness in Stockholm, and through the politeness of Count Platen my signals were introduced to the Swedish navy for trial.

Among other entertainments given for us after the admiral left was an evening reception by Commodore Adlersparre, Chief of the Marine Department, to meet the higher officers of the Swedish navy. The commodore resided at Shipsholm, the naval station, and had a large and beautiful family. He was very fond of America, and the walls of his residence were hung with sketches of its natural beauties and portraits of eminent compatriots. Why, I understood when I heard his romantic history, which is worthy of a brief repetition.

The commodore, it seems, was of noble birth, and his family wished him to gain distinction as a diplomat, —a career which had no charms for the high-spirited and romantic lad, whose love for the sea finally induced him to fly from home and board an American-bound vessel.

On his arrival in this country he was penniless, but still persistent, and at once shipped again on a United States navy vessel, Captain Percival in command, as a common sailor, and under an assumed name.

In a very short time the officers discovered that the young Swede had the manners and habits of a gentleman; and the chief mate having noticed his fine handwriting, called the attention of the captain to the lad, who was one day summoned to his superior's cabin and put through a severe catechism.

On being asked point-blank if he was not a gentleman by birth, he merely replied, " I hope you have no fault to find with me?" He was very restive under the examination,_ and the captain too good-hearted to press the point, but finally, knowing that he wrote an excellent hand, took him into his cabin as private secretary. The boy did his best, but could not conceal his longing to study navigation, and Captain Percival, pleased with his ambition, took pains to give him thorough instruction.

For three years young Adlersparre remained with the captain, and then returned to Sweden and made himself known. His family, conquered by his self-exile and wonderful perseverance, embraced and forgave him, and he was at once appointed to a position in the navy to which his rank and merits entitled him.

A few years later he was placed in command of a vessel to visit America, and landed in Boston. Of course the commander's position opened the doors of society to him, and he became a great favorite in the exclusive circle of which Mrs. Harrison Gray Otis was the leader.

While there the commander found that his old friend and chief, Captain Percival, dwelt in the city. As he was about to give a grand ball on board his ship, to which the captain, as a United States naval officer, would be invited, the commander decided not to bring about a meeting until that event, which he awaited impatiently.

When the captain appeared upon the deck of the ship, quite unaware that he was known to the titled host, whom he had not met before, he was astounded, on being presented to the handsome Swedish officer, at being literally embraced, and it was some time before he could realize that the little Swedish runaway and

the renowned Commander Adlersparre were one and
the same.

Captain Percival was made the distinguished guest
of the evening, and when he left the ship bore with
him some rich and beautiful souvenirs of the occasion.

When the commander sailed for home he took with
him a life-sized portrait of Captain Percival, and another of Mrs. Harrison Gray Otis,—gifts which he
prized greatly, and which hung in honored places in
his home.

CHAPTER XXXII.

THE TOMB OF THORVALDSEN.

On leaving the beautiful City of the Seven Islands
we proceeded to Copenhagen, perhaps the least interesting of the capitals of Europe, having few natural
and still fewer architectural beauties; even the Imperial buildings have fallen into decay. The Danes
themselves are not a fine-looking race, their irregular
features and bad carriage being accentuated, especially
in the women, by the sombre colors they are fond of in
dress, and which is seemingly at variance with their
passion for amusements, such as singing, dancing, fireworks, jugglery, seasoned with a great deal of drink, for
the average Dane consumes his fourteen gallons of
spirits during the year, I was told.

Nevertheless, we found much that interested us in the city, especially Thorvaldsen's Museum, with its remarkable collection of the works of this great modern sculptor, who is buried in their midst. A more extraordinary autobiography has never been presented to the world, for Thorvaldsen with his own hands chiselled his career in a language that all nations could read.

Forty large rooms, with their galleries and vestibules, contain a collection of national and artistic importance unparalleled by any other modern art collection; and it is strange to me that, as a rule, travelling Americans should evince comparatively little interest in it, for to them more than to any other nation, excepting the Danes, Thorvaldsen belonged.

During his life the artist was regarded as the actual representative of the first American of European blood, and in view of this was nominated a member of the Rhode Island Historical Society. The learned men of the society had established the fact that one Thorfinne Karlsefne had in 1007 led an expedition to Rhode Island; he had passed the winter at Mount Hope, and his wife, Gudrin, had borne him a son the following spring in that country. The child was named Snome. The genealogists having traced the descent from Snome, of Thorvaldsen, whose known ancestors in Denmark were descended from King Harold Hildetand.

In connection with Danish art and literature, we may hope for some valuable work from the pen of Professor Rasmus B. Anderson, our present minister to

Denmark, known in Europe as the father of Scandinavian literature in the Western world, and to his friends as a man of great force of character, simplicity, and warm heart.

Our minister in 1867 was the Hon. Mr. Yeaman, and he treated us with much courtesy, introducing for me the signals to the Danish government, and sending to France for some to make trial of. On our way home to Paris we spent a few days at Hamburg, and made brief visits at Berlin and Cologne; arriving at the French capital just in time to see something of the Exposition of 1867 before it closed.

When making preparations to leave Paris for Italy the year before, I saw Mr. N. M. Beckwith, the United States commissioner-general to the Exposition, and told him I had arranged a tableau of the signals to be shown at the Exposition, hoping that as they had been successful in America, and afterwards adopted by the French government, I might win a medal; but as I was obliged to leave Paris before the great Exposition opened, I was uncertain that the tableau would be properly presented.

Mr. Beckwith appeared to be interested, and said, "Send your exhibit to me, and go on your journey with an easy mind; I will take care of you." I thought this very kind, and thanking him heartily, did so, making, as it afterwards proved, a great mistake to trust him, for I found on my return that he had never hung my tableau until after all the medals had been awarded. My agent had, on missing it, applied to the commissioner-general, who said it was lost, and he therefore could not produce it; but when too late—the medals, as I said, having been distributed—the tableau was found, and with a great deal of flourish Mr. Beckwith had it hung with fine silk cords and tassels.

This was a great disappointment to me, as I had been told by eminent French scientists that if the tableau had been on exhibition in the French Department it would without doubt have drawn a medal of gold, as it had been adopted by the French government on the basis of its success in America. They were astonished that the American Department had not given it just recognition.

My niece returned home to America at this time, and I decided to spend the winter in Paris, hoping meanwhile to hear something from the different governments with which I was in negotiation. I had now a large number of acquaintances, and enjoyed visiting not only in the American Colony, but in exclusive French circles, which are seldom open to foreigners.

Soon after my return, the Minister of the Marine, Admiral Rigault de Genouilly, formerly commander-in-chief of the French Squadron, and who made the first favorable report upon the signals, sent me an urgent invitation to attend his weekly receptions while I was in Paris. This compliment was conveyed to me by General Hennequin in person, who added that he and his wife would be delighted to take me to the next reception.

We went in *grande toilette,* and found the minister's mansion to be almost royal in its magnificence, and filled with the *crème de la crème* of French society, re-splendent in lustrous satins, rich velvets, jewels, and lace of Brussels and Venice. The minister, a fine-looking bachelor, stood near the entrance to the main salon, in full uniform, with the royal sash, his breast covered with decorations, and surrounded by his ad-mirals.

As I entered, on the arm of General Hennequin, he left his place, and with exquisite *savoir faire* welcomed me, and, turning to the admirals, presented them one by one to me as "the lady who had *endowed* France." Of course, his reception was an intimation to the guests of my social rank, and throughout the entire evening I was treated with the most delicate and marked at-tention.

This did not escape the notice of Mr. Beckwith, for I was the only American lady present, and he sud-denly assumed a great pride in his country-woman, and came forward to claim my acquaintance with an insinu-ating smile. You who read may think me a little malicious, possibly rude; but you must remember the provocation I had received in regard to my exhibit at the Exposition. As he saluted me I said, coldly, "You have the advantage of me, sir."

Very obtuse, or affecting to be, he replied, "I am Mr. Beckwith, the United States commissioner-gen-eral."

"Oh!" I said, with the inflection a woman knows

how to give, " I have wanted to see you, Mr. Beck-with ; not here, but in your office : you must know for what reason." And with a slight inclination of my head I turned away.

I made many agreeable acquaintances that evening, the first of a number I spent at the minister's house, where I was also invited to the delightful musicales for which my host was famous, and where were to be seen the beauty, wealth, and aristocracy of France ; but in all those assemblies, the woman who made the most profound impression upon me was Madame Canrobert, wife of the Marèchal, whose radiant beauty and grace entranced me, as it did every one else.

CHAPTER XXXIII.

AT THE COURT OF NAPOLEON III.

DR. J. MARION SIMS and his family were also spending the season in Paris, and Miss Carrie, the eldest daughter, and I decided to avail ourselves of the kind offer of General Dix, then our minister to France, to be presented at the Tuileries. Our names were submitted to the Royal Chamberlain for presentation, and in due time we received a formal notification and invitation to the next court reception.

Of course the all-important consideration was the court dresses to be worn; indeed, I know of no costume, unless it be the wedding-gown, over which so much time, taste, and money is expended by woman. After consulting the best of the Parisian modistes, Miss Carrie decided upon a gown of white silk and tulle, festooned with pearls and marguerites,—charming for a young girl.

My own toilet was composed of a white satin skirt, concealed beneath clouds of gold-embroidered tulle; the long train of a vivid rich green velvet, also used in the *décolleté* corsage of gold-embroidered lace and satin, and the entire costume trimmed with a heavy fringe of green chenille and golden acorns; a long garland of delicate green velvet leaves gave the finishing touch. A jewelled comb and ornaments of gold and green were to be worn in the hair, and diamonds and pearls, family heirlooms, I decided to wear about my neck and in my ears.

Just before the important event, I was asked by Lord Lyons, the English ambassador to France, to chaperon Miss Bartlemore, a charming Lancashire lass of high degree, which of course I consented to do.

The day came, and I found myself utterly prostrated with a severe sick-headache, the horrors of which only those who have suffered in the same way can appreciate. At sunset I was no better, and the thought of the disappointment that my failure to appear would entail upon the young girls, who were depending upon me for a chaperon, made me all the worse.

At seven o'clock, as I lay ill and irritated upon the sofa, in walked my friend and landlady, Miss Ellis, whom many Americans will remember as the very kindest and largest-hearted Englishwoman they have ever known.

"Tut, tut! this will never do," she exclaimed, in her cheery way. "Those young ladies cannot be disappointed; we must get you up in no time." And with this she disappeared, to return in a few moments with a glass of old port and a dainty little dinner on a tray. Raising me up in her strong arms, Miss Ellis placed me in a large arm-chair, wheeled me in front of the fire to toast my feet, and then stood over me while I sipped the wine, giving me a morsel of chicken and roll now and then, as if I had been a child.

I felt myself improving, though still unable to stand, when the hair-dresser came; but Miss Ellis, without listening to my protest, set him to work upon my head, while she laid out upon the bed my toilet and its accessories. When my coiffure was finished, good Miss Ellis rang for her maid to assist her, and almost before I knew it I was dressed and brought before the mirror.

I was astonished to see the miracle that had been wrought in my appearance, through kindly care and my new finery. The thorough diversion of mind, the manipulation of my head by the hair-dresser, and the excitement enabled me to pull myself together, and when the carriage was announced I started off in good spirits to call for Miss Carrie Sims.

When the footman attended that young lady to the

carriage, she stepped in, greeted me in an almost inaudible voice, and took her seat. I thought something was wrong, and began questioning her anxiously, when I was answered with a merry peal of laughter, that revealed to me that it was Miss Fannie instead of Miss Carrie who was accompanying me.

It then transpired that Miss Carrie had a severe sore throat, and as she was gifted with an exquisite voice, her father would not listen to her endangering it by wearing a *décolleté* dress and going out in the night air. Accordingly Miss Fannie, who was about the same size, had donned her sister's dress, with the determination to take her place, and I must say she looked very beautiful in her borrowed plumage.

When we arrived at the palace, we found the usual bustle and excitement incidental to such occasions, although things were so admirably managed that there was no confusion. We passed up the fine Escalier de la Chapelle and were shown into the luxurious antechamber, with the celebrated ceiling of La Reine Blanche, where we uncloaked and joined our honorable minister, General Dix.

Meantime, Miss Bartlemore, lovely in her youth and simplicity of dress, had joined us, and we then passed into the grand Salle de la Paix, where, over the mantelpiece, hung a superb equestrian portrait of the emperor by Müller, and where I placed Miss Bartlemore in charge of Lord Lyons, with the understanding that after the presentation she would be returned to my care.

The emperor and empress, both being of fine appearance and magnificent in attire, were impressive as they made a stately tour of the hall, which was illuminated by twenty thousand wax candles, shedding a softened light, and perfumed with the fragrance that floated from the roses filling huge jars and graceful baskets.

As the imperial pair slowly promenaded, they paused from time to time to give the ministers and ambassadors an opportunity to make their presentations, each person being recognized, as their name was announced, by a gracious inclination of the head from the emperor and empress.

It happened that a few years previous to this event, Miss Sims, then a pretty child, spent a week at the palace of St. Cloud with her father, then in attendance upon the empress, who was for some time a patient of our illustrious physician. Accordingly, when the empress stopped in front of our group, she at once recognized in the charming young lady the pretty little American she had been so fond of, and saluted her warmly, indeed, as affectionately as the circumstances would permit.

When the presentations were over, the emperor and empress passed into the Salle du Trône, hung with dark red velvet, and carpeted with Gobelin tapestry that cost one hundred thousand dollars. The lofty throne was canopied with red velvet, powdered heavily with golden bees, and into this superb apartment the company slowly followed; gilded chairs being placed on either side of the throne for the guests of the evening, comprising those who had been presented.

General Dix seated us at the right of the throne, from which position we had an excellent view of the opening cotillion, composed of beautiful women and distinguished men.

Two of the ladies who took part in the dance were Americans, daughters of a well-known American, then abroad, and who sought every opportunity to render themselves conspicuous. They reminded one of a pair of exceedingly pretty and fragile French dolls, equally expressionless, and dressing alike, in a manner calculated to force attention. Affecting a fondness for the imperial color, they appeared every fine day arrayed in purple velvet costumes, and, seated in a high drag with their father, drove every afternoon out to the Bois, and, as long as the ice permitted, skated in the same showy costumes.

Their efforts to attract the admiration and attention of the emperor were so pronounced that they called forth not only public censure, but many a witty *bon-mot* from the empress, who had a quick eye and a keen sense of humor, and it is said used to joke with the emperor about the *poupées en pourpre.*

At all events, when practical jokes were being prepared for the first of April, the empress selected two wax dolls, adorned with the light brown hair and bright complexion of the young ladies. These she had arrayed in fine costumes of purple velvet, precisely like those worn by them, and with hats to match. When the morning came, Eugénie had the cards of the young ladies sent in to the emperor's private apart-

19*

ments, and while he was pondering on the questionable propriety of such an early call, his valet appeared, " by order of the empress," with the miniature dolls on a silver salver, and on to the tiny muff of one was pinned a morsel of a *billet doux,* with the inscription, " *Poisson d'Avril.*"

Not long after this, the names of the young ladies were stricken from the court rolls for " too much effrontery and boldness." Their father had taken pains to push them everywhere in society, and had succeeded better than he knew in making them the common talk of Paris. He felt this blow bitterly ; indeed, so much that when a grand ball was given by the Turkish ambassador, in honor of the sultan's birthday, he begged an influential American, then in Paris, to secure him an invitation for his daughters, that they might appear once more in society before leaving for America.

CHAPTER XXXIV.

THE EMPRESS EUGÉNIE.

I HAVE allowed these ladies to lead me far astray from my subject. *Revenons à nos moutons.* The first dance was over; the warmth, and heavy fragrance of the flowers, had their usual effect upon me, and I began to feel very faint. Having been advised that the supper-room was to the right of the throne, I took the young ladies with me and moved in that direction.

On approaching the entrance, I heard a voice say, "Voilà, Madame Coston!" and beheld an officer in full uniform coming toward me. It was my old friend General Hennequin, Tresorier Général des Invalides de la Marine. His wife and daughter were with him, and after the introductions had taken place the general said, "I am delighted to be able to give you the pleasure of entering the supper-room with the Diplomatic Corps and their Majesties."

He then gave me his arm; Madame Hennequin taking Miss Sims, and Mlle. Hennequin Miss Bartlemore. We waited for a few moments, when the great doors of the Gallery de Diner were thrown open, and the liveried lacqueys cried, "*Seulement le Corps Diplomatique.*"

The Prince Metternich with a royal princess, and the Princess Metternich with the Spanish minister, then entered, our party following, and after us the Diplomatic Corps, who were richly attired in varied costumes, and sparkling with jewels. We were given places at the upper end of the dining-salon, in the immediate vicinity of their Majesties.

I begged General Hennequin to get me a glass of water, but, much to Miss Sims's amusement, there was not a drop to be had, the cut-glass jugs being filled with iced champagne. Of course it is prohibited to touch the banquet before the imperial host and hostess; but on General Hennequin explaining to a powdered footman that I was ill, a goblet of foaming champagne was at once brought to me and revived me as if by magic.

Feeling now more in the spirit of the affair, I was able to observe with interest the superb banquet hall, through the entire length of which ran two long tables, decorated with Parisian skill and art; the table-linen, or rather lace, was fit to be worn on the person of a duchess; the exquisite cut glass, the silver, gold, and china, were each piece a miracle of art. The vast épergnes glowed with masses of rich fruit that seemed to spring from beds of velvety moss and brilliant blossoms; wonderful ices represented the royal arms and banners of France, pieces of statuary, and the frozen cascades of St. Cloud. Cakes and confections took form of flower, bird, and beast; and jellies, quivering in amber and crimson, representing marvels of architecture. Birds in their feather; frozen *consommé*, *pâtes de fois gras* on the backs of silver geese, were all there; but it would be impossible to enumerate the luxurious dainties which composed the repast.

Round the walls were ranged a line of footmen, in powder and gold embroidery, and as the guests entered to take their places they turned their backs to the table, thus forming an avenue through which the emperor and empress passed as they entered, smiling and bowing graciously right and left, then taking their places at the head of the room.

Almost immediately Lord Lyons stepped forward, and, saluting the empress, handed her a golden goblet of wine, which she and the emperor then touched to their lips. This was the signal for the guests to begin, and soon every one was enjoying the sumptuous supper.

For myself, I knew not what I ate or drank, so completely was I fascinated by the grace and beauty of the Empress Eugénie, whose every movement was a poem, and whose refined and delicate face absolutely sparkled with intelligence.

Always dressing in perfect taste, the empress looked her best in a long, rich robe of creamy silk, over which floated clouds of vapory tulle, attached to the dress by jewelled hoops of scintillating diamonds, emeralds, sapphires, and rubies; long sprays and garlands of yellow azaleas ran riot over the skirts. Round the tiny waist was clasped a girdle of the same precious stones; snowy shoulders rose from a dazzling berthe of gems, and her white throat was encircled by a band

p

of enormous solitaire diamonds. In her ears were fastened by fine wires—for she never would have them pierced—large solitaires, and in the wavy tresses of her hair were worn clusters and sprays of diamond flowers.

The effect of this charming toilet was indescribably enhanced by long scarfs of tulle, fastened to the shoulders of the corsage with bejewelled butterflies, and sweeping down the back, they floated over the end of the long train, giving an ethereal look to the beautiful, *svelte* figure.

Here was the fairy queen of my childhood's romance materialized, and by very force of contrast there arose in my mind the vision of Queen Victoria the first time I saw her. Will you forgive me if I pause to describe the occasion?

It was on the launching of the "Victoria,"—at which I was invited to be present by the Duke of Somerset, —one of a line of magnificent battle-ships; and the crown princess of Prussia, who was making her first visit to England since her marriage, was to do the champagne christening. A brilliant company had assembled, and were waiting for Her Majesty.

Presently there was a slight commotion. It is the queen, I thought, and looked eagerly, but no one savoring of royalty in appearance was to be seen; only a very stout and elderly lady, whose self and toilet I thought could be capitally caricatured by *Punch* as the British matron abroad.

She was very short, both in stature and of breath; her face was red and cross, and her toilet consisted of **a** large, gayly-plaided poplin, so short in the skirt as to expose the tops of a pair of heavy walking-shoes. A long loose velvet sacque fitted so tightly over the full dress that it gave the wearer's figure a barrel-like appearance; and a dark green hat of uncut velvet, its plumage draggled by rain and blown by the wind, was worn on a head that did not suggest familiarity with a crown; but the finishing blemish was a huge muff of royal ermine suspended round the lady's fat neck by a cord, and which, not being in use, wobbled helplessly back and forth over her well-rounded body.

"Who is that funny, fussy woman?" I asked laughingly of my naval escort, a British officer.

"Good heavens, madame!" said he, in a low voice, "that is our Gracious Sovereign!"

For a moment I was speechless, but not half convinced, until I noticed that all the gentlemen were standing, hats off, and a fine-looking man, whom I recognized as Prince Albert, joined the lady in plaid, also standing uncovered. The day was cold, bleak, and cheerless; the wind whistled around us, and great rain-drops fell. I really felt my first gleam of admiration for Her Britannic Majesty when she ordered the gentlemen present, including her husband, to put on their hats.

Since then both the fair Eugénie and the—no, plump—Victoria have been bereft of their husbands, and by some strange fate thrown together; but beyond their common sorrow, one can hardly imagine a congenial bond between them.

To return to the reception. When the supper was over their Majesties led the way to the ball-room, the rest of the company following, to join the three thousand guests assembled there. For ourselves, we felt that we had enjoyed the very cream of the entertainment, and were satisfied to retire with such delightful impressions of one of the most brilliant courts in Europe.

CHAPTER XXXV.

THE VISION IN FLORENCE.

THE following spring I sent to America for my son William, now developed into a fine young lad, to join me. On his arrival I placed him with a German professor, that he might acquire a thorough knowledge of the German language, as I intended to visit Germany again during the summer, on the strength of an intimation I received from the German ambassador to France, Baron Gerolt.

At this time war had not been declared, but was in the air, and Germany was watching with jealous eagerness every movement made by the French government to strengthen its navy and army, and was quite aware that France had adopted my signals.

When I left Paris, it was after all alone, as soon after his arrival my son had been induced by an American banker to enter his banking-house; and as he was himself obliged to go to the United States on business, he asked as a favor that I would not take William away until he returned.

On presenting my husband's invention to the German government, they wrote. at once to America for a large supply of the Coston Signals for trial. The order was sent to the manufactory which supplied the United States government during the war, and which during the absence of the proprietor in Iceland was managed by his brother-in-law. The order was promptly filled by this party, who corresponded directly with the German government, they preferring to deal with him, as he was a German, and they did not grant patents to strangers, so that I was left completely unprotected.

Very much discouraged, I returned to France, to find my son much upset in mind from some discoveries he had made as to the mode of doing business by the bank he was in.

In a short time this bank developed into a concern which his principals would not allow him to continue with, and he was very glad shortly after to accompany me to Italy, that beautiful land, associated with so much that was sad in my last visit there. [I would here state that the Marquise Bargagli married a lady the image of my niece, and brought her to see me on my second visit to Italy, and was pleased when I noticed the resemblance. This lady only lived a year and left him an heir. He had fulfilled his uncle's wishes in his will, which made him Marquise.]

20

When summer had passed I determined to return to my own country, and, having completed my arrangements, sent my son to secure our state-rooms. While he was gone on this mission, a letter was brought to me from the Italian government expressing its readiness to enter into negotiations for the purchase of the signals. Of course it was not only to my interest, but the height of my ambition, to place these signals in the European navies, and I concluded to go at once to Italy, that land to me so replete with sweet and painful memories.

We travelled rapidly over Mount Cenis pass, *via* Geneva, where the snow was falling fast, Turin, and Florence. We had hardly arrived at the latter place, however, when I was taken alarmingly ill, much to the despair and intense anxiety of my son, whose tears and prayers greatly affected me and caused me to make a violent effort of will to endure my suffering. God was merciful, for in a few days I was able to be moved to an American boarding-house, where I was treated with the utmost consideration. I was still ailing, and the first night after we moved I found it impossible to sleep ; and the fact that it was the 24th of November, the anniversary of my dear husband's death, roused in me many sad and tender thoughts.

I lived over the happiest, brightest, and most painful passages of my life ; and then finding myself drowsy, wondered if I should not see my husband in my dreams, as I often had, especially before receiving letters from my boys throughout their childhood.

The cathedral clock tolled twice, and counting the strokes aroused me; indeed, all at once every faculty seemed clear and my senses painfully sharpened. Suddenly I became aware that I was not alone. In the centre of the room, now illuminated with a soft and radiant light, stood a figure robed in flowing white. The face shone with the divinity from within; and the long, fair locks, parted in the middle and falling over the shoulders, the holy, blue, and inscrutable eyes, and the beard of pale gold completed the picture which we are early taught to love. Almost unconsciously I arose and cried, "Is this Jesus?"

No words came in reply, but with a smile of ineffable tenderness and pity, and hands extended as if in blessing, the vision passed away, and I knew that our Saviour had been revealed to me.

I am quite aware that those who claim to have seen what is usually denied the eye of humanity are summarized as impostors or the victims of a morbid imagination; and although I cannot expect that sceptics will show more kindness than to put me in the latter category, I must nevertheless affirm that I believe not only in the reality of what I saw, but that this Holy vision was vouchsafed me not alone as a solace for the bruises and wounds that the world inflicts, but to strengthen me to meet a painful shock that came upon me the next day.

It was at breakfast when a letter was brought to me, written in my son Harry's name, by a young officer, to the effect that Harry was dying with quick consumption, and in want of the common necessaries of life; and attacking me as a cruel, unnatural woman, living in luxury while her child was suffering for the means to sustain life; and finally demanding that money be sent at once to alleviate my son's misery, and the alternative of my being exposed in Washington and to the world generally; concluding that this letter had been written at my son's request.

I was stunned for a few moments, for I knew that of all the faults to be laid at my door, neglect of my children was not one of them. As I grew calm, I felt rather than knew that some nefarious plot lay at the bottom of this letter; and I enclosed it with a note to the uncle of the young officer who had written it, asking for an explanation. This gentleman lived in Washington, and had known me and of my devotion to my family for many years. The answer came by return post, full of grief and anger at this dastardly attempt to obtain money from me.

It transpired that my son Harry was in somewhat impaired health, and had left the B—— barracks, where he had been stationed with this young officer, and ordered to another station, where he was at the time the letter was posted. The wicked and unfeeling man, who had extorted money from his father and his uncle on false pretences, had hoped that in my alarm I would respond to his demands; but, like most sharpers, he overreached himself, and this exploit resulted in his expulsion from the marine corps, as such conduct richly deserved.

CHAPTER XXXVI.

THE PALACE OF PRINCE DEMIDOFF.

WHEN I was sufficiently recovered, I sent for my agent, Mr. Brown, and he immediately apprised the Italian government of my arrival. Negotiations were begun, and, after the manner of the government, kept open all the winter; during which, however, my old friends in Florence, including Mr. and Mrs. George P. Marsh, did all they could to make the time pass pleasantly for me.

Among other pleasures we enjoyed the exceptional one of visiting the Donati Palace, not far from the Porta al Prato, and the property of Prince Demidoff, renowned for his enormous riches and his brutal temper. The prince wedded the Princess Mathilde, a sister of Prince Jerome Napoleon, a charming and amiable woman.

Brought to reign over the most sumptuous palace in Europe, surrounded with all the riches and luxuries known to the civilized world, the princess was soon satiated with splendor and grew inconceivably weary of her magnificent prison and morose husband, who found his chief amusement in tormenting her. Finally she forgot everything, and fled from the palace with her music-master.

After a long time, and through the intercession of Napoleon III. and Victor Emmanuel, Prince Demidoff was induced to settle a large annuity upon his wife, whom, however, he never saw again. He deserted his palace, which was left in care of King Victor Emmanuel, and open only to very distinguished visitors on permission of His Italian Majesty.

It happened that I had a friend, an *aide-de-camp* of the king, who volunteered to gain for us the desired permission, understanding how anxious I was to see the unrivalled art collection, which attracted people from every part of the world.

The gentleman in question represented to the king that some very distinguished foreigners who were in the city were desirous of seeing the palace; and His Majesty granted him a permit, with an order for the palace to be properly prepared for our inspection. I learned later that the opening of it was attended with considerable expense,—that of several thousand francs.

A retinue of servants in the Demidoff livery were stationed throughout the grounds and palace, which was thoroughly dusted; the dark rooms brilliantly illuminated; the fountains in the gardens set playing, and the whole place garnished with flowers and branches of palm.

On the appointed day my friend came for us in a royal equipage, and after a delightful drive we reached San Donato, where we were received with a great deal of ceremony by the attendants, who escorted us up the main path, which was strewn with branches of roses, acacia, laurels, and palms. We spent a short time in the beautiful gardens, admiring the play of the colossal fountains, their graceful groups of statuary, and the Italian fancy which had scattered great clumps of Parma violets and orange-blossoms in the marble basins.

We wandered under laurel-trees and Indian palms, and passed into the conservatory,—the greatest private conservatory in the world. Here were collected plants from every quarter of the globe, from the little yellow dandelion that stars our grass to the giant exotics of the Indies and South America, towering from sixty to a hundred feet, under domes of glass; gigantic palms, stately tree-ferns, aloes, passion-flowers, orchids, roses of Japan; and thousands of plants and gorgeous parasites, the names of which were unknown to me, were massed in rich confusion.

The flowers were so brilliant in hue, the fruit glowing purple, golden, and red, the foliage so splendid in its vivid tints of crimson, russet, bright and deep greens, that I could have imagined myself in the heart of a tropical forest, had it not been for the glitter of gold, the glint of white marble, and the cool water flowing from the finger-tips of fair statues upon the blue, pink, crimson, and snowy water-lilies in the pond at our left.

The words of the Arab poet rose to my mind: " A palace of transparent crystal; those who look at it imagine it to be the ocean. My pillars were brought from Eden; every garden is the garden of Paradise; of hewn jewels are my walls, and my ceilings are dyed with the hue of the wings of angels. I was paved with petrified flowers, and those who see me laugh and sing. The columns are blocks of pearl by night, and by day perpetual sunshine turns the fountains to trickling gold."

On leaving the conservatory, we spent five hours in trying to grasp and appreciate the inestimable beauty revealed to us in the twenty-one grand apartments opened. It will be remembered that Prince Demidoff owned the malachite and most of the lapis lazuli mines of Russia; from both he had drawn liberally for the embellishment of the splendid suites of rooms.

In one, every article of furniture, even the mantels and mirror-frames, was of pure gold and malachite; in another of lapis lazuli and burnished silver. I was reminded by these apartments of the costly gift the Prince Demidoff made to the Emperor Nicholas, of Russia, for his magnificent Isaac Church, one of the grandest in St. Petersburg, the very foundation of which cost over one million of dollars.

The church itself is in the form of a Greek cross, with four chief entrances. The interior is barbarically splendid; its central columns formed of solid malachite. The small circular temple, or prestol, which forms the innermost shrine, cost more than one million of dollars. The steps are of porphyry; the floors of variegated marble; the dome is malachite, and the walls lapis lazuli, the whole gorgeously gilded, and the prince's princely offering.

To resume. We passed through gallery after gallery

of superb statuary, every piece the work of a master-hand, many of them priceless, and I was proud to recognize in this collection several works of our gifted Powers. The galleries of magnificent paintings were from the brushes of our greatest modern masters; one among them made an indelible impression upon my mind,—the head of a man, by Terburg. Demidoff cared little for the old masters as a rule, and few of their works were to be found on his walls.

A large sala, the walls of which were inlaid with rare marbles, precious stones, jade, jasper, and mother-of-pearl, was filled with rare curios and articles of vertu,—vases of Oriental alabaster, caskets of rock crystal; tables of Florentine mosaic, in which no less than ten thousand exquisite shades of color were used, and which represented the labor of half a century and fabulous amounts of money; urns cut with wondrous skill from blocks of lapis lazuli; carved chests of red Egyptian porphyry; cameos cut with such marvellous delicacy that a magnifying-glass was necessary to appreciate them; jewelled snuff-boxes, bouquets of flowers made of precious stones; ivory carvings so delicate that one almost feared to breathe on them; exquisite salt-cellars of Benvenuto Cellini; gold and silver plate that might have been the work of fairy fingers; diamond buttons; a vinaigrette wrought from a single emerald, and uncut jewels that in value amounted to several millions of dollars.

The Armory, a lofty hall draped with Eastern stuffs, was hung with suits of mail, beaten from silver, steel, iron, and even gold; Turkish poniards studded with precious stones, daggers and jewelled swords, with handles and hilts of silver and pearl, Toledo rapiers, Damascus blades, old and curiously wrought pistols, crude spears, and every implement of modern and ancient warfare, many of them the former property of the grandest warriors of the world, were collected here.

It would be impossible to give any clear idea of the riches of this palace, to be seen in every conceivable shape; and both dazzled and bewildered, we roamed from one apartment to another almost in silence, for the splendor was oppressive. On leaving we gave a liberal largess to the servants, who took great pride in the wonderful palace.

In 1880 this matchless collection was sold, and the enormous prices it brought may be remembered by the American public, who were kept informed of the sales by the cable. Among the lists I noticed that of my favorite picture by Terburg, which brought the sum of forty-two thousand dollars.

CHAPTER XXXVII.

ITALY ADOPTS THE SIGNALS.

I ALSO went to a court ball at the palace, and was surprised to find the Italian court so inferior in grandeur to either the French or English.

The king, Victor Emmanuel, was himself in appearance coarse and repulsive. The woman who made the most profound impression upon me was Madame Ratazzi, wife of the Minister of State, and a cousin of Napoleon III.; her beauty, grace, and magnificent jewels were the remark of every one. Since then Madame Ratazzi has become a widow, and has again married to a Spanish nobleman, who placed himself and his palace in Madrid at her disposal. She is now residing in the Spanish capital, and has given her husband an heir.

Winter was melting into spring before a price was agreed upon for my patent; but even then the Italian government, for some inscrutable reason, hung back, and made all sorts of excuses for not bringing the business to a close. Summer came, hot and unhealthy; both my son and myself began to suffer from the climate, and all travellers were leaving the city.

I became desperate, finding that my agent could do nothing, and made up my mind to call in person upon the Minister of the Marine,—the successor of the gentleman who had been so courteous to me on my previons visit. Etiquette obliged me to write first, asking for an appointment, and in reply I received a brief note conceding an interview.

At the hour named, having made a plain but rich toilet, and accompanied by Mr. Brown, I presented myself at the department and sent in my card to the minister. The official to whom I gave it returned with the reply that he was out. I answered that as Monsieur le Ministre had made an appointment with a lady, he would probably be in shortly, and I would wait. At this the man looked very much discomfited.

Intuition told me that the minister was in his private office, which opened out of the antechamber we were seated in, and that he wished to avoid seeing me. I determined therefore to wait where I was, in the hope that my persistence would have some result. Sure enough, after a half-hour had passed, the gentleman sent me word that he was ready to receive me, and we were ushered into his office, which I at once noticed had no other entrance-door than the one through which we had passed. Of course I knew the minister had been there all the time, and only my silent determination had made him concede the interview.

I met the gentleman with a coldness and hauteur that outrivalled his own, and as briefly as possible told him that I had made a second journey to Italy at the request of his government, and on his own representations; that I had waited the entire winter and spring for the negotiations to be closed, in vain ; and that I would spare him any expression of my own disappointment at the dilatoriness of the government and in the non-adoption of the signals, which, as they displayed the Italian national colors, seemed so eminently adapted to his country.

I had now, I continued, decided to leave Italy with my desire unfulfilled, and with the regret that the Italian government had been so lacking in courtesy in its treatment of a foreigner ; and that now I had merely come to take formal leave of him. As I uttered these words I saw my agent was very much alarmed, thinking that I had thrown the whole thing over, and accordingly that he would lose his percentage.

I motioned to him to keep silence while I studied the effect of what the late Lord Beaconsfield called his " baggage act." The haughty signor had remained seated when I entered the room, but now he rose to his feet a little excited, for he knew as well as I did that the American minister was my friend, and exercised a powerful influence over the king,—a fact that had led me to stake my all on this last chance.

He paced up and down the room as he urged me not to leave at present, and in such a frame of mind ; there had " been great interruptions and unforeseen delays ; it had been impossible for him to bring the matter up before," etc. Now would I not place it before Parliament ? I replied that I was aware that the next session of Parliament would not be opened before the following winter ; and were it otherwise, it was entirely out of the question for me to bring it before the Italian Parliament.

The minister knit his brows, and then said, " There will be a cabinet meeting of the king's ministers next Tuesday, and I, madame, though it is against all precedent to bring patent inventions before the cabinet, will present your affair to its notice, in the hope that they will authorize me to bring it to a close."

I was silent for a moment with surprise at this unexpected concession; but Mr. Brown spoke up at once, respectfully asking when he should call to inquire as to the results of the minister's proffered courtesy.

" Come here next Wednesday, when I may have a message for Madame Coston that will be acceptable to her," answered the dignitary.

We then took leave with quiet dignity, and descended the stairway in silence. When we reached the street, my agent could not refrain from laughing as he said, " Mrs. Coston, I would not have missed that interview on any account; the way in which you reversed the position with the minister was simply masterly."

On returning to my hotel I began preparations to leave Florence, for I was most anxious to get into the mountains on account of my son, who was threatened with a nervous disease superinduced by the intense heat of the city; indeed, on our way to Lucca he began to wander in his mind, and I was thankful when we arrived at the celebrated baths some twelve miles from the city of Lucca, and in a region remarkable for its fertility and pure air.

To the baths the fashion of Tuscany resort, and at the Hôtel de New York, where we stopped, we were pleased to find a number of English families. The delightful atmosphere, lovely mountain scenery, the daily use of the baths, which bubbled hot from the earth into tubs of marble, the long donkey-rides, and excellent cuisine soon had the most happy effect upon my son, who rapidly began to recover his nerve and strength.

On the following Wednesday I received a telegram from my agent, to the effect that the council had authorized the Minister of the Marine to close my business, and asking me to return to Florence the following Monday to facilitate the long-desired end.

On my arrival Mr. Brown told me that the minister was ready for a settlement, provided that Minister Marsh would receive the money for me. On this being repeated to him, Mr. Marsh at once sent word that he would be "most happy to receive the money for Mrs. Coston, and to hear that her business had been most successfully closed." Surely, I thought, there can be no further delay now.

I was mistaken!

The Marine Department, to my utter surprise, expressed an unwillingness to receive my recipes, demanding certified recipes from the United States government. Knowing the length of time required to write and receive an answer from the Navy Department, I asked if certified copies from the French government would answer, expressing at the same time my willingness to write to both countries. They replied that either would do.

In answer to my letter to the French government I received a prompt reply, enclosing certified recipes, which proved satisfactory to the Italian Marine Department; and the government agreed to pay Minister Marsh one-half the sum for my patent on the recipes being delivered, the other after testing them and finding them practical and reliable.

It was most fortunate that France had shown me this courtesy, for it was quite six weeks after my business had been closed, and when I had left Italy, that I received a reply from the United States Navy Department. It was from Commodore Case, Acting Chief of the Bureau of Ordinance, acknowledging my letter and *refusing* me certified copies of the very recipes I had furnished them, on the ground that " the United States government having purchased this invention, there was no reason why it should give me certified copies of the recipes;" so if France had not come to the rescue, my own country would have prevented me from obtaining my rights."

Later I was informed that Captain Henry A. Wise had in his visit to Italy, taken the opportunity of hinting to the Italian Marine Department that I had caused trouble to the United States government by furnishing false recipes, etc., and, naturally enough, the Italian government hesitated to bring to a close the negotiations. Now their long delay was explained.

As for Commodore Case, notwithstanding his refusal to give me certified copies of the recipes which I had given to the United States government, shortly afterwards copies of them were given to A. P. Cooke, commander of the navy, who published them in full in a book on ordnance, etc., and thus gave to the world what had been denied me, and what should have been kept solely for the United States navy.

Nevertheless, beyond the injury to my feelings, the want of common courtesy displayed in the conduct of Admiral Goldsborough, Captain Wise, and Commodore Case did me no harm, but added zest to my triumphs.

21*

CHAPTER XXXVIII.

À BERLIN!—KING WILLIAM.

HAVING been successful in Italy, my thoughts again turned to Austria, for which country I had taken out a patent, and I made arrangements to have the French government supply the Austrian navy with signals for trial. The reports sent in were most favorable, but, as usual, the government was slow in taking action, and I returned to France in the autumn of 1869, and again placed my son under his former German professor.

The year 1870 dawned; mutterings of war were in the air, and I was loath to leave; but I felt under the necessity of returning to America, to recover if possible six thousand dollars I had lent to my late manufacturer of the signals to invest in an enterprise from which he expected to make his fortune. Before sailing I left enough money with my banker to send my son home should war be declared.

My ocean trip proved to be in vain, and I found on my arrival in New York that I should never recover my six thousand dollars, and I never have. After spending a few months in my own country, I sailed again for France in July, taking with me the box of signals intended for the "Franklin," and now presented to me by the Secretary of the Navy. The box was a handsome affair of rosewood, highly polished, securely screwed down, and not unlike a music-box in appearance. This I intended to take with me to the north of Europe.

While we were *en route* war was declared between France and Prussia, but this we were of course in ignorance of until we arrived off Brest and the news was brought to the steamer. Great excitement ensued, and a commander in the French navy, who was on board, with a magnificent air ordered champagne for us all, as he said he would now have a chance to win the title of admiral.

Many of the passengers landed at Brest, but understanding that the Prussian fleet was lying in the English Channel, I determined to remain on board until we reached Havre, in the hope of seeing something of it. In this I was disappointed, but on landing met some American friends, who were stopping at Frascatti's, and decided to stay with them until my son, whom I telegraphed on leaving the ship, came to escort me to Paris.

My box of signals caused me no little anxiety, as it was, in a season of war, a delicate thing to carry them with me, especially as they were made to fire from a pistol, and had a suspicious look. However, our consul got them through the custom-house safely for me; and as soon as my son joined me we started for the capital, now in a state of terrible ferment.

A day there convinced me that it would be wise to

get out of Paris while we could ; and deciding to go on to Berlin and remain there until the war was at an end,—for I thought it would be speedily terminated,— I left all my wardrobe excepting what I needed for the summer, together with all the objects of vertu,—paintings, statuary, embroideries, and various odds and ends I had collected during my sojourns, covering ten years abroad,—in the rooms occupied by my son in the house of his German professor.

I felt perfectly safe in doing this, as a son of Minister Washburn was also under the tutelage of the same professor, and he had the American flag displayed over the building.   I looked at our colors and believed my treasures secure.

The evening before we left Paris, the emperor and the National Guards passed down the boulevards, off for the seat of war.   An enormous throng of people surged along with them ; and so wild were the soldiers in their manner and appearance, many of them half drunk and frenzied with excitement, that they made one think of troops of uniformed devils.

The emperor had given permission to the bands to play "La Marseillaise," the magic air that fires the French blood ; but the sound of the instruments was drowned in the deafening cries of the populace, who took up the refrain, dancing and shrieking as they sang, like demons.   Worst of all were the women, who ran along swearing, sobbing, screaming, and praying.

As one company passed I noticed a soldier, on whose

knapsack was perched a great green and yellow parrot, that with ruffled feathers and glittering eyes screeched out, "À Berlin! à Berlin!" at which the gamins became wild with delight.

There was something so dreadful and so revolting in the whole spectacle that I involuntarily wondered if God would permit success to an army like this.

That night we drove to the station, and found that every train had been taken for the militia; it was impossible to go North, the railroad officials said. However, I had made up my mind to go, and finding that a train started at midnight for Geneva, I concluded to wait, and reach my destination by way of Switzerland.

We travelled all night, but on our arrival in Geneva I found myself so prostrated that we were obliged to rest for an interval, resuming our journey by way of Berne, Zurich, and Prague, and having in consequence to pass through many custom-houses. Every time our baggage was examined I grew very nervous, for fear my box of signals would get us into trouble. Fortunately, the lid was well screwed down, and as a screw-driver was never forthcoming, and I was not unwilling to let them think the contents were nothing more than "a music-box," they would, after severely scrutinizing me, let it pass; so that after all I managed to take the box, contraband of war, into France and out of it through the other countries, *via* my roundabout trip to Berlin.

On our way we fell in with a Prussian family of distinction who were going home to put their son into the army, in order to save their property from being confiscated. Already twenty-five of their horses had been seized by the government, and they were impatient to prevent any more such forced loans. They were exceedingly kind people, and offered to take us into Berlin with them, which offer we were very glad to accept.

At one of the stations where we stopped I was approached by a bright-looking young man, who told me he was a special correspondent of the New York *Herald;* asking as a favor if he might join our party, as he was most desirous to get into Berlin and join the Prussian army. To this my new friends consented, and we resumed our journey, travelling sometimes in luxurious carriages, and again in cattle-cars with boards placed across for seats.

We entered Berlin through the little town of Gorlitz on the 27th of July, and just in time to see King William and his army off for the seat of war. Was this not a strange coincidence?

The day had been set apart by the king as one of humiliation and prayer for the success of the Prussian arms. A solemn silence pervaded the city, broken only by the ringing of the church-bells and the hushed voices of the people, who quietly and reverently passed into the places of worship.

All places of amusement were closed. Most of the women we met upon the street wore the red cross of the society for succor for the wounded; and even the children seemed imbued with the atmosphere of the day, and forgot their toys. In such a solemn and religious spirit did the Germans enter upon that terrible conflict. What a contrast to the wild, almost demoniacal frenzy of the French !

During the morning, while I sat in the window of my hotel watching, much impressed, the reverent observance of the occasion, I noticed a crowd assembling in front of the hotel, attracted by a carriage emblazoned with the Royal arms, and attended by servants in rich livery. I summoned a waiter and asked him what was going on. He replied that the king had come to visit the old blind Duke of Mecklenburg-Strelitz, a brother of Queen Augusta, and who had brought his son to place him at the disposal of King William during the war.

I found that by sitting in a secluded part of the corridor below, with my son, we could see the king in his exit from the duke's reception salon. We had not waited long before His Majesty appeared on the threshold of the salon, with the venerable and totally blind grand duke leaning upon his arm, his hand clasped in that of his sovereign.

The king looked well ; erect and animated ; his uniform, with its broad sash and helmet hat, became him, and his broad breast glittered with decorations. His manner to the grand duke was touching in its gentleness, and he positively refused to let the old man accompany him to his carriage as he wished. They embraced, and with moist eyes the king strode through the hall.

At the door he was met by two old women, both poorly dressed and weeping; they hastily thrust petitions into his hands, perhaps to save their sons from the war. His Majesty nodded kindly to them, stepped into his carriage, and rolled away, while murmurs of love and admiration went up from the waiting populace and the two old women, who remained sobbing.

At three o'clock that afternoon I was expecting a visit from our minister, the Hon. George Bancroft; and the landlord, who had not been able to give me a private parlor, placed at my disposal the large reception-room, which had been vacated by the grand duke a few moments before, and was beautifully decorated with garlands of roses and golden baskets filled with the king's favorite blue corn-flowers. So it came about that I had the pleasure of receiving my distinguished countryman in the salon ornamented for a king.

CHAPTER XXXIX.

FRANCE WAS LOST.

MR. BANCROFT pronounced me a heroine for having reached Berlin at a time it was thought inaccessible, and running the gauntlet of so many custom-houses with my box of signals. He told me that all Americans had left the city, and laughingly added that he hoped I had brought money with me,—coin instead of a letter of credit,—as there was no connection with banks outside, and he had almost bankrupted himself helping Americans to get away.

Fortunately, I had brought nothing with me but gold, and was able afterwards to dispose of every twenty-dollar gold-piece I had at a high premium, the American metal being so much richer than the foreign gold.

Mr. Bancroft very kindly offered to call upon the Minister of the Marine for me, and bring to his attention the value of the signals for the use of the German navy during the war; which he did, but the excitement was then too great for them to receive proper attention.

That evening, escorted by my son, I mixed in the populace that filled the broad Unter den Linden in front of the royal palace. The crowd was immense, orderly, and quiet, every eye being fixed upon the balcony draped in flags. Presently the king and the crown prince came out to take leave of the people, many of whom fell on their knees, while others wept; but not a sound interrupted His Majesty as he uttered a few words of affectionate farewell.

That night the king and his army left, and for days and nights afterwards troops marched through the streets, bearing their standards on high, while bands played the "Vacht am Rhine," for the seat of war.

A few days after this I descended to the dining-room for breakfast at an unusually early hour, but was

22

scarcely seated at the table when the hotel proprietor came up to me in great excitement to ask if I had heard the news.

" What news ?" I asked.

" That the first blood has been shed ; they have had the first fight at Saarbrucken," he replied.

I at once sent for the correspondent of the New York *Herald,* who was calmly sleeping, and by the time he appeared I had managed to get for him the telegram from the seat of war, and which was embodied in the first despatch sent to our great *Herald* of the memorable fight that opened the war.

While in Berlin I made myself thoroughly acquainted with the strength of the Prussian army, its numbers, Uhlans, ammunition, guns, etc.

Seeing that our stay in the city was perhaps to be prolonged beyond our desire, I tried to make arrangements to leave, though I was told that there was no opportunity, all trains being taken for the militia. Still, letters came and letters went all the time, and it did not require much sagacity to suspect the existence of a mail-train. I went to the general post-office and found that one started *via* Flensborg, the Schleswig-Holstein country, by which we could reach Copenhagen that night.

On returning to the hotel I paid my bill, and we were soon packed up and steaming toward the capital of Denmark. Once there, I wrote to the daughter of General Hennequin in France, my old friend, and gave her all the data I had collected relative to the strength of the Prussian arms. Miss Hennequin translated my letter and sent it to the Marine Department at Paris.

There they were completely staggered by my information, the reliability of which General Hennequin vouched for. France had entered upon this war without the faintest conception of the power and strength of her opponent.

Miss Hennequin wrote me in reply :

"DEAR MADAME COSTON:

"If what you write is true,—and we have not the least doubt of it,—papa says ' France is lost.' "

And the sequel proved that France was lost.

CHAPTER XL.

DANISH DELIGHTS—AN INTERVIEW WITH CHARLES XV.

DURING our brief stay in Copenhagen I had the pleasure of renewing my acquaintance with a number of the naval officers that I had met in Paris, among them Count Bouet de Wilaumy, commander of the French fleet lying at this time in the Baltic, for the purpose of blockading Prussia ; and the officers were glad to come on shore for society and diversion. The fleet was well supplied with the Coston Signals, and their frequent use afforded the Danes excellent opportunity to judge of their utility.

One evening during our stay we went out to take a walk, when I observed that the people seemed to be crowding into the cars, and all going in the same direction ; and curious as to their destination, we got into a car, and after riding some distance stopped in front of large, illuminated gates, through which the populace surged.

After paying our entrance fee we followed, and found ourselves in the Danish paradise, a description of which I recently read by Mr. Robert P. Porter, and I cannot do better than quote his language :

"The Tivoli consists of an enormous garden or park, laid out and arranged so as to afford every possible amusement to all classes of people. The place is divided into a labyrinth of romantic walks, shaded with trees and dotted with vine-entwined bowers and rose-thatched pagodas to eat, drink, rest, or chat in.

"Some of the 'rambles' were overarched with climbing foliage, rich in blossom, and at night lit up with myriads of tiny lamps which blazed like fairy jewels. This mixture of natural and artificial beauty is so bewildering that it is only when people are fatigued that they discover they are lost in a classical labyrinth. A curious feature of the place consists of telescopic tunnels of luxuriant vines, so bent in training as to form tubes richly verdant within and without, and illuminated with innumerable colored lights.

"There are also footpaths completely overarched by a skilful growth of vines and young trees, forming pleasant retreats. At the extreme end of these walks is an ingenious arrangement of many-colored glasses and powerful lights, producing the effect of a monster kaleidoscope. Other out-door amusements are found in whirligigs, roundabouts, sailing boats, tunnels, and immense octagonal platforms which make the most airy of ball-rooms. Here the gallant Danes with their sweethearts held in grip of steel, hats on, cigars between their teeth, start a giddy whirl which ends only when the music stops.

"On the evening I was at the Tivoli the platforms were packed with human beings, dancing and perspiring. Girls with bonnets on their shoulders and hair down their backs, men without coats,—but still they danced oblivious to all save the strains of the music.

"Then there is an open-air theatre, in front of which thousands stand in a sort of amphitheatre and witness the performance. There are spaces allotted for acrobats, rope-walkers, and jugglers. There are booths, bazars, side-shows, and drinking-places. Numerous music-stands, including one large concert hall, are scattered about the grounds, and under the trees in the vicinity of the music the people sit.

"On what is called the island is a song and dance house in which the 'bald-headed' and 'front row' may engage in conversation with the 'artists,' entirely consisting of ballet-girls in tights and singers in short dresses. There are two of these places, patronized by both sexes. The artists mix with the audience and drink with them during the intervals.

"By eleven o'clock Sunday night the Tivoli is in full swing, and a pandemonium it is. Music from many bands, the clinking of glasses, the popping of corks, the fizzing of beer and wine, the bustle of waiters, the ribaldry of the open-air theatre, the songs from the concert halls, the rushing of the whirligigs, the rattling and crushing sounds of the falling boats on the inclined plane, the hissing of fireworks, the noisy talking from many thousand throats, combined with the sparkling, dazzling, undulating light, make up a scene the equal of which I have not yet witnessed anywhere in Europe."

One feature of the concert which struck me was the wild applause of the Danes at every friendly allusion in song to the French, with whom they sympathized;

and their finally joining *en masse* in singing " La Marseillaise."

When we decided to push on to Stockholm, we made
our arrangements to go by way of Gothenburg and the
beautiful lakes, that we might see the celebrated Falls
of Trollhätta, a magnificent volume of water that leaps
and plunges in descents of from ten to seventy feet at
a time, and then dividing to embrace an island, reunites
in a resistless flood.

We spent the night at a comfortable inn near the
Falls, or perhaps I should say, a portion of it, for we
were obliged to rise at two o'clock in the morning to
drive twenty miles across the country to Lake Wetter,
to meet the train *en route* for Stockholm. I never shall
forget that drive. Comfortably wrapped in warm rugs,
and seated in an open carriage drawn by a pair of stout
and spirited horses, we seemed to rush through the
bracing air and dawning light of a clear Northern
morning.

We reached the train in good season, and arriving
in Stockholm, drove to the Hôtel Rydberg, where I
had stopped with Admiral and Mrs. Farragut on a
former visit. The good people seemed pleased to see
me again, and did all they could to make me comfortable.

In the course of a few days I called on General
Andrews, who represented our government, having succeeded General Bartlett, who was a very great favorite
at court, so much so, that when he was recalled by
President Grant, who wished to make room for his

friend, the king sent a special despatch to President Grant asking that, as a favor, General Bartlett be continued in office. The reply came " that General Bartlett, or any other person that the President thought fit, would be minister to the Swedish court," or words to that effect; and General Andrews was sent to succeed him.

This snub from our government so incensed the king and his cabinet that for a long time nothing American was acceptable; General Andrews was received with much coldness, and was obliged to step very carefully before he gained the confidence and regard of the Swedish government; which state of things of course had a disastrous effect upon the adoption of the Coston Signals. I presented my letters of introduction to our minister and explained my business to him, and the fact that when in Sweden two years before I had, through the kindness of Admiral Farragut and the courtesy of Count Platen, presented a number of my signals to the Swedish government for trial, and having understood they had been favorably reported on, was anxious to ascertain whether a satisfactory conclusion could not be reached.

The general received me very politely, and at once offered to do anything for me in his power, finally suggesting that he should obtain for me an audience with the king, Charles XV.,—of course the highest compliment he could pay me.

I thanked him, and was much pleased when, a few days afterwards, I was formally notified by His Majesty's private secretary that an audience would be granted me at the palace the following week, for which a day and hour were appointed; the king to receive me in the *konungen's mindre eller enskilda vaning* (the king's private apartments), in the northwestern angle of the palace.

At the time set, half-past one in the afternoon, having made a proper toilet, and escorted by my son, we drove to the palace, arriving punctually at the moment. We were shown into a charming little antechamber and given seats while my card was sent in to His Majesty, who was then giving audience in the adjoining boudoir to a distinguished general of the army.

Presently a gentleman entered, and making me a profound bow, said, "The king desires to know if Madame Coston converses in French before seeing her." I replied in the affirmative, and a moment afterwards the silken tapestries were thrust aside, revealing the king, who not only rose, but advanced towards me (an unusual courtesy) into the room where we were sitting.

He received me most graciously, and then invited me into the private audience chamber, a perfect bijou of art and beauty, addressing me in French at the time. I then recognized the fact that between his foreign accent and my own slight confusion I should be unable to converse with him on my affairs in the language of the courts, and thought it best to say so frankly, with an apology.

"Your Majesty has the reputation of speaking English with great fluency, and as I can express myself with more assurance in my native tongue, may I be permitted to do so?" I asked.

The king, with great good nature and courtesy, at once addressed me in English, motioning me to be seated; then asking with great interest many questions about America and the distinguished people he had met from there, especially Admiral and Mrs. Farragut, of whom, fortunately, I was able to give him the latest news. His Majesty also inquired with affection in regard to General Bartlett, but studiously avoided any reference to General Grant, whose brusqueness in regard to the change of ministers he had never forgiven.

As it is not permitted to introduce any topic in conversing with a monarch, my own remarks were very much in the nature of replies, though Charles XV. of Sweden had so much tact that he made me forget for the moment the king. He referred to my signals with interest, and I gave him all the particulars he asked for, referring him finally to a commander in the Swedish navy.

I rose once to take leave, but the king requested me not to cut short the interview; and settling himself comfortably in the deep recess of the window, before which stood a table laden with rare and beautiful roses, chatted on about his own country, asking me for my opinion of its social customs, etc.

It happened that His Majesty wore on his cravat a curious brooch that fascinated my eye. An Ethiopian head of gold and-enamel, with diamond eyes and pearl teeth; a marvel of fine workmanship. To my horror, the king, who must have noted my glances at his ornament, said, "I see you admire my brooch; it is curious, is it not?" He then suddenly unfastened it, and, with the grace of an Italian, was about to present it to me. I was intensely mortified that through my inadvertence I had placed myself in such a position; but though it is against etiquette to refuse a king's gift, my own self-respect would not permit me to accept of this; and the king, seeing he had embarrassed me, kindly desisted from any persuasion.

A few moments later I withdrew with my son, and a very happy impression of the manner and amiability of the reigning monarch of Sweden.

CHAPTER XLI.

THE QUEEN DOWAGER'S PALACE.

At this time the queen dowager, mother of Charles XV. and grand-daughter of the Empress Josephine, to whose portraits she bore a striking resemblance, was living at Drotningholm; and with a very distinguished Swedish gentleman and my son I made a visit to the palace, and greatly enjoyed a view of the finely-furnished and interesting apartments thrown open to the public.

To our pleasant surprise, just as we were about to

leave, a message came from the queen mother to the effect that as she was going out for a drive, we were at liberty to inspect her private apartments. Of course we were glad to avail ourselves of this permission, and accordingly we were ushered into the cosiest, prettiest, and most home-like suite of rooms I had ever seen occupied by royalty.

The low, frescoed ceilings, the walls padded with satin, the cheerful crackling of wood fires in the fine fireplaces, all conspired to the same effect. In the boudoir the velvet hangings and chair-covers had been exquisitely embroidered by the queen dowager's own white fingers, and were admirable not only as specimens of her industry, but for the beauty of their design and coloring. A thousand interesting trifles were scattered about the rooms, which were hung with water-colors, old engravings, and occasional gems in oil.

On a dainty table lay a piece of unfinished work, and beside it, left open at the place where the reader had evidently laid it down, the "Life of Prince Albert," on the fly-leaf of which was written in a bold hand, "To Josephine, from her friend Victoria R."

Frequently after this visit, when driving through the park, we would hear the merry tinkling of bells, and a moment after would encounter the queen, seated in her low sleigh, and always received a pleasant smile and bow in return for our salutations.

One pleasant incident of my sojourn in Stockholm was an invitation I received from a lady of position, an intimate friend of the late queen and of Fredrika

Bremer. The latter had given such enthusiastic descriptions of travel and people in America, that she had inspired Madame B—— with the desire to meet and entertain me.

Madame B—— resided on one of the thousand beautiful little islands about Stockholm, which she had converted into a tiny kingdom of beauty, in which art and nature rivalled each other.

To reach it we stepped into one of the wonderfully swift little omnibus-steamers, which for a trifle ply between the islands, and are to me one of the most amusing features of life in the Swedish capital. Miniature in size, jaunty in style, holding only six or eight people, they dart hither and thither on the water like dragon-flies; and at night myriads of them, illuminated with colored lights, speck the water, and shoot from one point to another with marvellous rapidity, barely escaping collision, and presenting a kaleidoscopic spectacle.

Our toy boat speedily wafted us to our destination; and after a short walk through paths overarched by stately trees, and bordered by the most brilliant flowers and plants, glittering with the spray flung from the fountains that sparkled in the sun, we reached the stately chateau, standing on a lofty promontory.

Our welcome was most cordial and unaffected, and after being presented to the guests, most of whom were eminent in the world of art and letters, we were led on the different balconies and verandas, which commanded magnificent panoramic views of the picturesque islands and the city in the distance, which we enjoyed through colored glasses.

The dinner was served in the manner of the country, which to me was a novelty, for at most of the entertainments given me in Sweden the fashion of France was affected.

We were first ushered into a very pretty dining-room, to partake, standing, of the " smorgasbord," or appetizer, a national institution that not only precedes dinner, but figures in almost every act of business or passage of social enjoyment during the day. It consists of every possible variety of salted and smoked fish, from sprats to raw salmon, served with Swedish brandy, which is white, tastes something like a cordial, and is most insidious; and little cakes of knackebred, a flat, hard cake of a black-brown color, and the staple food of the Swede, both rich and poor.

When we had done justice to the smorgasbord we were ushered into another room, where the dinner proper began by the serving of soup from a table set with exquisite Nymphenburg china, and lavishly decorated with flowers. A great deal of pleasant chat mingled with the supping of soup, and then the guests quietly wended their way into a third apartment, where fresh fish was served from a table ornamented with wild grasses, ferns, and rare sea-weeds.

In this fashion we passed from room to room as the different courses appeared, the guests standing, until finally we found ourselves in a lovely little drawing-room, furnished in the style of Louis XV., where at last we were seated while black coffee was served us, in tiny porcelain cups, and some native artiste rendered fine music.

Long before we reached the climax of the dinner I had been forced to give up even the pretence of eating, and I could not help thinking of poor Mary Woll-stonecraft, who travelled in Sweden nearly a hundred years ago to escape and forget the horrors she had already witnessed in France, only to fall into those "terribly long Swedish dinners," with their sideboard prefaces and infinite variety of drink.

It does seem to a stranger that the middle and upper classes of the country do nothing but eat and drink. One cannot escape from the little bottles and glasses and cold lunch; they are in the air, they appear at the most unexpected moments; while you are admiring your host's cattle, his orchard, or his flowers. They confront you at the places of public entertainment; while you are listening to the sweet strains of music in the public gardens; and even in the theatre, the pit is almost peppered with little tables, and in the boxes of the rich they appear again covered with little silver trays laden with small spirit-bottles, sandwiches, smoked and salted fish, pickles, etc.

However, at this particular dinner I tried to conceal my lack of capacity by joining freely in the chat, while I inwardly wondered if the anatomical arrangements of the Swede were not similar to those of the camel. After a really delightful evening, accompanied by our kindly host, we returned to the little omnibus-boat, laden with a profusion of flowers and much pleased with our visit.

After fifteen years of life abroad, I must confess that in many respects Sweden has remained to me in memory the most delightful country I have visited, and my recollections of it are pleasantly devoid of cheating cabmen, swindling hotel proprietors, thieving chambermaids, and roguish shop-keepers, the evils, to a greater or less extent, that the traveller is called upon to endure in other countries.

The Swedes are, as a rule, fair-minded and industrious, good linguists and musicians, and most hospitable; they also take an honest pride in those of their countrymen who have won distinction. In the grand collection of statuary at the king's palace, and in the museums of the city, they would point out to you with pardonable pride the marble busts and portraits of Bellman, their great poet; Treidman, the watchmaker, "without workmen, watches, or shop;" their great violinist, Ole Bull; Ericcson the inventor, Jenny Lind, and Christine Nilsson.

Stockholm itself is fascinating in its unique beauty; partly due to its being built upon a number of islands, some of which are filled with the great public buildings and imposing palaces; others, covered with luxurious foliage, are dotted with handsome houses and beautiful chateaux, against a background of bold cliffs, and surrounded everywhere with glittering water.

There is a great deal to see in the city, and the suburbs are extremely lovely.

Stockholm in summer and Stockholm in winter is, however, a very different thing. During the latter it is indeed a frozen Venice; as far as the eye can reach sparkles ice, and the streets and buildings are half hidden in great coats of snow. The fountains no longer tinkle, the blossom of bush and plant has vanished, and the stately trees are turned into weird snow giants, with outstretched arms, threatening the passer-by to let fall their cold white drapery upon his head.

From the window of the Hôtel Rydberg we could see the equestrian statue of Gustavus Adolphus, surnamed the Great, transferred into a mighty caricature, his epaulets, cocked hat, and the tail and mane of his charger banked up with snow. Beyond lay the frozen river; and the lines of little shops on either side of the bridges which spanned it, and where the curiosities of the country are sold, looked like veritable toy shops of Jack Frost.

Farther on we could see the royal palace, its granite walls and hanging casements piled with snow and glittering with fringes of icicles, the palace of an ice-king. Sometimes at night we were surprised by seeing a horseman coming at full tilt, and carrying on high a flaming torch. This we knew was the warning that the royal carriage was *en route* for the opera. Then we slipped on our own warm wraps and sallied forth over slippery pavements and often through blinding snow to the little bijou theatre, near our hotel, where Jenny Lind made her début, and which on these winter nights was alive with color and gayety. The king himself contributed seventy-five thousand rix-dollars annually to the support of the theatre, where only the very best talent appeared.

There was to me, however, besides the drinking, another great blot on the beauty of Sweden,—the degradation of woman; equally painful and mortifying, and more thorough and complete in Stockholm than in any city of Northern Europe. Here she practically supplants the beasts of burden, being exclusively employed as hod-carrier and bricklayer's assistant. She carries bricks, mixes mortar, and, in short, does all the heavy work about the building.

At the dinner hour you see groups of women sitting on piles of wood and stone eating their frugal repast. They wear a short gown, coming a trifle below the knees, home-knitted woollen stockings, and wooden shoes. Over their heads a kerchief is tightly tied. Those engaged in tending plasterers, mixing mortar, etc., wear aprons. They are paid for a day's hard work of this kind of toil, lasting twelve hours, the munificent sum of one kroner (equivalent to twenty-six cents).

Women sweep the streets, haul the rubbish, drag hand-carts up the hills and over the cobble-stones, unload bricks at the quays, attend to the parks, do the gardening, and row the numerous ferries which abound at Stockholm. The entire dairy business of this city is in their hands, and here they take the places of horses and dogs, carrying on their shoulders the heavy cans of milk from door to door, to say nothing of acting as barbers to men. Now and then one sees a Dalecarlian peasant in their peculiar but rather pretty toilet, who seem a thrifty and well-to-do class. But may we never see American women thus abased by being brought into competition with the pauper labor of Europe is my prayer !

While women thus slave in Stockholm, man parades. You will see him in a sort of uniform, in the market-place, lounging all day " for hire," to run on errands or do light porterage. Whenever any light work that pays fairly well is to be done, there is the genus man. On dress parade you see him as a soldier; swaggering about beer-gardens, loafing in the barrack yards, or fishing on the outskirts of the town. "It is a pity," says a recent traveller, "that some of the scatterings of soldiers of these little European powers could not be crystallized into expert hod-carriers or skilful mortar-mixers, instead of weighing woman down under the yoke of a double burden,—viz., the hardest toil and mother-hood."

CHAPTER XLII.

PUTTING OUT MY LIGHTS.

A SHORT time after we left Sweden, three naval officers were sent to the United States with instructions to thoroughly look into the Coston Signals. They returned with the most disparaging reports. Unfortunately, they had come in contact with General Albert J. Myer, who at that time was prejudiced against the signals, though he afterwards wrote a very commendatory letter of them.

Why? you will ask.

Because he had offered during the rebellion, provided that I would throw off the name of Coston on the patent stamp from my signals, to employ them freely in his corps. I applied to a patent lawyer to see if doing so would jeopardize my interest, and he replied that such a step would render my patent void.

General Myer was obliged to use the signals in his army corps in order to exchange intelligence with the United States fleets at night during the war.

As if to complete my misfortune in this case, the Swedish officers also met two or three United States naval officers, who underrated the worth of the signals, and completed what General Myer had begun.

We hear much of the chivalry of men towards

women; but let me tell you, gentle reader, it vanishes like dew before the summer sun when one of us comes into competition with the manly sex. Let a woman sit, weep, wring her hands, and exult in her own helplessness, and the modern knight buckles on his imaginary breastplate and draws his sword in her behalf; but when the woman girds up her loins for the battle of life, ready to fight like a lioness, if need be, to put food in the mouths of her children, let her select for her field the school-room or the cooking range.

To me it was a most bitter thing to find in that lofty institution of our country, the navy, men so small-minded that they begrudged a woman her success, though achieved after long years of struggle and patient industry. And this notwithstanding the fact that many of the officers had been benefited personally by the use of the signals,—for not a few of them were made rich through prize-money won by capturing the blockade-runners at night, which they did not do in a single instance without the aid of the Coston Signals. That they were a "powerful auxiliary of incalculable value" during the whole war wrote Gideon Welles, then Secretary of the Navy, in the letter he sent me on my departure to deal with foreign governments. So it came about that while the great men and the great minds of the navy appreciated my labors and gave me good words and encouragement, others left no stone unturned, both abroad and at home, to defeat every effort I made, notwithstanding these efforts had been of such benefit to the navy of the United States that they ought to have been glad that the navies of the old world should have the advantage of them.*

That they sometimes succeeded in their designs was shown in this instance, and I blush to record it of my countrymen that they so prejudiced the foreign officers that the latter returned to Sweden without being willing to recommend the adoption of the only signals known to the world enabling ships to converse through the darkness and terrors of the night.

CHAPTER XLIII.

AN INTERESTING TRIP—PALACE OF PETER THE GREAT.

WHEN we left Stockholm it was for St. Petersburg, and we started in the cosey little steamer " Dagmar," named for the Danish princess, now the Empress of Russia. A more delightful journey could hardly be imagined. Skirting the hundreds of beautiful islands covered with a luxurious growth of verdure, many of them crowned with picturesque villas surrounded by beautiful cultivated grounds, we were suprised to find

---

* This probably was at the time the signals were manufactured so imperfectly at the Government Naval Laboratory.

ourselves so soon at Abo, the ancient capital of Finland.

Most of the passengers, including ourselves, went
ashore to enjoy a drive about the quaint city. At this
time the Societats Haus was considered the most
northerly hotel in the world,—latitude $60\frac{1}{2}°$,—and its
cathedral, decorated with frescoes illustrating Finnish
history, was the first Christian temple erected in this
northern land. We rambled through some of the
pretty tea-gardens, climbed the high cliffs looking over
the great waters, and backed by superb forests of fir
and birch, gathered handfuls of the wild heather, and
returned to the "Dagmar" to retire for the night, much
pleased with our little excursion.

Early in the morning the little steamer resumed its
tranquil course, and by the time we repaired to breakfast—a delicious one served *a la carte*—we were again
threading lovely little islands, between coasts bristling
with huge granite rocks, green-tipped with fir, and
turned to gold and emerald in the brilliant sunshine.
We had good music on board, and never I thought
was a journey so like a perpetual gala-day.

Our next stopping-place was at Helsingfors, the
modern capital of Finland, and a town curious for the
number and similarity of its yellow-washed houses and
broad streets. It had also a fine university and library.
The day was enchanting, aud we enjoyed our tour of
the town and our visit to some beautiful country-seats
in the suburbs beyond. Then we repaired to the public
gardens of Brunnsparken,—a surprise to us, with our

crude idea of the Finns; for it would have required no great strength of imagination to have thought ourselves transported to *la belle France.*

The grounds were laid out with great taste, the flower-beds assuming a thousand fantastic forms, and the plants so disposed as to produce the richest harmonies and most striking contrasts of color. A number of light and airy pavilions were scattered about, and in one of these we enjoyed an excellent supper of fresh fish and wine, admirably served, while soft strains of music floated through the air.

Later the band struck up livelier airs, and soon the platforms under the spreading boughs of the great trees were covered with people elegantly dressed, and who danced with ease and grace.

Another night of tranquil repose, and another day's feasting for our eyes, brought us to Wiborg. Here again we went ashore, and found the Russian military in barracks. In the course of our peregrinations some familiar strains were wafted to us from the public garden, and on entering it we found there a troupe of American negro minstrels. Their dancing and singing, though the audience did not understand a word, amused it very much; but for us to hear "'Way down upon the Swanee River," "Buffalo gals, come out in de night," away off in this foreign land had something touching in it, and I felt indeed sad when I discovered that these wandering minstrels were Southerners,—men of good families, who, impoverished by the war, unable to dig, and ashamed to beg even in a

foreign land, had chosen this way to earn their liveli-
hood in the regions of the far North.

Another night on the water and we reached Cronstadt, the great naval port of Russia; and an hour
later the vast and glittering domes of St. Petersburg
loomed up before us. Supreme among them St. Isaac's
reared its lofty crest; the sun turning almost into fire
its great dome plated with pure gold.

On our arrival we had to go through the usual tire-
some formula over our passports, knowing it would be
a matter of perhaps three weeks before we should be
able to regain them. Then we drove to an English
hotel opposite St. Isaac's, where we found our American minister, Governor Curtin, and his family established.

On my late visit to America, Admiral David D. Porter and the Russian minister to our country, M. Cata-
cazi, had given me letters of introduction to Admiral
Lesofsky, the Grand Admiral of Russia, who commanded
the Russian fleet that visited the United States during
the war, and was handsomely fêted in New York.
Since then the admiral had been made governor of
Cronstadt, and afterwards given place in the emperor's
cabinet as Minister of the Marine, and was, I learned,
then living in the summer palace of Peter the Great,
on this island.

I forwarded my letters and card to the admiral, and
the next day he made me a lengthy call, extending a
most cordial invitation for myself and son to spend the
following day at his home at Cronstadt. I knew that

in Russia no higher social compliment could be paid me, and accepted the invitation with pleasure.

The next morning we took a brisk little steamer and puffed down the Neva to Cronstadt, where we found on landing our host's carriage and servants awaiting us. We soon reached the palace; the massive gates were swung open, and the spirited Russian steeds fairly danced up to the marble steps where the admiral stood waiting to receive us; a stately figure, admirably set off by his fine uniform.

He escorted us into an antique salon, where we were gracefully welcomed by a cousin of the admiral's, the Countess E——, as the wife of our host was away. The countess summoned a maid to remove my wraps, and the admiral then presented me with a superb corsage bouquet of orchids, as he informed me that as governor of the island he had given command to his officers not to call on him that day, which he intended to devote to my pleasure.

A walk through the splendid conservatories and gardens of the palace was then proposed, and for an hour we sauntered among rare plants and trees, through forcing-houses rich with ripe fruits; finally rambling through the broad flower-lined garden paths intersected with exquisite statuary, and fountains spouting over groups of carved marble figures.

On returning to the palace we passed through the different apartments, which were truly Russian in lavish decorations of Siberian jasper, malachite, porphyry, and lapis lazuli, precious metals and stones.

There were also many things of interest to be seen: extraordinary Chinese paintings; a globe of the world mapped out in diamonds, emeralds, and turquoise; old Russian and German armor; some splendid portraits of Catherine II. and Peter the Great; rare porcelains, bronzes, and a thousand objects, each one of which was a treasure in itself.

Late in the afternoon dinner was served à *la Russe*, and with all the elegance of a state banquet. We were at the table three hours, but so entertaining was our host, and so witty the pretty countess, who chatted gayly in French, that when we reached the stage of Spanish plums and mellow pineapples, which the admiral proudly remarked were the same we had seen growing and were plucked for me, we were not in the least fatigued.

This day was certainly a white one in my Russian experiences; and our minister, Mr. Curtin, informed me I ought to feel greatly flattered, for he as yet had not been entertained by Admiral Lesofsky.

Mr. Curtin treated me with great consideration while I was in St. Petersburg, and before I left gave me a very handsome dinner at his residence, where I met among other people of note the remarkably able secretary of the legation, Mr. Eugene Schuyler, who has since distinguished himself, as he gave promise of doing at that time.

We loitered in Russia for some time, but in spite of the fact that the Russian navy had only a flash signal for use, and that I had introduced to a number of officials the Coston Signals, I could not succeed in making any headway; and wearied with waiting for the Franco-Prussian war to come to an end, we decided to return to Stockholm before navigation closed in the North.

CHAPTER XLIV.

PERILOUS TRAVELLING.

WE made our journey without mishap, but had scarcely arrived at the Hôtel Rydberg before a balloon letter from Paris was printed in the London *Times*, and from it I learned that the building in which I had stored all my possessions had been sacked because it was the residence of a German, and notwithstanding it was under the protection of the American flag, which Mr. Washburn had placed over the building.

It seems that a passing regiment of Mobile Guards had been incited to the act by a man crying out, "Voilà une maison de deux Prusses!" That was enough; the doors were at once broken in and the place plundered. Minister Washburn reported the matter to Jules Favre, who ordered the regiment to be drawn up in front of the house and the officers reduced to the ranks and reprimanded. The professor was compensated for his loss, but on presenting my own list of losses to Mr. Washburn, he calmly informed me that he could do nothing for me; I must suffer the loss.

While we were in Stockholm I received an intimation from the Danish government that the trial of the Coston Signals had been thoroughly satisfactory, and that their adoption was decided on. The weather was now bitterly cold and a terrible storm raging, but for fear we should be frozen in altogether, we started for Copenhagen at once. The railway carriage was crowded to excess, and entirely with men; but in spite of the number, the atmosphere was intensely cold; and being unused to the climate, I found to my dismay that we were not properly provided with sufficient fur wraps.

However, there was an English captain in the carriage who had two Russian coats of fur with him, and he very kindly insisted on my son making use of one of them; while a gentleman who had some extra wraps placed them at my disposal. In fact, the attention we received was rendered with such *empressement* that I was puzzled, until I discovered later that I had been mistaken for the great Swedish actress Vassar.

We travelled all day, stopping but once to get some coffee, when, much to my amusement, we were obliged to hire snow-shoes in order to reach the restaurant, as the snow was piled so deep that not only the paths but the fences were obliterated. At midnight we arrived at a primitive inn, where huge log fires burned a cheerful welcome and a hot supper was awaiting us. At four in the morning we again started off in the train, nor did we stop until we reached Gothenburg late in the afternoon.

Everything was frozen up, and I smiled at the idea of taking the steamer, as we had expected to do. Nevertheless we did take one, but to do it had first to walk a long distance on the ice to take the small boats and row out to the steamer. It was so cold that I was unable to speak when we reached it. At Elsinore, so associated with the name of Hamlet, again we took the train to Copenhagen, and arrived there on the last day of the old year and drove at once to the Hôtel de New York.

The same evening we called on Mr. Cramer, our minister, and the brother-in-law of General Grant. Mr. Cramer was a Swiss, but spoke German so fluently and was so friendly to the Germans that the Danes, who were no longer able to sing " La Marseillaise," were prejudiced against him. Mr. Cramer was, nevertheless, very polite and kind to his travelling country people, and assisted me materially in bringing my business with the government to a prompt conclusion. Very happy I felt to know that in one more country the language of the Coston Signals would be spoken, and that especially in Denmark, one of the oldest maritime powers of the world, and one of the most generous, for in proportion to its size and exchequer its compensation was more just than that of any other country.

Just at this time somewhat of a sensation was caused in Copenhagen by a little *faux pas* on the part of Mr.

24*

Cramer, who was invited to a state dinner and reception given by the king and queen on New Year's Day. At the dinner the king in the most flattering manner singled out Mr. Cramer, as the representative of the United States, to take a glass of wine with him. This Mr. Cramer refused point blank to do, on the grounds that he was a temperance man.

According to foreign etiquette, a greater insult could hardly be offered to royalty. Mr. Cramer, though a little proud of the moral courage he had displayed, I thought should have complied with the custom to at least the extent of touching the glass to his lips,—in other words, accepted the king's compliment.

A pleasant little incident occurred to me one day while in the city, when with my son I visited the grand skating-rink which Jackson Haines had taught the Danes to establish. The officers of the club were very polite, made us honorary members, and gave us badges. My son put on his skates and shot away to try the ice while I seated myself on a chair with runners to watch him. Suddenly some one came up behind me, and taking hold of my chair, pushed me swiftly round and round the rink. I did not know whether to be amused or alarmed, when suddenly we stopped, and the unseen propeller presented himself in the shape of a gallant gentleman, who with a deep bow and a foreign accent said, "How der doo, Madame Coston?"

It was Count Rasshof, the former Danish minister to the United States, whom I knew well in Washington. I much enjoyed this pleasant meeting, and the count seized the opportunity while we remained in Copenhagen to show us many courtesies.

Before we left the capital, Mr. Cramer bought a very fine statuette, a copy of one of Thorvaldsen's famous groups, and asked me to take it to Mrs. Grant as a remembrance from him, which of course I was glad to do, and packed it in my trunk. We now became very anxious to leave Copenhagen, but the feat seemed impossible: so severe was the winter that the usual watercourses were blocked up with ice; but fortunately our kind landlord told us that if we had the courage to undertake the journey there was one route by which we could go, viz., by way of Korsoer, across the island of Funen, through Fredericia, down the Schleswig-Holstein country; and that several parties were already waiting to go that way, and that he would telegraph to Korsoer and find out when the next venture would be made.

The telegram was sent, and day after day we waited for a reply, which we really began to despair of, when the message was flashed to us one day that a party would start the next morning; and if we wished to join them we must reach Korsoer that night. Our preparations were hurriedly made, and we left on the next train and arrived at our destination at ten o'clock that night, with the impression that human beings could not be colder and survive.

At four in the morning we were called to a warm breakfast, and then got into carriages provided for the travellers, including one other lady beside myself and eight gentlemen.　We drove several miles through the keen, biting air, getting out when we reached the beach, and walking what seemed to me an interminable distance on the ice until we came in sight of two row-boats waiting for us.　Into one was put our baggage, and into the other we very thankfully climbed.

The brawny fishermen in their gay woollen jackets put all the strength of their muscular arms into their oars, and we shot through the water until we reached a solid field of ice, to cross which we left the boats and walked over the slippery, undulating mass.　We began to feel like Arctic explorers, and suffer like them, too.

Taking boat again, we rowed until the highway closed up before us and again obliged us to walk, while the boats were pushed across the ice.　Four times in all this performance was repeated; but the last time I succumbed, for my feet were without feeling, my wrists swollen up under their fur coverings, and I could not articulate: the ice seemed to have struck at my very heart.　Seeing that I was incapable of moving, the kind-hearted Danes motioned me to stay in the boat while they drew it out of the water across the last field of ice, and launched it again.　This time the work was so great that the passengers were obliged to help.

When we reached the open sea, we rowed for several miles, the coxswain continually blowing a trumpet; for, to add to our misery, a heavy fog had risen and completely enveloped us.　The gentlemen were alarmed as we rowed round and round, and one by one stopped talking until we all sat in perfect silence, trying to make the steamer. For myself I was too cold to care, and crouched down in the boat in a state of numb indifference—I thought—until we heard the cheering sound of the steamer's whistle; then hope animated us all.

Never did the voice of lark or prima donna carry such music in it. In a very short time, guided by the sound, we reached our haven, and, exhausted and half frozen, we were lifted on board. We were several hours in making the passage to the island of Funen, and it took us all that time to get thoroughly warm and recuperated. When we landed it was again to walk on the ice to get to the train, which we boarded to cross the island; and when we got off we had good appetites for the rough dinner and sour wine made ready for us.

Then followed another ice promenade, with a biting wind blowing right in our teeth, to the steamer, which carried us over to Fredericia, where, thoroughly exhausted, we remained for a night's rest, starting off next morning and not stopping again until we reached Hamburg, which seemed a very paradise.

Never shall I forget that trip, nor the suffering that it entailed, and which I could not have endured but for the unceasing kindness and attention of my fellow-travellers, who, Dane, Swede, German, and Englishman, were alike thoughtful and even chivalrous, for many of their kindnesses were at the cost of personal comfort, and appreciated the more because the only other person of my own sex in the party was a handsome, fast peasant, the Countess ——, whom it was known was the old king of Denmark's left-handed wife, and who took a malicious delight in trying to embarrass me because I would not accept any overtures of friendship.

CHAPTER XLV.

BEAUTIFUL AMERICANS ABROAD.

WE spent a week resting in Hamburg, and a great deal of that time I amused myself by watching through the windows of my hotel sitting-room the grand Basin, which, frozen over, had become the fashionable skating-rink of the city. There was something fascinating in the wonderful evolutions of both the men and the women, whose heels seemed fairly winged as they flew over the smooth, glittering surface, barely grazing it; dancing in a thousand fantastic figures, gossiping, flirting, laughing aloud in their gayety, and dressed for the most part in bright colors, the scene was indeed a pretty one.

When we left Hamburg, it was in an immense stage drawn by six horses, and filled and covered by thirty people and a goodly quantity of luggage. With much cracking of whips, prancing of horses, and blowing of horns, we travelled over the frozen ground for several miles, when all at once I discovered that we were crossing the river. It was evening; lights were put up on posts along the route to show the way. I thought of our great weight, and shuddered, as I felt the ice tremble beneath us. Could it bear such a burden? became a momentous question with us all, and once or twice as the great vehicle swayed, exclamations of "Ach Himmel!" and "Mein Gott!" went up all round. However, we scrambled up the bank on the other side, and in a few moments rolled into the station, where we took the train for Hanover and The Hague.

On the way we made the acquaintance of a Greek priest from Russia, who conversed easily in French, and told us that he had been called to The Hague by his sister, whose husband, the Russian minister, was supposed to be dying. They were at the hotel to which we were going, and on our arrival we learned that the Russian gentleman lay dead in the house.

As we entered the corridor, the queen of Holland was descending the stairs; she had been to visit the wife of the late minister. Her Majesty looked well at me as I did at her, wondering who she was, and whom I was guilty of the rudeness of turning my head to look at again. To my amusement she had done the same thing, and as our eyes met she smiled faintly. I was told afterwards that the queen was struck by my likeness to herself, which had been previously remarked in Paris.

At dinner that evening we met the American minister, Mr. Gorham, and his wife, who were seated opposite us at the table and addressed me; Mr. Gorham knowing that we were Americans, was anxious to inform us that smallpox was raging in the city, and that there was one case in that very hotel,—the English husband of an American lady whom I knew well.

After dinner we were invited to the parlor of our minister, and while there the doctor arrived to vaccinate the family, who were anxious that my son and self should also submit to the operation; but we declined, for I had no fear of the disease. They thought me rather reckless to stay, for the deaths averaged forty and fifty a day, and we could see from our windows men going from house to house in a sort of beadle's dress of black, and knocking at the doors to inform the inmates of the deaths, as is their custom.

The next morning Mr. Gorham, who was exceedingly kind to me, gave me a letter to the Minister of Marine, which I delivered in person, accompanied by my son. I was received with the greatest courtesy, thanked for bringing the invention to the notice of the government; and the minister added he would take steps for its adoption; finally asking me for some signals for trial and the necessary instructions, which of course I was glad to supply.

One evening during our stay Mr. and Mrs. Gorham invited us to accompany them to the opera, which we enjoyed greatly. In the next box to our own was seated a lady whose face seemed very familiar to me;

and I was not surprised when Mr. Gorham told me that she was the wife of the Minister of State, and formerly Miss Belle Cass, the lovely daughter of General Cass, who had met her Dutch fate in Washington when her father was Secretary of State, in the person of the Dutch ambassador to the United States.

There were also present that evening the Italian Minister to The Hague, Chevalier Bertinatti, and his wife, formerly the famous beauty Mrs. Bass, of Mississippi, of whom Ben : Perley Poore wrote as follows in one of his pleasant letters :

" Probably the most superbly beautiful woman ever married in this country to a foreign diplomat was Mrs. Bass, of Mississippi. After having passed several winters here [in Washington] she married the Chevalier Bertinatti, a man of rare accomplishments, but in no ways good-looking. Her beauty was so celebrated when she was the widow Bass that the mere mention of it suffices to recall to many throughout the country the vision of her superb presence. ' A daughter of the gods, divinely tall and most divinely fair.' The Chevalier Bertinatti, after his marriage, went to Turkey, where he was the minister of Italy for some years, and the sultan presented Madame Bertinatti with exquisite and valuable jewels. He died, and she returned here to recover from the United States government a considerable sum of money for cotton destroyed on her Mississippi plantation. When afterwards she came here she was accompanied by her daughter, Miss Bass, who inherited her mother's fair, sunny face, wealth of light

N   t   25

brown hair, and imperial person." Not long after, both Madame Bertinatti's lovely daughters died, and her son has joined the Royal Guard of Italy.

The presence of these two lovely Americans and the admiration they attracted made us, their countrywomen, very proud.

We remained in The Hague long enough to enjoy the beauty of the famous drive to Scheveningen, to study the superb collection of paintings in the National Museum, and to visit the palaces, especially T' Huis im't Bosch, or House in the Woods, where the unhappy queen of Holland lived, and once a year received a visit from the king. The place is very charming, and situated in the midst of a beautiful park.

Before leaving Holland I played a game of cards with the English gentleman whose wife I knew, and whom we had found ill with smallpox on our arrival at The Hague.

From Holland we made a brief and rapid trip to France *via* Brussels, and went on to England safely by way of Calais and Dover, notwithstanding the Franco-Prussian war was raging, passing on to London, where we drove to the Victoria Station Hotel, delighted once more to hear the sound of our native tongue, and to enjoy the comforts of English life.

We heard from our friends in London,—which, by the way, was crowded with refugees,—who were in communication with relatives in Paris, the latest news, to the effect that the war was raging more fiercely than ever. This decided us to return to America, though we had to go without the few boxes I had left with my bankers in Paris.

CHAPTER XLVI.

"HOME AGAIN! HOME AGAIN!"

OUR voyage was tempestuous and disagreeable, and glad enough we were to forsake the delights of a life on the ocean wave and tread once more the stone pavements of dear old New York.

Soon after we landed I received a letter from Holland, which country was about to enter upon a war with the Achinese and wanted their fleets well supplied with the Coston Signals, which, said the Minister of the Marine, M. Broc, in his letter, "they intended to adopt officially in the navy." The order, filled in New York, was for a large amount, and very gratifying to me, as my efforts at The Hague had been comparatively slight. I insert the following notice of this order from the New York *Tribune*, June 6, 1873: "Thirty-one boxes of the 'Coston Telegraphic Night Signals,' containing about one hundred and sixty signals each, were shipped to Rotterdam yesterday on an order of the Dutch government, for the use of the fleet about to be despatched to Sumatra, and to be employed in the blockading operations against the Achinese."

Not long after my return home I went to Washington

on business. General Grant was then President. I wished to meet the Secretary of the Navy; and Admiral Joseph Smith, who had always regarded me as a benefactor of the navy, offered to escort me to the Navy Department and introduce me to him. When we entered the office we found the dignitary we were in quest of tilted back in his chair, his feet high up on his desk, and a lighted cigar in his mouth.

When Admiral Smith presented me, the Secretary did not trouble himself to change his attitude, but said, as distinctly as the cigar between his teeth would permit, " What do you want, Madam ?"

My gallant old friend, who knew that I was accustomed to be treated with courtesy both at home and abroad, felt so keenly the Secretary's manner that he replied, brusquely, " Mrs. Coston wants nothing, sir," and led me at once from the room.

I now opened correspondence with the Chief of the Bureau of Navigation, in reference to the inferior quality of the Coston Signals being manufactured by the government, and also in regard to an improvement on the original patent made by my son, H. H. Coston, now an officer in the marine corps and just then absent on duty.

This improvement enabled a flight of colored stars to be thrown up from a pistol or gun which my son planned for the purpose, instead of burning the signals from a holder held in the hand and showing light on deck. Fortunately, my son took the precaution of filing a caveat at the Patent Office for this improvement before he left, and when he came home he made it over to me and I at once obtained a patent covering it.

Meantime, a Lieutenant Very applied for a patent on this same improvement, which he called his own, but was refused, one only being granted him for a certain sort of cartridge. Nevertheless, through the influence of Commodore Ammen and Captain Walker, his successor, this form of signals, called the Aerial, has been adopted by the United States navy and known as the Very signal.

Naturally enough, this caused me great concern and annoyance, especially as the adoption of the so-called Very signals was proclaimed in the newspapers, having emanated from the Navy Department, and accompanied by disparaging and erroneous remarks on the Coston Signals.

Finally my son William, to set the public right, sent the following communication to the press; it appearing in a number of prominent journals, including the New York *Tribune* of July 11, 1879, from which I now clip it:

"THE COSTON MARINE SIGNALS.

"William F. Coston, the proprietor of the Coston marine signals, has sent the following statement to the press for publication:

"'The proprietors of the Coston signals, in reply to a Washington despatch of July 8, relating to the contemplated substitution of the Very signal lights in place of the Coston night signals, state that the description of the latter given in the despatch, and the statements that they have been condemned both by the proprietors of the patent and the chief signal officer of the Navy Department, are erroneous. The Coston signals, and the signals described in the account referred to as Coston signals, are not the same. The Navy Department, in attempting various alterations and improvements of the Coston signals, have caused the invention to deteriorate. The Coston signals, as furnished to the merchant marine and used in the Life-Saving and Revenue Services, are not liable to deteriorate in any way by long storage, hot climates, or dampness. The Navy Department is itself to be blamed in the matter, and is accountable to the public for allowing an invention which was purchased at the public expense to become worthless. No effort has been made by the Department to acquire the improvements that have been made since the conclusion of the late war. The proprietors of the Coston patent furnished the night signals to the United States Navy throughout the war, and of twelve million signals used, not one was returned as damaged. The signals furnished to the Life-Saving Stations have been in use since 1872, and are kept at the stations, North and South, all the year round, and have seldom been found imperfect.' "

Finding my letters to the Chief of the Bureau of Navigation (then Commodore Ammen) ignored, I determined, repugnant as the effort was to me, to call upon the Secretary of the Navy and set before him my claims, though I had written to him and received no answer.

I went to the Navy Department, and through old Lindsay, the faithful colored man who for more than fifty years had been door-keeper to the different secretaries, sent in my card. He gave me a seat in the corridor while he took it in to the Secretary, returning with the answer that he would send for me as soon as he was ready to receive me. For three long hours I waited silently, watching people who had arrived after me, even young midshipmen, called in one by one; but no message summoned me.

Old Lindsay looked mortified and uncomfortable, for he remembered the cordiality and courtesy with which I had been received in other days; and finally he went of his own accord to the Secretary, but returned much discomfited to say that he could not see me that day.

I said rather sadly, "Lindsay, you are not accustomed to see me treated in this manner, are you?"

"Fo' de Lord, dat's so, Missus Coston," said the good-hearted man, shaking his gray head, but prudently adding no commentary; and just then the Secretary, with a superb bouquet in his hand, walked out, and the old door-keeper, with a grimace, slyly pointed to the flowers.

I tried in every way I could to protect my interests in the Navy Department; and again I wrote to the Secretary of the Navy. He referred the letter to Admiral Ammen, who wrote a curt reply, and pigeon-holed it with mine in the Navy Department—and it was found there some time after by a member of Congress, never having been sent to me.

I went to the White House, hoping that as I had made the acquaintance of President and Mrs. Grant through the medium of a warm letter of introduction from Mr. Cramer, the minister to Denmark, and had also been invited socially to the White House on delivering the statuette which I had brought over to Mrs. Grant, that I might possibly gain, through the President, the justice of a hearing in the Navy Department; but I never succeeded in even seeing General Grant, Babcock his secretary always excusing him. I wrote to him in vain, no answer came; and in silence I was obliged to see my signal used in the United States navy under the name of the Very signal.

Lieutenant Very, however, sold out his invention at a low price to Messrs. Hartley and Graham, of New York, and they were unable to make use of their new

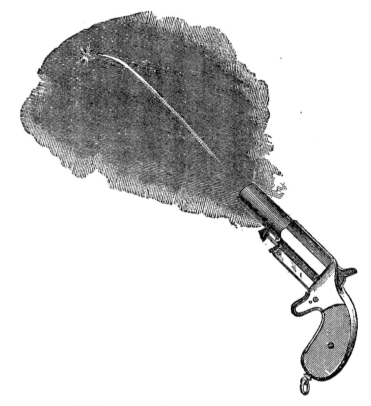

THE COSTON AERIAL NIGHT SIGNAL.

purchase; and for fear of my patent have never made use of it. They sent an agent to see me, who began with an air of cool indifference to tell me that he was about to put on the market a new and attractive toy, to make which successfully he wanted to use parts of a patent that he understood I owned, and which separated I would never find occasion for; and he was willing to pay me a small sum for the use of it; so much clear gain to me, he added.

I thought of Lieutenant Very and was on my guard, but I did not let the man suspect that I divined from whom he came, but promised to meet him the next day at my lawyer's. When we met, I found the gentleman more eager than before, and he agreed to pay five hundred dollars.

The temptation to turn the weapon of the enemy against him was too strong, and I asked my lawyer to draw up a bill of agreement, and make it so binding that the parts of the patent asked for could be used *only for a toy*, in no case for signalling; and that there should be no evidence in number, letter, sign, or color placed on the outside of these "toys" to indicate the color to be shown on ignition.

This clause I knew would prevent the "toy" from being used for signalling; and in addition I added another to the effect that they should not be used either by the manufacturer or the party he sold them to, or any third or fourth party they might reach, for signalling. My lawyer was not a little amused at my stringency, which he thought unnecessary; but the lieutenant was still fresh in my mind. The agreement was accepted by the agent, who thought he would be able to find a loophole in it; and I received the five hundred dollars in cash. He returned to his business house, who found he had nothing for it.

CHAPTER XLVII.

AN APPEAL FOR JUSTICE.

FOR a great many years I had burned under a sense of injustice and injury in regard to the adoption of the primer which my husband had invented, only to be appropriated, as I claimed, in the Dahlgren gun.   His widow claimed the invention in the claim which she presented before Congress for the Dahlgren gun, of which Mr. Coston's primer, in my judgment, was one of the chief merits.   This was in 1874, and I then determined to present my claims to the primer, of which I had ample proofs, before Congress in the shape of a bill.

For this purpose I embodied in my petition numerous letters, documents, etc., in the form of a small book, which also included a statement of the full particulars of the Coston Signals furnished to the government during the war, at rates I knew to be ruinous, but on the understanding from the Secretary of the Navy that in the future I should receive full compensation for them, which I never did.*

Some of the letters referring to Mr. Coston's inven-

---

* The details regarding the furnishing of the Coston Signals to the government, the war taxes under which I labored, etc., may be found in previous chapters.

tion of the primer may be found in previous chapters of this book; and of the others which were included in my petition, the following were of importance, showing reply to my letter to the Secretary :

"NAVY DEPARTMENT,
"WASHINGTON, June 19, 1873.

"MADAM:

"I herewith enclose a copy of a report dated the 13th instant, from the Chief of the Bureau of Ordnance of this Department, to whom was referred your letter of the 5th instant on the subject of percussion primers.

"Very respectfully, etc.,
"GEO. M. ROBESON,
"*Secretary of the Navy.*

"MRS. MARTHA J. COSTON,
    "*New York.*"

"BUREAU OF ORDNANCE, NAVY DEPARTMENT,
"June 13, 1873.

"HON. GEORGE M. ROBESON, Secretary of the Navy :

"SIR,—In reply to the letter of Mrs. Martha J. Coston, of June 5, 1873, relative to the number of percussion primers manufactured in the government laboratories, referred to this Bureau, I have to state (without conceding the claim therein made, that B. F. Coston was the inventor of the percussion primers in use in the navy of the United States) that the record shows that two million six hundred and sixty-two thousand three hundred and sixty (2,662,-360) percussion primers have been manufactured in the Ordnance Department of the Washington Navy-Yard between October, 1847 (the earliest data of which we have any record), and May, 1873.

"I am, sir, with high respect,
"Your obedient servant,
"WILLIAM N. JEFFERS,
"*Chief of Bureau.*"

When my claim was presented to Congress it was referred to the Committee on Naval Affairs, of which the Hon. Glenni W. Schofield was chairman; and that gentleman placed my affairs in the hands of a member of a sub-committee, who, however, left the matter unattended to during the entire session. On finding out his incompetency I appealed to Mr. Schofield, who very kindly placed another member on the sub-committee with him,—the Hon. Leonard Myers, of Philadelphia, a man of great ability.

It happened that in my petition I alluded to the action of Captain Henry A. Wise, and his efforts to prevent my receiving proper compensation from the government. Captain Wise had been dead for some time, but it transpired that Commodore Jeffers, his successor as Chief of the Bureau of Ordnance, had been a friend and sympathizer of the deceased captain.

Constituting himself the opponent of my claim, Mr. Jeffers covered seventy-five pages of foolscap with evidence, which he had scoured the navy-yard to get, in his endeavor to prove that I had no grounds for claiming the invention. He even did not hesitate to show his feeling in a personal way to the extent of speaking derogatory of me to my young son, for which, however, he apologized. So great a task did Commodore Jeffers make for the sub-committee that they advised me to forego my claim to the primer before that Congress, and present only a bill claiming indemnity for the war taxes charged on the Coston Signals.

Much against my inclination I deferred to the judgment of those gentlemen, and waited while they wrote to the Bureau of Ordnance, demanding a statement of the number of the Coston Signals furnished the Navy Department during the war. I was surprised and pleased that the amount was greater than I supposed; but so much the better for me, as the bill was made out accordingly, and, with accumulated interest, amounted to twenty-one thousand dollars.

The Hon. Leonard Myers took up my case with energy and decision, but it required all his skill to work against the tremendous odds of malicious influence brought to bear against my claims, and at the same time to drag along with him the member above referred to, whom he did not want to offend by taking the matter entirely out of his hands. With great difficulty Mr. Myers succeeded in getting this gentleman to present the bill a day or two before Congress adjourned; the Speaker having promised to recognize him on presenting it. The bill passed the House unanimously, and now there was but one day left to get it through the Senate before Congress adjourned on March 4.

Through Mr. Myers's influence, the chairman of the Naval Committee of the Senate had it considered in the morning and was authorized to present it that day, all of which I passed in the Senate gallery anxiously awaiting the event so important to me. Midnight still found me sitting there, when the friends who accompanied me were obliged to return home, and I could not remain there, the only woman.

Reluctantly I left the gallery and came down-stairs, when I met Vice-President Wilson, who had seen me leave, and left his own chair in the Senate to speak to me. "Surely you are not going now, Mrs. Coston?" he said.

I replied that I felt obliged to leave with my friends. Mr. Wilson then asked me a few questions in regard to the bill, which showed me he had informed himself upon it, and as we were then joined by the Senator who was to present it, he added, kindly, "Go home in peace of mind; we will take care of you."

I was then stopping at the Arlington Hotel, and about two in the morning I was roused from a fitful sleep by a violent rapping at my door,—a telegram to tell me that my bill had passed the Senate,—from a friend who wished to be the first to inform me. My readers may imagine how relieved and delighted I was, and how rose-colored my early morning dreams.

In the morning, womanlike, I took unusual pains with my dress, and feeling in a very happy frame of mind, drove to the Capitol to thank my friends for their exertions on my behalf. First I looked for the kind soul who had telegraphed me the night before; when he, to my consternation, told me in a faltering voice that he had made a mistake; my bill had not passed.

For a moment I was speechless, overcome; and then went to the Senate chamber, determined to find out who had defeated it, and on what grounds. I found Mr. Myers, and he told me that the great objector was

Senator Robertson, of South Carolina, who when the bill was brought up objected to its consideration; and under the rules during the last hours of Congress, the objection of a single Senator prevents the bill being considered.

It was now eleven A.M., and the next hour held a very small and slim chance for the passage of my poor bill, for Senator Robertson not only positively refused to give the reasons for his opposition, but turned a deaf ear to his brother Senators, who begged him to withdraw his objections as a personal favor to them, or to give his reasons for not doing so. In vain; and he made brusque replies to men like Mr. Justice Field, Vice-President Wilson, and even ministers of the gospel who were in sympathy with me and urged him to do this graceful act of justice in the last moments of a dying Congress; and amidst their pleadings the hammer fell. It was twelve o'clock, the Senate adjourned *sine die*, and my bill was lost through the hard-hearted obstinacy of one man.

I was most anxious to discover whether Senator Robertson thought he had any real basis for the stand he had taken, and I made several endeavors to see him, but without success, for he refused to see me in such a manner that his servant apologized for him. I returned to my hotel ill with disappointment, and locked myself in my room.

In the course of the afternoon the member with whom I had had so much trouble sent up his card. He had come for a recompense, and had not been informed that my bill had not passed the Senate; partly, as I sent him down word, through his dilatoriness in not presenting it to the House until the eleventh hour.

The next session all had to be commenced over again; but Senator Robertson was no longer there to oppose the bill; another man filled his chair on the floor of the Senate, for nature had laid a heavy hand on the Senator from South Čarolina, and at the same time his constituency deserted and refused to re-elect him; and Senator Edmunds, who had not been favorably disposed towards the bill before, had meantime investigated its merits, and now gave it his support, so that after it had been cut down to thirteen thousand dollars,—the government refusing to pay interest,—the bill passed without opposition.

This experience, although I have spared my readers many disagreeable details, will give them some idea of the trials of a claimant before Congress; and at the same time I beg to call their attention to the distinction to be made between a claimant and a lobbyist. The latter may be a person of either sex; and often is, I regret to say, a woman, employed to use influence to secure the passage of a bill, or, in common parlance, to "lobby" it through for a certain party or company as the case may be.

A claimant is a person who may or may not have a just claim on the government, but who is presumably honest in the belief that he has, and who does not sell his own services to push the interests of another.

A great proportion of this class are the widows of army and naval officers. I could name many instances of such women, who have exerted themselves to procure for their children and selves the provision which the government usually makes in such cases; and certainly none of these ladies could be classed as lobbyists, —a name rendered particularly odious because the typical lobbyist is one who hesitates at nothing to carry out his or her purpose.

CHAPTER XLVIII.

WHAT MY SON HAS DONE.

A FEW years later my son, William F. Coston, who had now grown to manhood and had received a thorough business training, was enabled to take in hand the business of manufacturing the Coston Signals. He originated and established a plan to provide distinguishing signals for different lines of steamers and other craft, yachts, etc., which proved a great advantage in introducing the signals to the New York Yacht Club, of which Commodore Kingsland was then in command.

The Club appointed a committee to revise their signal-book, which had only flags for a day signal chart, when the Club adopted the Coston Night Signals, and instructed the committee to confer with my son to arrange a letter code chart for night signalling. This was the first letter code for that purpose ever put into use, as heretofore numerals had been used. The Club spent several hundred dollars in perfecting this work, and after the code was adopted they unanimously elected my son a member of the New York Yacht Club.

About the same time the signals were brought to the attention of the New York Chamber of Commerce, and approved by it in the report from the Committee on Inventions, which report was sent to the Secretary of the United States Treasury; a great testimonial to the signals, as the Chamber had never before nor since cared to introduce a patent invention.

The New York Board of Underwriters also gave the signals an unqualified vote of approval, and asked the Secretary of the Treasury to take action in aiding my son and self by some law that might establish their use in the merchant marine.

The New York Board of Pilot Commissioners gave the signals their warm approval, evinced in the most practical way by their adoption of a Coston Signal to call a pilot. The colors of this signal are white, red, white, burned in succession, and can be recognized whenever seen.

The New Jersey Pilot Commissioners endorsed them, and the United States Board of Inspectors of Steam Vessels, in their report of 1875, approved of the use of the Coston Signals by the merchant marine generally, and passed a resolution stating " that it is the opinion of our Committee on Inventions that had these signals been adopted before, many lives and much valuable property would have been saved."

The New York *Herald* inserted a paragraph under " Shipping News," stating " that the *Herald's* steam yacht would be known by all vessels entering the port of New York at night by the use of the Coston Signals, and would receive any shipping news from them." This paragraph was daily in the *Herald* for six or seven years; so highly did that journal think of these signals that it took this way of promoting their usefulness, without any pay or solicitation on our part; but the New York *Herald* is always a pioneer in the application of science for the benefit of humanity.

There were in 1885 some sixty or seventy different interests using the distinguishing signals, among them nine yacht clubs,—New York, Eastern, Brooklyn, Sewanaka, New Bedford, St. Augustine, Chicago, American, and Atlantic.

Through the efforts of myself and son, the United States government has established in the Treasury Department a Bureau of Registration of funnel-marks, house-flags, and distinguishing night signals; so that a record can be kept and published of the same for a guide to the signal and life-saving stations, light-houses, light-ships, and mariners at large. This cannot fail to meet with the approval of all " who go down to the sea in ships, or do business in great waters."

This system of registration is superior to anything of the sort in the world. The English Board of Trade publishes the signals of several steam lines, and charges for registration; this of course puts great limitations on their register, which cannot be so comprehensive as that of the United States Treasury Department. This register does double duty,—answering as a guide to those who wish to obtain a distinguishing signal for day or night, and who can thus avoid confusion, as well as informing those who wish to know what signal is being shown.

The name of Coston is now so well known in the marine world that it is the synonyme for night signals showing colored fire, and is the only name known in connection with night signals in the English Board of Trade register.

My son then endeavored to introduce the signals upon railroads as headway and danger signals. His plan was to have a signal burned, each color in turn to burn several minutes, to show any train following the distance between the two and thus avoid collision. The signals can be shown from the rear of a train or left to burn on the track. In the terrible Spuyten Duyvil Hudson River disaster, if the brakeman on the train wrecked had been in possession of one of these signals, he could have stopped the rear train; the little hand lantern carried by him was not powerful enough to be seen.

The signals would also be of great service at a wreck on a railroad at night, being readily and quickly ignited,

and, while burning, giving out a great amount of light.
Time means life in such cases. The signals will burn
in any sort of weather, and neither long storage nor
dampness destroys them. The yacht "Mohawk,"
which was sunk off Staten Island some years ago, and
in which the owner and his wife perished, had some
Coston Signals on board. These signals were under
water until the vessel was raised, and were not at all
damaged.

Professor Doremus, of New York, as I have already
said, analyzed the signals and found they were not
subject to spontaneous combustion. As further proof:
while the French government was testing them to see
how much heat they could stand without explosion,
they caused a box of the signals to be put in a chimney-
place against a wall of bricks, on the other side of
which there was kept a constant fire, so that there was
only a single thickness of brick and the side of the
box between the signals and fire. At the end of a year
this box was taken out, and it was found that the side
of it was so charred that it fell to pieces, but the signals
had never ignited.

Later, in the United States Life-Saving Service,—of
which the Hon. Sumner I. Kimball is superintendent-
general, to whom much credit is due for the efficiency
of that great service,—every patrolman was ordered to
carry what is called the patrol Coston signal light.
This signal warns off any vessel that may be seen
standing in danger. Every year the Life-Saving Service reports issued from the Treasury Department men-

tion the numerous occasions upon which, through warnings given by these signals, hundreds of vessels, thousands of lives, and millions of property are saved; Superintendent-General Kimball being always careful to give full credit to the Coston Signals whenever used.

Mr. Kimball having found it difficult and in many cases impossible to make the captains of vessels in distress understand what was and would be done for them by the crews of the life-saving stations, thought he would arrange a code of night signals, using the Coston Signals. Of this endeavor, in which my son William assisted, the New York *Herald* published the following account:

"IMPROVEMENT IN THE CODE OF INTERNATIONAL MARINE SIGNALS.

" The chief of the revenue marine division, Mr. Sumner Kimball, is engaged in preparing an appendix to the code of international signals which will enable communication to be maintained between vessels at sea and the life-saving stations along the coast. The urgent need of such an extension of the code was felt last month, when a German bark was wrecked on the Virginia seaboard just below Cape Henry. The life-savers fired the ball across the vessel and the line dropped on her deck, but her captain was in utter ignorance of its use, and the vessel lay for many hours at the mercy of the waves before the rest of the apparatus was hauled on board. Had the contemplated code been in existence, conversation could have been established at once and the captain instructed to do promptly what was necessary to further his rescue. It is true that all captains are not likely to prove so stupid. In this case he probably thought the life-line was the beginning of a movement for his rescue to be wholly conducted from the shore, and waited what was nearly a fatal time before he comprehended the meaning of the lights and the shouts on the beach. It is the intention of Chief Kimball to make the shipwreck code available at night as well as in the daytime, for which purpose he will use Coston signals. The code will comprise two letter combinations, and when completed will be translated into the leading foreign languages and published as an appendix with all future editions of the international code."

After considerable study, a perfect code for night signals was arranged. Mr. Kimball knowing that the Navy Department published the commercial code of Day Signals, which should be done by the Treasury Department, thought it proper to call their attention to this new chart, that it might be adopted in the same code, so that all mariners carrying the commercial international code would be benefited. The Navy Department replied to Mr. Kimball that they already had a code. I may add that at this time Admiral Ammen was Chief of the Navigation Bureau, and claimed the jurisdiction of signals and codes.

Some time later my son, after several years of work, obtained the approval of many different important bodies, dreaming—for it proved only a dream—that he would meet with encouragement from the Navy Department, the branch of the government that had been so greatly benefited by these signals, and that it seemed could hardly refuse, when so strongly endorsed, to approve and adopt this code.

Two bills were introduced in Congress, one by Mr. Clayton, of California, but nothing came of it; and two years later the second was introduced, which set forth all the reports and endorsements from shipping merchants and vessel-owners; a bill asking "that a night signal of distress be established for the use of the commercial marine, and said signal to be a Coston light, showing while burning the colors red, white, red, in succession; also that a signal for a pilot be established for night use by the commercial marine, said signal to be a Coston light showing the colors white, red, white in succession; and that a code chart of night signals for communication between vessels at sea and stations on shore be established; and that the Secretary of the Navy shall cause the said code and charts to be published in the international day signal code of flags, and that the Secretary should cause the fact to be made known to other maritime powers through the Secretary of State."

The Hon. Hereford, Chairman of the Committee on Commerce, H. R., appointed a sub-committee when the bill reached his committee. Mr. Reagan, of Texas, was made chairman of the sub-committee, and he at once communicated with the Navy Department, and received a very inconsistent reply, quashing it, over Mr. Robeson's signature, but written in the Bureau of Navigation, to the effect that "the Secretary of the Navy had no jurisdiction over vessels of the commercial marine; that it was more properly a matter for the Secretary of the Treasury to act upon, and any statement or action by the Navy Department might be considered obtruding upon the province of the Treasury Department;" also stating "that anything of this nature being placed in the international day

INTERNATIONAL CODE

OR OFFICIAL DANGER OR DISTRESS SIGNALS.
U. S. COAST SIGNAL SERVICE.

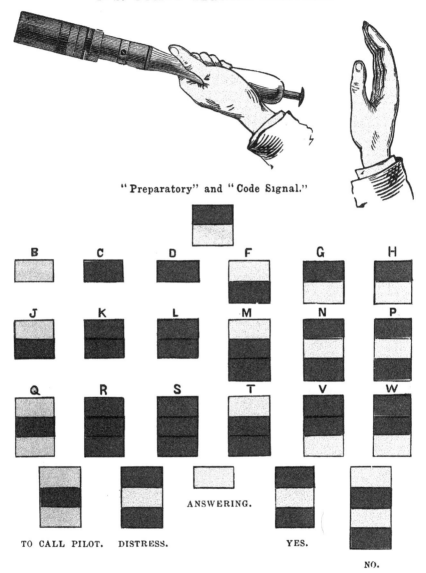

"Preparatory" and "Code Signal."

ANSWERING.

TO CALL PILOT. DISTRESS. YES.

NO.

Any message contained in the International Code or Official Danger or Distress Signals can be signalled by exhibiting, in their proper order, the Coston signals corresponding to the letters of the International Code found opposite the message. The plain white light will be used as the ordinary answering signal.

signal code would be considered tampering with the code."

Mr. Reagan showed this communication from the Navy Department to my son, who told him not to act upon the bill, that he would withdraw it. Mr. Reagan should have addressed the Secretary of the Treasury on mercantile matters.

Soon afterwards a large number of ship-owners, shipping merchants, and others adopted the Coston distress signal, in the absence of anything else, and instructed Mr. Kimball, Chief of the Life-Saving Service, to recognize it. The pilot signal, without Act of Congress, has also been put into use by the untiring efforts of my son.

After this, to show the injustice to which we were subjected, the Navy Department submitted to the Hon. S. J. Kimball a code containing the same questions and answers as that of my son's compiling for night signalling, and showing the same colors adapted to them, under the title of the "Coston or Very" Signal Code, thus claiming for Lieutenant Very a part of the Coston Signals.

Mr. Kimball submitted this to me, and I was justly indignant that this lieutenant should presume to place his name beside mine, and at once applied to the Secretary of the Treasury to prevent the publication of the code, and succeeded. The Navy Department, it will be observed, did not think it wrong in this instance "to tamper with the commercial code."

Years ago the chief signal officer of the army, General William B. Hazen, for the benefit of the commercial and agricultural interests of the country, caused a board to meet to adopt a code and chart of Coston night and day signals, called the "Official Danger, Distress, and Storm Signal Code," for the Signal Service, seacoast stations, and mariners generally.

General Hazen ordered signals to be supplied to the signal stations; and it now remains for the merchant marine and others to supply themselves, that they may have perfect means of communication at night; in fact, it is shameful that any vessel should court death for its crew and loss for its cargo with such simple and powerful means of averting collision, summoning help, flinging a silent cry of distress to the shore.

Every experienced mariner knows that there is nothing for signalling at night so effective as a colored pyrotechnic fire; and the Coston Signals, as I have said before, are not common fireworks, but a fine combination of chemicals, made to change suddenly and distinctly from one color to another, or by throwing colored stars; and these colors fix themselves upon the memory, simplifying the interpretation, and not to be confounded with the flash of a gun, as is the case in the flash system used in Russia and England.

Any one not color-blind can read them, and it is not necessary to have a regularly-educated signal officer, as any common sailor, in the absence of an officer, can make or read these signals. We have not introduced our aerial system, such as is used in the United States navy, because we cannot say that the aerial signals are as safe. The pistol-holders are very expensive, and in the long run not as satisfactory.

The Navy Department made, I think, a serious mistake in causing a bill to be passed through Congress named the "Rules of the Road at Sea," in which is recommended "the throwing of a star into the air which shall be recognized as a distress signal"; hence every signal the navy makes may be reckoned as one of distress; and for the United States Navy Department to cause the passage of such a bill in the face of what is known about the adoption of the Coston Distress Signals, by such a large number of our merchant marine, was of course intended as another blow at the Coston system, and an imitation of the inefficient plan of signalling used in England, always half a century behind the times.

The great advantage that the adoption of the signals would be to the merchant marine of England is shown by the fact that at present all ships entering ports where they have to enter docks, such as at Liverpool, are obliged by law to transfer their fireworks, rockets, etc., to some magazine, or else to throw them overboard, and consequently have to provide themselves with fresh supplies when they again go out to sea. What an unnecessary expense and tax this is, when the Coston Signals, which are guaranteed against spontaneous combustion and against injury from damp, need not be renewed until the supply is exhausted!

CHAPTER XLIX.

SUNSET COX ON THE LIFE-SAVING SERVICE.

IT is an exceedingly sweet thought to me that the work to which I have given my life has been not only a means of support, but a benefaction to my fellow-creatures ; and I feel this especially in the use to which the Coston Signals have been put in the United States Life-Saving Service,—one of the noblest institutions our country can boast, and the elevation of which was due largely to the efforts of the Hon. S. S. Cox, who made before the House of Representatives, June 4, 1878, a powerful and eloquent speech, from which I cannot resist the temptation to quote the following extracts :

" It is not my purpose to go into the history of the organization and development of this Life-Saving Service. It is of comparatively recent origin. It dates only from 1848, since which time up to 1872 four thousand lives have been saved. It was limited for twenty years to the New Jersey and Long Island coast; it had small appropriations, a few shanties, no discipline, and very indifferent apparatus. In 1872 a new era was inaugurated. Discipline was evoked out of chaos, by the employment of regular crews and a patrol system. The line, which is attached to a ball and shot from a rocket or mortar and thrown over the disabled vessel, then came into more frequent use. Since then the car, fastened upon the rope extending from the vessel to the shore, has been the vehicle of safety to thousands of lives. The first use of

work to which I have given my life has
a means of support, but a benefaction to
creatures; and I feel this especially in the
the Coston Signals have been put in the United
Life-Saving Service,—one of the noblest institutions
our country can boast, and the elevation of
due largely to the efforts of the Hon. S. S.
made before the House of Representatives
1878, a powerful and eloquent speech, from which
cannot resist the temptation to quote the following
extracts:

"It is not my purpose to go into the history of the organ
and development of this Life-Saving Service. It is of compara-

SIGNALLING WITH COSTON'S AERIAL SIGNALS.

this car resulted in the saving of over two hundred lives on the Jersey coast.

"Since 1872, as will be seen in detail hereafter, nearly five thousand lives have been saved, and not less than seven millions of property. During the year ending June 30, 1877, one hundred and thirty-seven vessels were driven ashore within the scope of the operations of this service. Of the fifteen hundred persons on board, only thirty-nine were lost,—about two and one-half per cent.

"Of the cargo and vessels, estimated at $3,266,612, more than half was saved."

Since this time this service has been rendered vastly more efficient, especially since the sad fate of the "Huron" and "Metropolis," thanks to the very able services of Superintendent-General Sumner I. Kimball, to whom the country and all humanity are deeply indebted.

Mr. Cox proceeded:

"The ineffable glory of life-saving!

"I have said, Mr. Speaker, that we have one beautiful statute which has a sacred halo around it. It makes a sunshine in the shadow of our selfish, sectional, and patriotic codes and laws. It is that which preserves human life. It is not merely a sentimental humanity, but a real benefaction. Like the orange-tree, it bears fruit and flowers at the same time. No language can make more emphatic that which every member must feel in contemplating its inestimable beauty and beneficence. It is no exaggeration to say, in view of its object, that it gives us a glimpse, though dim, of the Golden Age. The world's heart clings to it as if it were a memory of a past Paradise, or the hope of Paradise regained. The sea itself plays its mighty minstrelsy in its honor.

"No reward can adequately remunerate for the saving of precious human life. 'Men,' as Bacon has said, 'fear death as chil-

27*

dren fear to go into the dark, and in proportion as they fear, so is their appreciation of its sacredness.' There are a thousand deaths in the apprehension of losing life; it is the one terrible enemy; we are used to contemplating it, even in the most loving surroundings of home, as the arch foe of mankind. The silent closing of the flower around the insect is, however, none the less a death-agony, even in the gardens of home.

" Life is precious because its loss cannot be repaired. Jeremy Taylor has told us that while our senses are double, there is but one death,—but once only to be acted, and that in an instant, and upon that instant all eternity depends. Other losses may be recompensed by genius, but loss by death, never; no one is so lordly or powerful as to stay this irreparable loss; every day puts us in peril; while we think, we die. Can any legislation be too ample or adequate for its protection?

" To you inland legislators, far and aloof from the stormful perils of the sea, who sit happily in the blooming circles of household loveliness, it is the one hard lot of life to you to see the silver cord loosed and the golden bowl broken. None but the stoic— and he perhaps is a myth—can sing that sweetest of canticles, ' Nunc dimittis.' But there is a peculiar terror connected with death by shipwreck, amidst the leap and clash, boiling and battling of the tempestuous coast.

" Who can picture the poignancy of such death, in the company of those whose piercing shrieks and prayers typify the worst of agonies of human despair? Who can picture the joy beyond all joys, when, in such despair and amidst the double darkness, the cry of ' life-boat' rises above the weight of water, yet insubmergible, and now leaping above on the feathery plume of the wild wave?

> " 'The life-boat! oh! the life-boat!
> We all have known so long;
> A refuge for the feeble,
> The glory for the strong.'

" It is a part of the progress of our civilization that death shall be, whenever possible, robbed of its sting, and even the watery grave robbed of its victory; nay, the very stone removed from the sepulchre as if by angel hands, in the revivification of those only not drowned. Who can describe the terror of the long absent, sacrificed at the threshold of home, in sight of the dear native shore? Think of Margaret Fuller Ossoli; think of her at Rome, the lover of Italy; the synonyme of all that was first fair, first good, first beautiful.

"What a romance was her life! In Rome, more than a Roman; in Italy, more than an Italian; in America, the emblem of our best thought in intellect and taste, no parallel except herself. What infinite and strange forebodings had she before she sailed on the good ship 'Elizabeth,' out of the flowers, sun, and sympathy of Italy, along with her noble husband and beloved child! She sailed all unwillingly to her home; to her mother, sisters, friends, passing through pestilence and at last past the terrible trials of our coasts in midsummer, she lost by wreck her sweet and benignant hold on our mundane life. She went down with her husband and child, in sight of home. Her written thoughts perished with her manuscripts. There was no life-boat to save. She sat in her death-robes twelve hours in sight of the Fire Island sands on the Long Island beach. Ossoli and her child and her noble self, they perished as one. She went from the storms of time and sea to the Infinite One, who opened the door-way to the White Throne.

". . . It is within the memory of men present when the name 'wrecker' was a synonyme for the 'storm pirate' upon the Cornish and the Jersey coasts. He preyed upon the dangers and calamities of the sea. Much has been done in England from time to time by her shipping acts to mitigate the barbarities, cruelties, and wrongs which have for so many ages added to the perils of the sea. The most terrible penalties have been enacted against despoiling the wreck and murdering the shipwrecked. It was the disgrace of centuries. But happy change: the world rolls on; the footfall of progress is audible; every form which the inventive mind can adopt is called in requisition by humane government to rescue life. . . .

"It has always been a law among nations that salvage should be allowed for the rescue of property in ships. It was but the other day that an English court gave a large sum to the heroes of the sea who brought the floating obelisk of Egypt safely into port. It is but a year ago the Life-Saving Service on the Jersey coast saved two millions of bullion for our treasury. But it is of more recent date and from a better spirit that the savior of human life not only can be rewarded with a salary under government, but by medals of honor and the laudation of the good.

" It was but the other day that I picked up a volume by a minister of the gospel, about the life-boat work on the Goodwin sands. He pictures a familiar scene of a century ago ; with the skill of an artist he surrounds a company of low-browed villains with the environment of darkness, wildness, and storm, on a cliff near the sea.

" They plot for the destruction of a vessel. It is the story of Nag's Head over again. A white horse is led along the edge of the cliff; a lantern is tied upon him, the light sways with the movement of the animal not unlike the mast-head light of a vessel rocked by the sea. A ship is making steadily for the land. The captain grows uneasy ; he will put his vessel round. The lookout man reports a dim light ahead.

" ' What kind, weather away ?'

" ' Aye, aye, sir ; 'tis a ship light, for it is in motion.'

" ' Yes, it must be a vessel standing on the same course as this.'

" The captain will go on. There is a lull in the storm ; a hoarse murmur is heard. It is the sound of the sea beating upon the rocks. Lo ! a white gleam upon the water. Breakers ahead !

" Down with the helm ! Round her to. Too late ! too late ! Crash ! a shudder from stem to stern ; the shriek of voices in agony ; the sweep of the seas over the vessel. Broken timbers and cargoes, and lifeless bodies lie along the beach. No ! one living body is thrown among the rocks. Dead men tell no tales ; murder closes the tragedy.

" Think ! all these pirates of the tempest have given way to the Storm Warriors,—the life-boat, the howitzer, the rocket's flash, the *Coston hope Signal* of safety, the salvation of human life ! Can there be a nobler object for legislation ?

" Imagine a wreck upon our coast in January : a steamer of

three thousand tons' burden is steaming through the rain, cold, and darkness. Unconsciously she approaches the land. She has a pilot on board, but there is an error in sounding. There is a southeast wind and heavy sea. Her immense dusky hull is shadowed against the night like a living monster. Her gloomy lights are shades; they glimmer as faint stars gleam through clouds. How can words paint the scene? If there be one artist whose genius alone could do it, it is Turner,—he who has portrayed the tossing sea and its wild crests; the desperate passengers and reckless crew; the broken rudder and general menace of the wreck. Add to his genius the obscurity of a Rembrandt, with his shadows unbroken in the blackness save by little flashes of lustre; and fill the dim object with the throbbing enginery of man trying to mate the surging sea, and you have all that the eye can see of this unspeakable terror.

"Hardly do we discern her hull, her smoke-stack, her masts and yards, projected in black against the gloom, when we hear the noise of her steam, the mighty clank and throb of her engines, mingling with the rustle of the rain and the weltering shock of the sea as she rushes on with vast undulations.

"On the deck are a few muffled figures; below in the berths are two hundred or more sleeping forms. Suddenly there is a tremendous shock; every one on board is thrown down, and the sleepers below are dashed about pell-mell. Then above the din is a storm of screams. The ship is in a strong convulsion, pounding upon the sand. The engines stop, but the bell is still ringing, the whistles are shrieking; but amidst and above the hissing of steam, the swash of the ocean, the shouts of command and the human yells of dismay.

"What does all this mean?

"It means that the steamer is hard aground on a bar, plunging and writhing with an ominous straining and cracking through all her huge bulk, as if in the gripe of some vast hand. Gradually she settles, with slanting deck, over which, to and fro in the darkness, run half-clad tottering figures.

"The rain matters little, for around her like a shoal of monsters are the bounding seas, and there on her lee, a few hundred yards

v

off in the gloom, up-shaking and down-falling, pallidly, with ominous uproar, are the breakers. She is stranded on the Jersey shore.

"Well may there be horror and confusion and dismay. Between her freight of souls and the land is that unstable wall of surf. The storm increases, and the heavy coils of water, whirling round her, rise and lick off her oaken planking as if with the tongue of Hydras; and the great surges club the bottom with her hull until they break her keelson. This is the wreck!

"Where is the savior?

"Suddenly amidst the confusion and alarm there is a whiz of ruddy light, and there vivid, in a sort of orb of ruddy bloom, stands a figure holding high above his head a baton from which flies the red fire of a Coston Signal. It is the patrol of the Life-Saving Service. They stare at him from their unsteady deck; a cheer bursts out from them. God be thanked! we are seen; help is at hand. Then in the last flicker of the expiring Coston Signal their hearts sink again, as they see the patrolman race away. He bounds off to the station; it is near three o'clock in the dark January morning. By four he is back again, and now as one of a crew of seven whom he has summoned.

"They are all hot and blowsed, and splashed from head to foot with the mire of a winter road, through which for a mile they have dragged the life-boat. They pause only to take a look; then they bend all together to the launch.

"Along the beach is a wall of ice three feet high, over which they clamber, slipping and floundering with the heavy boat. Once over the barrier, they drag on, over great jags and boulders of ice which pave the beach to the edge of the water. There before them is a boiling surf full of enormous ice-cakes. Whitening, thundering, crashing and rising, spreading and tumbling incessantly the slabs of ice with deafening uproar, looms that appalling abatis of breakers through which they will force out the boat to the vessel. In vain! Drenched and bruised, blown and reeking with the effort, they again clamber over the ice barrier. Another crew from a more distant station arrives, and the keeper in command gasps out the order which sends the men to the station for the mortar apparatus. Boats are useless now, for ordnance, the wreck artillery, arrives and prepares for action.

"Suddenly the keeper sees a light near the water alongside the steamer. His heart bounds with fear. It is the old folly: a boat from the ship to the shore. The deep-water sailors see only the smooth line of the shore, instead of a swarm of enormous turbines, whirling all under and into the caverns of the brine. Keeper and beachmen rush forward with their warning cries, by voice and trumpet.

"In vain! The light starts on its phantom passage. It is borne in a boat with twelve sailors. Like a spectre from the shadow of the steamer, they see the little white craft emerge upon the summit of a huge wave. One moment's pause, and it flies smoothly towards them, so swiftly, so lightly, that it seems in one second more it will be upon the shore; and then in another instant, as if by some deft magic, it has feathered over, crewless, and keel uppermost; caught in the turbine wheels of the surf.

"Has the crew perished? No! dark spots are seen struggling in the fuzz of the foam, and the voice of the keeper bursts forth with, 'Come on; over the ice wall, men.' They plunge into the undertow. There they are, braced on legs of bronze, resisting with all the might of hip and loin the hideous suck and swirl of the waters; staving off the ice-slabs, and clutching for the drowning men.

"Four of these figures are dragged from the surf. They are heaved upwards over the ice barrier. Another powerful tussle in the foam, and they master four more. Another desperate struggle, and one more is saved. Two more are seen but cannot be saved. Another struggle, and the gallant keeper totters, gripped by a drowning man; the undertow, like an accomplice, winds around him and throws him down; the mad body clings to him and he cannot rise.

"In a moment of awful extremity the sea floods in upon them with its deathful roar, lifts and throws them inland; but before it can wash them back the keeper catches at a pile of ice and holds on. This enables him to resist the fearful siphonage of the undertow, and with a desperate effort he regains his feet and makes for shore. It is his last chance for life; a single second's delay and the sea may wash him down; but in that moment he does not forget that there is another life to save beside his own, and furious, with the sea upon his heels, he seizes his man and staggers on, dragging this human weight behind him. A mate rushes to his assistance; the surf falls in a crushing flood behind them. They are safe, and one more body rescued. Of the twelve men of the boat's crew, three have perished; nine have been drawn from the ocean by this little band of heroes.

"Is this a fanciful picture? No! This is what took place at the wreck of the French steamer 'Amérique' near Seabright, New Jersey, on the 11th of January, 1877. The day was Sunday, a Sabbath day for a Sabbath deed. That heroic keeper, whose breast deserves to be covered with decorations, was Abner H. West, of Station No. 3. Those three men deserving of equal honor, who wrought with him, in the ice and undertow, to save those lives, and whose names I regret I do not know, were members of the station crew. How they and their mates toiled later, and achieved that splendid rescue of all on board the French steamer, with which the country rang, is a matter of public record.

"Such labor and danger! Is there a splendor equal to its heroism? How that day they traversed the shore between the station and the wreck, lugging their heavy cart, before they could get the mortar apparatus and life-car to the rescue. How after two hours of hard pulling and hauling they were there with it, drenched with sweat, clothed with mire, alive with energy. How with thug and gun-flash their shot lines fled swishing to the steamer; the hawser and the hauling lines dragged aboard; how day broke, and again with desperate labor the effort was made to launch the boat through the surf and ice-floes.

"How difficult it was to get near to the vessel, to make her foreign officers understand how to attach the life-lines. How at last the launch was achieved, and, despite the breakers and currents which engirt the steamer with a circle of hell pools, the boat's crew got near enough to make their instructions known; and the slender bridge of rope for the life-car, narrow as the line

Mohammed saw floating across the gulf to Paradise, was drawn taut from the vessel to the shore.

" These were a few of the incidents of that night and day.

" To and fro, hung by its rings to the hawser, and hauled backward and forward by those arms of brawn, sped the life-car with its burden of human lives ; six or eight at a time ; men, women, and children, till all were landed.

" Then the baggage of the passengers, the trunks with their wealth of apparel and adornment; the mails, with their written weight of more than wealth, and the bullion of the Treasury followed the delivered lives in the same car.

" First, as I have said elsewhere, we save the man, and then his gems and gold. Is there salvage enough to recompense such service ?

" The ' Amérique' was seen by the patrolman at three o'clock in the morning. They toiled incessantly, never pausing for a mouthful of food or to change their soaked clothing ; stern, pale, unflagging, bemired, bedraggled, rough, weary, indomitable, and magnificent. Such were they, and such in very feeble outlines and faint colors have I endeavored to display their heroic work at the wreck of the ' Amérique' on that Sabbath day, which they thus kept holy. ' *Laborare est orare.*' . . .

" In conclusion, Mr. Speaker, it is impossible personally not to felicitate myself upon having given much earnest study to this Life-Saving legislation. It would not perhaps be in good taste to boast of having been instrumental in its organization and improvement. The inspiration for what I have done, however, came out of a storm upon the Scilly Isles in the winter of 1868, when a great steamer barely escaped shipwreck. It was the worst tempest in thirty years upon that coast. When we arrived in port the day after the peril, the English journals were full of the glorious exploits by rocket and signal and coast-guard and mortar and lifeboat.

" I wondered if so much could be done in England, with her forty-five hundred miles of coast-line, why should not our country, with double that number of miles, have a similarly efficient service ? It was this that led me to propose what the Superintendent of the

28

service called the efficient beginning of the patrol of the Jersey coast. Since that time how much has been done for the well-being and rescue of imperilled human life! How much of comfort and joy has been vouchsafed to families and friends and beneficiaries of that mercy which droppeth as the gentle rain from heaven in this warm-hearted legislation, blessing and blessed!

"Mr. Speaker, I have spent the best part of my life in this public service; most of it has been like writing in water. The reminiscences of party wrangling and political strife seem to me like a nebula of the past, without form and almost void. Gladly I would if I could, for many reasons growing out of personal inconvenience and party competency, reverse much that I have done here.

"Confessing so much inadequacy, recalling so many who have come and gone from this House,—gone, many of them, to another sphere, and I hope and trust to a better world,—I would gladly lay down my commission and turn to other duties which the lapse of time admonishes me should have attention; but what little I have accomplished in connection with this Life-Saving service is compensation 'sweeter than the honeycomb'; it is its own exceeding great reward. It speaks to me in the voices of the rescued; aye, in tears of speechless feeling; speaks of resurrection from death,—

> 'In spite of wreck and tempest's roar,
> In spite of false lights on the shore.'

"Speaks of a faith triumphant over all fears in the better elements of our human nature, it sounds like the undulations of the Sabbath bell ringing in peace and felicity.

"It comes to me in the words of Him who, regardless of His own life, gave it freely that others might be saved. Humanit and civilization should walk white-handed along with government. They strengthen and save society. In the perils which environ our country from passion and prejudice, from old animos ities and new irritations, let us do good deeds,—pray hopefully that our vessel of state be free from leakage, collision, wreck, and loss. Burn the signal; send out the life-boat; fire the line over the imperilled vessel ; free the hawser from the life-car ; and then, with stout hearts and thankful souls lift up our prayer to Him who holds the sea in the hollow of His hand.

> " ' Jesu, bless our gallant boat,
> By the torrent swept along ;
> Loud its threatenings,—let them not
> Drown the music of a song,
> Breathed thy mercy to implore
> Where these troubled waters roar.'

> " ' Guide our bark among the waves ;
> Through the surf our passage smooth ;
> Where the whirlpool frets and raves,
> Let thy love its anger soothe.
> All our hope is placed in Thee.
> Miserere, Domini.' "

CHAPTER L.

WOLVES !

FROM a long and interesting article on the American Life-Saving Service, published in *Harper's Magazine* of February, 1882, I cut the following :

" The life-saving stations on the Atlantic seaboard are now within an average distance of five miles of each other. Each crew consists of a keeper and six surfmen. At sunset two men start from each station, one going to the right and the other to the left. They are equipped with lanterns and *Coston Signals*, and each pursues his solitary and perilous way through the soft

sand, in spite of flooding tides, bewildering snow-falls, over-
whelming winds, or bitter cold, until he meets the man from the
next station, with whom he exchanges a check to prove to the
keeper on his return that he has faithfully performed his allotted
task."

PATROLMAN SHOWING SIGNAL.

The life-saving capacity of the Coston Signals was
curiously demonstrated a number of years ago in
Schwatka's search in the Arctic regions in quest of th
" Franklin" records. When the famous explorer, wh
was accompanied by Colonel Gilder, was preparing fo
his travels in unknown regions, the greatest interes

and excitement were shown by New Yorkers in the expedition, and every one was anxious to do his quota to aid in the bold undertaking.

My son, William F. Coston, presented the party with a box of signals, knowing their usefulness in the exigencies of travel.

When the explorers left the "Eothen" in Hudson Bay, and began the longest sledge-journey on record, they wisely took with them the box of Coston Signals. One day in the month of April, when they were suffering from a degree of cold appalling to us, the party, which had killed a number of reindeer and cut them up, went into camp not far from the abandoned carcasses, and in consequence were roused during the night by the peculiar low barking of the dogs, which announced the presence of the dread enemy,—wolves. They came boldly and in increasing numbers into the camp, approaching the igloos, or snow huts, with the evident determination to destroy them and banquet on the dwellers therein.

How to fight them off was the question. Powder and shot were precious, and the men were aware that as fast as they could shoot the hungry beasts the smell of blood would attract others of the pack, until there would be no limit to the use of powder and shot.

A happy thought struck Lieutenant Schwatka; he had not carried the Coston Signals thousands of miles in vain, and now he sent Toolooah, the intelligent dog-driver, outside to observe the effect of burning one. A Coston Signal was put through a hole in the side of the

28*

igloo and ignited. Toolooah reported that on stepping outside he found the wolves, who were now **howling** for their feast, circling around the igloos, their dusky bodies plainly discernible against the frosty white surface and their ranks being constantly recruited.

When the signal suddenly burst upon them in a blaze of color that displayed the whole landscape, the beasts were transfixed with terror, and when the color suddenly changed, becoming as green as it had been red, they turned tail and fled in dismay, and every transposition of color seemed to lend wings to their flying feet.

Colonel Gilder in his interesting book called " Schwatka's Search,—Sledging in the Arctic in Quest of the Franklin's Records" describes this incident, and adds : " We saw the wolves prowling around during the next day's march, but they kept at a respectful distance. Through our entire trip the Coston Signals served us a good purpose in keeping the wolves from our doors, though I do not remember that the prospectus mentioned this application as one of the advantages of keeping the signals on hand."

Soon after the return of Lieutenant Schwatka, he was invited by the Geographical Society to give some account of his travels in a lecture at Chickering Hall. Invitations were sent to my son and self among others to be present, and we listened fascinated to the description of his explorations, extending over three thousand two hundred and fifty-one statute miles, and the party being absent from their base of supplies seven months and twenty days, during which time they relied for their subsistence and the subsistence of their dogs on the game which was found in the locality.

This was the first time that an expedition had relied upon itself for subsistence, and the first expedition in which the white man of the party lived as and with the Esquimaux, passing through hardships that seemed to us incredible.

When the lecture was concluded, many of the audience went upon the stage to shake hands with the lieutenant, my son and I among the rest; and I could not resist remarking to him, " Lieutenant Schwatka, I am happy to say to you that in the Arctic regions you carried out my original idea when you used the signals to drive away the wolves from your igloos; for my principal object in perfecting the invention was to keep the wolf from my own door."

At this the lieutenant for the first time that evening broke into a laugh, and gave me a more detailed description of his use of the signals, adding that they had occasion to use them again and again for the same purpose, one signal generally sufficing, and had found them invaluable.

I need hardly say how exceedingly proud I was to know that my husband's name and the results of his brilliant genius had reached to the limits of civilization, and nearer the North Pole than the foot of man had ever trod before.

THE PRESENT.

As I write the last few pages of this book, I am reminded of how life runs on in infinite circles, even unto

Eternity; for the sound of martial music fills the air; I hear the shouts of the populace, and looking from the window, see the troops of handsome young men who compose the New York Seventh Regiment marching up our broad avenue; for they have come to Washington to celebrate the twenty-fifth anniversary of the entrance of that regiment into the nation's capital.

The sight brings back other days,—days a quarter of a century ago, when, with the whole of that brave and gallant regiment for an escort, I came on from Philadelphia to do my woman's share of the fighting. Alas! among these fresh young faces, unscarred, unblemished, I see none of those who answered their country's call to march to the defence of its seat of government.

Later in the day I am asked to view a fine painting by Fosberg,—a faithful picture of a large house of dull red brick, with an old-fashioned portico, supported by fluted pillars and surrounded by the snowy tents that tell of an encampment. I recognize the present home of General John A. Logan; but a quarter of a century ago the headquarters of the officers of the Seventh Regiment, when it encamped on Meridian Hill. This picture was presented to the present gallant Captain Daniel Appleton, in memory of the old days, by Mr. C. W. Spofford, of the Riggs House, who as a friend sheltered and fed the Seventh Regiment in Philadelphia on their memorable trip to this city.

Well, time has somewhat powdered my once golden hair, which still will curl; but as yet no frost has reached my heart, and I find it hard, even when I gaze on the charming faces of my little grandchildren, to realize how rapidly the years have stolen away; for they have left me young in heart, in health, and the capacity for happiness.

A golden glow hangs over the past, for, with all its sorrows and disappointments, I feel that it has not been wasted. I have been permitted to carry out the brilliant thought of the husband of my youth; to keep his name alive and without a blemish before the old world and the new; to watch the signals that bear his title burn bright in the dark nights of France, Italy, Denmark, and Holland, as well as in the great night that fell upon our own country with the war; while they are employed in saving thousands of lives and millions of property annually; to see my sons grow up into useful and honored manhood; and to find myself able to maintain the position which has always been accorded me in society, and to enjoy life in the pleasant home I have made for myself, and known to my friends as the " Villa Coston."

Now I am called upon to maintain my rights, and to demand from the government the erasure of the name of Very from the Coston Signals, now being used in the United States navy. But I know no fear nor hesitation, for I have found in my experience of life that Right proves Might.

THE END.

AWARDS GRANTED

TO THE

COSTON SIGNALS

BY THE

DIFFERENT EXHIBITIONS THROUGHOUT THE WORLD.

1873—VIENNA, AUSTRIA.

DIPLOMA AND MEDAL.

1875—CHILI, SANTIAGO DE CHILI.

DIPLOMA AND MEDAL.

1876—U. S. CENTENNIAL, AT PHILADELPHIA.

MEDAL AND DIPLOMA.

1886—INTERNATIONAL EXHIBITION FOR NAVIGATION, COMMERCE, AND MANUFACTURES, LIVERPOOL, ENGLAND.

GOLD MEDAL—HIGHEST AWARD.

CPSIA information can be obtained
at www.ICGtesting.com
Printed in the USA
LVHW081327290119
605650LV00035B/626/P